Radical Process Change

Radical Process Change

A Best Practice Blueprint

ASHLEY BRAGANZA

JOHN WILEY & SONS, LTD

Chichester • New York • Weinheim • Brisbane • Singapore • Toronto

Published 2001 by   John Wiley & Sons, Ltd,
                        Baffins Lane, Chichester,
                        West Sussex PO19 1UD, England

                        National   01243 779777
                        International   (+44) 1243 779777
                        e-mail (for orders and customer service enquiries):
                        cs-books@wiley.co.uk
                        Visit our Home Page on http://www.wiley.co.uk
                                or http://www.wiley.com

Other Wiley Editorial Offices

John Wiley & Sons, Inc., 605 Third Avenue,
New York, NY 10158-0012, USA

WILEY-VCH Verlag GmbH, Pappelallee 3,
D-69469 Weinheim, Germany

John Wiley & Sons Australia Ltd, 33 Park Road, Milton,
Queensland 4064, Australia

John Wiley & Sons (Asia) Pte Ltd, 2 Clementi Loop #02-01,
Jin Xing Distripark, Singapore 129809

John Wiley & Sons (Canada) Ltd, 22 Worcester Road,
Rexdale, Ontario M9W 1L1, Canada

British Library Cataloguing in Publication Data

A catalogue record for this book is available from the British Library

ISBN 0-471-48630-2

Typeset in 11/15.5pt ITC Garamond Light by Footnote Graphics, Warminster, Wiltshire
Printed and bound in Great Britain by Biddles Ltd, Guildford and King's Lynn.
This book is printed on acid-free paper responsibly manufactured from sustainable forestry, in
which at least two trees are planted for each one used for paper production.

Contents

Series Foreword

I am delighted to be able to introduce to you the *CBI Fast Track Series*. The book you are holding is the outcome of a significant new publishing partnership between the CBI and John Wiley & Sons (Wiley). We intend it to be the first in a long line of high quality materials on which the CBI and Wiley collaborate. Before saying a little about this partnership, I would like to briefly introduce you to the CBI.

With a direct corporate membership employing over 4 million and a trade association membership representing over 6 million of the workforce, the CBI is the premier organisation speaking for companies in the UK. We represent directly and indirectly, over 200 000 companies employing more than 40% of the UK private sector workforce. The majority of blue-chip organisations and industry leaders from the FTSE 250 are members, as well as a significant number of small to medium sized companies (SMEs).* Our mission is to ensure that the government of the day, Whitehall, Brussels and the wider community understand the needs of British business. The CBI takes an active role in forming policies that enable UK companies to compete and prosper, and we ensure that the lines of communication between private and public leaders are always open on a national scale as well as via our regional networks.

The appropriateness of a link between the CBI and a leading business publisher like Wiley cannot be understated. Both organisations have a vested interest in efficiently and effectively serving the needs of businesses of all sizes. Both are forward-thinkers; constantly trend-spotting to envision where the next issues and concerns lie. Both maintain a global outlook in servicing the needs of its local customers. And finally, both champion the adoption of best practice amongst the groups they represent.

Which brings us back to this series. Each *CBI Fast Track* book offers a complete best practice briefing in a selected topic, along with a blueprint for successful implementation. The aim is to help enterprises achieve peak performance across key disciplines. The series will continue to evolve as new and different issues force their way to the top of the corporate agenda.

I do hope you enjoy this book and would encourage you to look out for further titles from the CBI and Wiley. Here's to all the opportunities the future holds and to *Fast Track* success with your own corporate agenda.

*Foreign companies that maintain registered offices in the UK are also eligible for CBI membership.

Digby Jones
Director-General, CBI

About the author

Ashley is a senior lecturer and Director of the IT Directors' Forum at Cranfield School of Management's Information Systems Group. He directs all major Business Process Orientation (BPO) initiatives at Cranfield. Ashley has consulted with a number of organisations, including Vauxhall Motors Limited, McDonald's Restaurants Ltd, Coca Cola & Cadbury Schweppes, United Distillers, The Environment Agency, Midland Bank, Mars – Europe, Glaxo, and AT&T ISTEL. He has advised them on a variety of strategic, business process, and knowledge management and systems issues.

He joined the IS Group at Cranfield in 1991 to research the managerial aspects of Electronic Data Interchange (EDI). Ashley also carried out a study for the European Commission's TEDIS programme. This pan-European project (12 EC and 6 EFTA countries) involved examining the use of electronic banking and financial EDI, and their development over the five years.

Ashley has published two books and over twenty articles and working papers covering a range of topics on process orientation, knowledge management, governance, and organisation structure. He has co-edited three special issues of the leading international journal *Knowledge and Process Management* (Wiley). Ashley recently completed his doctorate, which focused upon the implementation of radical process oriented change.

Ashley completed an MBA at the Strathclyde Business School, specialising in corporate strategy and finance. His most recent interests include the integration of process management e-business.

Acknowledgments

This book is brought to you by endeavours of the many channelled through the one. My foremost thanks are reserved for Radhika, Anazia and little Lara, without whose support this work would not have been completed. They afforded me something that I can never fully repay: time. I would also like to thank my parents for raising me with the belief that I should only stop learning when I am dead. It will be an unceasing sadness that my father did not live to see me reach this milestone in my life.

My thanks go to my colleagues in the Information Systems Group, especially Professor Chris Edwards, at the Cranfield School of Management. They provided me with the space in which to complete this work and the feedback to improve my understanding of this area.

I would also like to thank Phil Janes for his Downs Tools contribution, which characterises many of the lessons in the book. Humour is essential on the road to change!

Introduction

Sixty-five million years ago, most of the dinosaurs which might have borne Hollywood ambitions – the big photogenic ones – died out after a huge meteorite struck the Earth towards the east of the Gulf of Mexico, and its effects spread almost instantaneously around the globe. It was not that the big dinosaurs were inefficient carnivores or herbivores; most were quite the opposite, which was what had allowed them to grow to their great size and to prosper. As a class of animal they survived for millions of years; much longer than human beings have so far walked the planet. They evolved, along with the planetary conditions, into the most successful group of animals there has ever been. Then they died, practically overnight. Why? Because after the meteorite strike evolutionary change was suddenly not enough. The plummeting global temperatures and the restriction in sunlight devastated plant life. Numbers of herbivores were the first to dwindle, followed by those who fed on them. The dinosaurs faced a revolutionary change in their environment, and they could not adapt with anything like the required speed to the new world. The radical change that they needed required more time than they had left.

Of the animals which did survive, the insect class did best, because the speed of their reproduction allowed them to maintain a phenomenal rate of alteration so that their own evolution kept pace with that of the world around them.

The analogy in a book considering change in the world of commerce is not subtle. The rate of change in today's business environment has been increasing for many years. In the more recent of those years the internet, e-business and an organisation-led recession have hit the business world much like the meteorite which devastated that of the dinosaurs, this time impacting first just north of the Gulf of Mexico but spreading their effects around the globe with almost the same speed. Long-established companies which continue to make small evolutionary changes in reaction will disappear much as the giant lizards did. New companies will emerge just as new species emerged on the post-cataclysmic Earth. The existing ones which survive will be those which can make radical changes quickly.

One point where the analogy diverges is that 65 million years ago there was only one meteorite and one cataclysmic change with which to contend. If an animal made it over the transition, it was set. Today's business world is constantly changing, and doing so ever faster. If a company is continually going to survive, it must continually change. It must be in a position to react quickly to what is happening around it, and it must be prepared to do so.

This is not to say that every company today must be constantly changing in a radical way in order to keep up and survive. Once conditions have been created whereby continual change is possible then continual prosperity is also possible. It is the creation of those conditions which represents the required radical change; the prerequisite leap across that transition.

It is a pretty safe bet that the dinosaurs took little time out to contemplate conditions in the wider world around them, being concerned solely with their internal needs – centring around the next meal and carnal satiation. In the same way, many companies even today have a largely inward perspective, if not in the minds of the board, then certainly in those of the staff, and this is largely created by the organisational structure. The further inside a company's departments one delves, the more will the gaze be found to be turned inwards. To be fair to the lizards, there is not much that a Tyrannosaurus Rex could have done about its perilous situation even if it had taken due note of its surroundings, but few of today's companies have the excuse of only possessing a brain the size of an orange!

This book considers radical change, based on the assumption that a company is only able to stay in business as long as it addresses the expectations of its stakeholders – for example customers, shareholders, suppliers, employees and pressure groups. Any company which loses sight of that prime requirement, and which concentrates on its own internal workings, whose individual staff concentrate only on their own departmental and personal goals, will quickly fail. That which forms the heart of a successful organisation is its business processes and the way they are designed to meet and exceed stakeholders' expectations. It is, as we shall see, only processes – as defined in the next chapter – which can achieve that expectation or requirement satisfaction. Hence this book looks at how radical business change can be achieved based on a company's processes.

This is not the first book to consider such change. Since the early 1990s, and the work of, among others, Michael Hammer, James Champy, and Tom Davenport, process orientation and process-based changes have been part of the landscape of company management theory. What this book does is to consider the real world, because theory is all right so long as everybody – all the staff and all the stakeholders – is conversant with it, believes in it, and does nothing to disrupt it. Yet people are people and they do not naturally conform to whiteboard-based generalisations. Taking that fundamental truism into account, this book addresses the implementation of radical process-based change in a way that gives the greatest chance of success for any company undertaking it. Any company not undertaking it must either already have successfully done so, or should be preparing to see the blurred shapes of their competitors racing past, taking mission critical stakeholders with them.

Positioning Radical Process-based Change

There is nothing new in highlighting the need for radical change if a business is to survive. The last few years have seen a number of approaches which addressed the same problem. In the 1980s Total Quality was mooted as the way forwards, with each of the company's activities being subject to scrutiny and designed to reach sometimes officially benchmarked levels of accuracy, or whatever definition of quality was adopted. In the same decade came the notion of Matrix

Management. The organisational structure was changed with the appointment of matrix managers, whose role was to focus on the cross-functional activities that delivered value to the stakeholders. Line managers therefore had dual reporting lines; one to the functional director and one to the new matrix manager. Yet by the end of the 1980s matrix managers were being withdrawn and the matrix structures disbanded. In practice, matrix organisations proved unmanageable: dual reporting lines led to confusion and conflicts; committees were formed, each with its own set of reports to the management team; overlapping roles and responsibilities created turf wars and budget battles; and people were able to avoid accountability.[1]

The 1990s saw the advent of Re-engineering, which diverged from the more incremental approaches advocated in the 1980s. The underpinning idea was that organisations should stop doing what was akin to 'rearranging the chairs on the decks of the *Titanic*'. Senior managers needed to make radical changes to the organisation, breaking through functional walls and even disbanding functions altogether if necessary. Since the idea was to make major productivity gains and achieve radical benefits, only such radical change could be the key to success.

Downsizing was another approach used in the 90s, wherein a company intentionally reduced the number of personnel. It sometimes featured removing whole functions, such as marketing or finance, and might also have included delayering, as well as voluntary or compulsory redundancies. Its aim was almost exclusively to achieve a rapid and significant reduction in costs, especially people related costs.

All these types of change initiative (or 'project' – we use the terms interchangeably) were designed to make the company more effective and efficient, and more able to prosper in the increasingly competitive modern marketplace. As such they can be seen as initiatives which were designed to stave off failure – they were reactions to pressures which threatened the company's position.

In the first decade of the new millennium we have the emergent phenomena of e-business, which can be seen as a possible approach to change which can be adopted in the same way as those of the previous two decades mentioned above. It can also, as we will see, be considered as a potent driver for change, and in this e-business differs from earlier approaches in that it is both driver and medium.) Along with this, though, there is the change approach with which this book is primarily concerned – the process-based change. As we shall see, this approach requires a company to consider and implement stakeholder-facing processes which satisfy specific stakeholder expectations.

These two approaches – adopting e-business and adopting a process-based approach – both differ from the earlier change initiatives in that they are not basically defensive in nature. Instead they strive to achieve success in the marketplace through accentuating positive factors, either in the way the customers are gained and serviced or in the reinvention of the internal processes such that the customers' expectations are specifically targeted. Figure I.1 illustrates that point graphically, and adds a further element, that of positioning the type of change.

As Figure I.1 suggests, both Total Quality and Downsizing can be seen as tactical approaches to fend off the spectre of failure. They do not seek to change the overall strategy or internal construction of the company. Nor for that matter does establishing a Web front end affect the core of the organisation; although it suggests that the

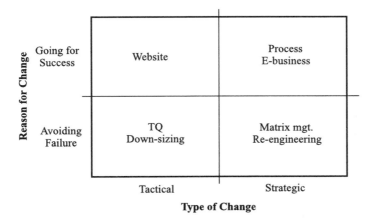

Figure I.1 *Proactive change: positioning process-based initiatives*

organisation seeks to be responsive to the marketplace. Matrix Management and Re-engineering can be considered more strategic approaches, in as much as they do fundamentally address the company's internal operation. They are more elaborate ways to address the fear of failure, but they do not, as do E-business and Process approaches, take the fight to the marketplace and actively seek to gain competitive advantage through the change initiative.

Furthermore, as we shall demonstrate later, e-business initiatives will depend for their success on following a process-based change approach. The new ways of doing business must be integrated with a company's existing activities such that the processes of which they form a part address the stakeholders' expectations. If they do not, then e-business is just a hi-tech way of waving goodbye to the customers, and with the costs involved, a spectacularly effective way of removing any profits!

'Business change' will mean different things to different people, and indeed there are many levels of change which differ from each other in the degree of change which they seek to initiate. Figure I.2 indicates where process-based change is sited in relation to other potential change initiatives, in terms which refer to the reaction to today's new technology. The minimum level of change, assuming some change reaction is made at all, is the creation of a static website.

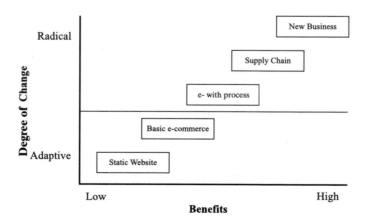

Figure I.2   *Positioning process-based change by degree of change*

Basic e-business would be the next higher level, wherein the technology is used as an active front-end, a gateway to the company, as well as an advertising medium, and so on. But at this level there is no integration of the technology into the company's processes.

Such integration identifies a further level of the adaptation to the new technological environment. The company must identify its processes, and which stakeholder expectations they satisfy, and must interweave the technology into the further development of those processes. The technology must be more than a 'bolt-on' accessory, a further departmental creation or merely a doorway into the existing activities of the company; it must be integral to the organisation's database applications and infrastructure, and a part of everything which the company does. It is at this level of change where this book is aimed. We will see how the new technology not only provides a driver for change and an enabler of it, but how that enabler must be used to support the processes which are required to satisfy fundamental stakeholder expectations in order for the company to survive and thrive.

The levels above 'e- with Process' in Figure I.2 go beyond the study which is presented here. Inclusion of the complete redesign of the supply chain as a result of 'e', or the creation of completely new business, based on core competencies when combined with 'e' or on quite new ventures, are not the subject matter of this study. Whenever such changes are made, however, they too must be based on the new and complete business processes which are required, and not simply on a subset of them. In order to provide the greatest assurance of success in today's marketplace, and in that of tomorrow, the business process must be the building block.

The Basis of Change

As described in the section above, this book concerns itself with process-based change, and we shall see in the next chapter exactly what we mean by the word 'process', because without that all the positioning in the world will still result in different interpretations.

We shall discuss in later chapters how process-based changes are identified, managed and implemented, and how they may be judged effective or otherwise. Much of this can be done through 'whiteboard' theory, and the logical arguments derived in such a way can often be backed up by statistical evidence. But all the identification and clarification of the unit of analysis and of the micro-econometrics of the changes would not allow us to get to grips with the fundamental basis of change, and that is *the people involved*.

It is people who identify changes, people who determine what they are, who implement them and are affected by them, and people who manage them, resist them and even thwart them. Many studies have considered the importance of change management, and that management is of the people who are involved in the changes, but such studies and theories generally concentrate on the implementors of changes. They do not consider the earlier identification of the changes, over which people have just as much influence and which require just as much management.

Taking that thought to its logical, and true, extremes, it is people who create the conditions which demand that change is needed in the first place. And even the external factors which influence those conditions are themselves shaped by real people as manifested in customers and other stakeholders.

Structure

Because change is about people from conception to conclusion, this study of process-based change makes extensive reference to two in-depth case studies, researched over a period of several months through interviews with the people who were most closely involved with the changes in their companies, from the managing directors down through the hierarchy to the staff performing administrative and manual tasks. Those interviews were taped and transcribed to ensure accuracy of interpretation. Some are in part reproduced in the following chapters to provide real illustrations of radical process-based change in action.

The first study is of 'Carton Carrier', a parcel distribution and delivery company. The second is 'Foundry Insurance', an inspector and insurer of boiler, mechanical and electrical plant. The case study companies both implemented radical process-based change, and did so successfully. In each case it was following the implementation of the identified changes that the studies were undertaken.

As we explore these case studies, there are two points which should be borne in mind regarding the study companies and the characteristics which they exhibited at the start of their initiatives. First, we should be wary of throwing the first stone in the direction of their problems, lest it crack a window in our own glasshouse! Second, as we said above, the implementation of radical process-based change in these companies has been successful. They no longer exhibit those traits which became their change drivers, and as a result they are now far better placed than most other companies in their markets.

A third case study is included in rather less depth where it provides further clarification in the area under discussion. This company – 'Software Inc' – provides computer software facilitating the collection of external data. The case study was undertaken using the same interview techniques.

Through the use of these case studies we ensure that the conclusions drawn and change axioms posited in the following chapters are based upon the actual experiences of real people, and sufficient research has been undertaken to ensure that those people are fully representative.

Every company has people within it, be it the oldest established manufacturing or financial services company, or the newest dot.com, and the characteristics and motivations of those people will largely be similar. No particular aspirations, anxieties, or behaviours are exclusively associated with any one industry or company profile, including those in which you, the reader, participate. The findings herein apply to companies which are considering or undertaking radical change, and to those where such change is becoming or may become necessary. In today's rapidly changing market, that covers just about every company on the planet, including yours.

We also make introductory reference in each chapter to a further case study, within the company 'Downs Tools'. This case study is not quite as well assigned as the others, in that it is not entirely based on one particular company. It may even appear to some readers to be purely fictional. Be warned, however, that the situations encountered and the opinions expressed in Downs Tools are drawn not from an overactive or fevered imagination, but from experience of many change initiatives in many real businesses. The staff and management of Downs Tools have been and can be found in practically every company in which one cares to look. That, too, includes your own!

Layout of the book

Change projects or initiatives are, as we shall see, extremely difficult to tie down in terms of a structure which must be adhered to. It is not possible to identify explicit and unchanging steps which lead in well-behaved sequence from initiation to completion. However, there are broad, distinct elements within each project which must be addressed, and these are explored in the following chapters. Discussion of the researched evidence will then provide insights for others, both in terms of examples to follow, and pitfalls to avoid.

The first chapter clarifies the most important term in the study, clarifying what we mean by 'process'.

Having established that, we consider what can be seen as the 'Commencement phase'. The elements covered in Chapters two and three are those drivers which contribute to the initiation of a radical change project, and why process-based change is chosen as the way forward, as it was in our case studies.

'Identification of the changes which need to occur' is the heading within which lie the next elements of the projects. Chapters four to six cover this topic and will investigate:

- How the organisational elements should be addressed, arguing that a physical change to process orientation – much vaunted in past literature – will usually damage the change project.

- How it is vital to gain acceptance of the actual changes which need to occur, rather than seeking easier alternatives.
- How people's preparedness to allow change to affect them will determine the overall success or failure.

'Management of the issues which arise' describes the third set of elements, and these are considered in chapters six to nine. We will investigate the following:

- Linking the issues to the changes which have been identified, such that they can be individually managed and resolved.
- How adopting a mode of implementation of the changes which is either radical or evolutionary, as proposed by differing experts, is a recipe for failure.
- The new concept of people's willingness to implement the changes required.
- How people do not – and should not – split into change 'implementors' and change 'recipients', as much current wisdom suggests that they do.

Finally we discuss the results of the initiatives, and what must be considered in order to determine whether success has been achieved.

At the end of each of the ten chapters described above, we put forward a summarising axiom which encapsulates what we should learn from the evidence and put into practice in any future change initiative. We also include a set of questions which the reader might ask of his or her own company. At whatever stage of a change project you might be, answering those questions in the light of the axioms which precede them will provide guidance as to whether the project needs some remedial or additional actions to ensure its success.

We apologise in advance if the axioms outlined below provide insights into why your particular project went horribly wrong or petered out and achieved nothing. But change is not something which will happen to your company just once and then go away, so the chance will certainly come again to get it right.

ONE

What is a Process?

Arnold Tomb looked up from his terminal as his young colleague came into the room, looking over his shoulder as though he were being followed. 'You look excited, Jester. More so than usual.'

Jester Harrold nodded. 'There's something going on. Big board meeting this afternoon.'

'And those two go together, why?'

Harrold frowned in puzzlement. Tomb was nearing retirement, so knew much more than did Jester of life in Downs Tools. 'Well, you know, a *board* meeting.'

Tomb shrugged. 'Whenever managers get bored they have a meeting. That's where the name came from. Meetings are the perfect substitute to actually doing something. If there was really anything going on, they'd be busy making it go on rather than sitting around in a room talking.'

Harrold looked dubious. 'My new boss, Alan Parsons, has called the meeting, and he seems different. Almost as though when he says something he actually means it. I think he wants ...' He looked round furtively and dropped his voice. 'He wants *change*.'

'Change?' Tomb did not, as Harrold had half feared, clutch his chest and slump over his desk. Instead, he smiled and shook his head. 'Here? In Downs Tools? Don't be daft; nothing changes here.'

'It doesn't?'

'No. Every now and then someone brings it up, but it never happens. You just make all the right enthusiastic noises and keep your head down until it blows over. It always does. Don't worry about it; it's not in the managers' interests to have change, and if Parsons is serious he'll soon find that they didn't get where they are today without knowing how to stop it.'

'What do they do?'

'Well, the favourite method is to analyse any proposal to within an inch of its life, then just wait for it to run out of steam. And if that doesn't do the trick you just suggest building a new computer system. Or even better, buying one and then spending three years customising it and fitting it into your existing legacy systems. That's marvellous; it gives the impression of frantic activity and all it changes is the size of the IT contractors' cars.'

Harrold shook his head uncertainly. 'I don't think Parsons is going to suggest computer systems. Or not yet anyway. He's talking about *processes*. He wants us to focus on what the customer wants.'

'Which customer? We've got hundreds. Well, dozens, now.'

'All of them, I think. He wants to identify what their expectations are and exceed them.'

Harrold wondered for a moment if he had slipped into his native tongue, such was the look of incomprehension on Tomb's face. But then his colleague rallied.

'Well at least that leaves us out. Finance haven't got anything to do with exceeding customer expectations.' He reflected for a moment. 'Or meeting them for that matter.'

'Parsons doesn't seem to think that way. He thinks we're all involved. He says that we all have an interrelated impact on the customer. He's talking about cross-functional changes.'

'Well if he tries that he's going to run up against some very cross functional managers!'

'I don't think that would put him off.'

'Courageous bloke, is he?'

'He seems to be.'

'Okay, good luck to him, I say. Identify expectations and exceed them, eh?' Harrold nodded. 'Well if he manages that with our customers and he wants to move on to the big league, he can try it out on my wife!'

*   *   *

In order to consider the successful implementation of process-based change, there is a fundamental question which needs to be answered. What is a process? Many change initiatives have floun-dered because that one simple question has been inappropriately answered. The reason for this is that for the most part the question has not even been asked, largely because everybody *knows* what a process is, don't they?

The appropriate answer to that, of course, is 'No'.

A dictionary definition mentions 'a series of actions or events; a sequence of operations …' In this book we are not trying to enforce any particular definition of the word, but to gain a common under-standing of it such that the discussion which follows can be received in the context in which it is intended. The dictionary definition aids that objective in that it distinguishes a process from a single action or activity. But in terms of a business process it still allows for *any* collection of activities to be somehow arbitrarily bound together and given the 'process' title.

A Traditional, Bottom-up Approach to Processes

Such an arbitrary boundary is often imposed using the logic that there is indeed a boundary, and that is the one at the extremity of the department within which the process is defined. Consider Figure 1.1.

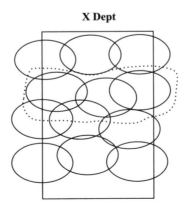

Figure. 1.1 *Activities within a functional department*

This depicts a department within which a large number of activities are taking place, each represented by a separate, but overlapping ellipse.

Those within X department have identified a set of activities – represented by the dotted line – which begins with the receipt of an item of work and passes through several distinct and identified 'tasks' or 'operations' before it passes out of the department. As far as X department is concerned, this is a bounded set of activities, and is therefore classified as a process. Should the department decide to 're-engineer' its processes, it is this set of activities that will be addressed. However, X department is likely to have, on at least one 'side' of it, another department, one which passes the work item to it, or one to which it passes that item. It will probably have both. There will probably be other departments which have some input to the work item but which do not have a direct hand-off to or from X department. But the process definition in X department will not take the activities in these other departments into account. Similarly, the other departments will have their own process definitions based upon their intradepartmental activities. But none of those definitions actually captures the process.

As an example: one of the country's leading life assurance companies – and it is very far from being alone in this respect – has, within one of its pensions administration areas, an assembly of activities which are collectively known as the 'claims process'. A claim request is received by the department, which, using computers and manual methods, calculates the amount of the claim to be paid. There are various different parts which make up this claims process, such as the loading of the data, the manual checking of the computer output, and the creation of a letter containing the answer. The conclusion of the process comes when that letter is placed in the 'out' tray for onward transmission.

Consider the end customer, though. For him or her the claims 'process' starts with the first contact with the life assurance company to make the claim request. The process is only completed when the quotation or the cheque (whichever has been requested) arrives in the customer's hand.

Unknown to the customer, the request, made via a company representative, has first to be passed to the head office, and transported to the administration department. Part of their work is completed before the preliminary answer is passed to the actuarial department for approval. The finished letter is transported back to the company representative who delivers it to the customer. (And this assumes that an Independent Financial Advisor has not acted as an intermediary between the customer and the company rep.)

The claims 'process', as it is called within the administration department, is but a part of the overall process which begins with a customer requirement and ends with the satisfaction of that requirement. It is this wider interpretation of the business 'process' that is the appropriate definition when we are considering process-based change. The change initiatives we shall study in this book are those which are concerned with the totality of the activities required to satisfy customer requirements (or as we shall see below, stakeholder expectations). What we must ensure in using the 'process' definition is that we are not taking an arbitrary, unbounded collection of activities and calling them a process, nor using as a boundary the internal organisational structure of a company. A process, generally, starts and finishes with a customer as with the claims example and as in Figure 1.2.

The customer on the left of the diagram initiates the process by having a requirement, and that same customer on the right defines the conclusion of the process when that requirement is satisfied. The process consists of a set of activities, each of which must be completed in order to satisfy the customer's requirements. This definition is that a process will always start with a customer requirement and conclude with the satisfaction of that requirement. There may be exceptions to the rule – for example when a process is initiated by a date, for some sort of renewal process – but for the vast majority of processes the customer is involved at start and finish.

This traditional approach to understanding business processes suggests that the chain of activities defines the process. This is quite the wrong way round. It is the process which defines the chain of activities. What, then, defines the process?

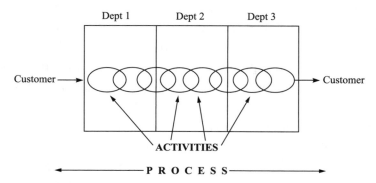

Figure. 1.2   *The process 'chain' of activities*

A Top-down View of Business Processes

We have started this chapter by considering the view which is taken by most people within an organisation – that from the centre of a mass of interrelated activities which make up their 'day jobs'. In order to answer the question we have just posed, however, we must take a view from the more rarefied atmosphere breathed by the business strategists, and work downwards, for it is only through examining strategy and its interaction with stakeholder expectations – of which the customer requirements are a single example – that we can identify viable business processes. Business processes, as we shall see, should be the bedrock on which the success of the company is built. Those processes, binding together their component activities, should support the business strategy which itself should be aligned towards the satisfaction of the most important stakeholder expectations. Let us consider each of those terms – business strategy, stakeholders, expectations, processes and activities – to see how they all fit together in a process-oriented company.

Business Strategy

All commercial and, increasingly, not-for-profit organisations operate in a competitive environment. Such an environment can be considered in two disparate forms, in terms of chronology and characteristics. The 'current' form consists of products and services that already exist, competitors that are identified and whose relative strengths and weaknesses are understood, customer demands that are known, and trading relationships that are in place and which operate with little friction. In effect, the boundaries and structures of the competitive space are well defined.

The 'future' form of an organisation's competitive environment is as unknown as the future itself. In this form, the boundaries and structures of the environment are indistinct. Companies look to develop products and services that deliver superior value and delight both existing and new customers. The demands of those customers become ever more sophisticated. Organisations attempt to revolutionise the very basis of competition to steal a march on their competitors. Traditional business relationships are open to reinterpretation where, for example, suppliers can be vendors, customers, competitors, and partners all at the same time. While the shape of the environment is unknowable, it can both be estimated – for example through scenario planning – and, to a certain extent, influenced.

Organisations need strategies that address both the current and envisaged future competitive environments. Business strategies that address the current environment are generally based upon a consideration of meeting customer needs, securing a strong position in the industry, optimising financial returns, enhancing existing competencies, and developing employees. Business strategies that deal with the shaping of the future environment must set aside the current assumptions about the industry. Instead, business leaders combine imagination and acumen to shape and craft the future sources of competitive advantage in ways that best suit the organisation's resources and competencies.

Business strategies tend to be broad statements of direction and intent. Hence, starting with those strategies, business leaders identify the business objectives to be achieved. Business objectives should be specific, quantified and have timescales by which they are to be achieved.

Business leaders monitor, evaluate and agree the strategic direction and business objectives that the organisation is to pursue. They also prioritise the business objectives so that resources can be directed appropriately. They ensure each objective is quantified with measurable outcomes and timescales.

Stakeholders

Stakeholders are individuals, groups or organisations that are interdependent with the organisation's strategy and can exert power over whether or not the strategy and objectives are achieved. The sources of stakeholder power can be financial resources, knowledge, access to the media, or critical competencies and capabilities. Stakeholders can be external to the organisation, for example customers, suppliers and regulators, and internal to the organisation, for example the parent company and the staff. Organisations identify their stakeholders by assessing which groups are likely to impact business objectives. However, some stakeholders are self-justifying. For example, many organisations and institutions may not select pressure groups such as Greenpeace as a stakeholder, but that does not stop Greenpeace from appointing themselves as a 'stakeholding' wielder of power.

Organisations rarely have an explicit prioritisation of stakeholders. That can lead to implicit prioritisation taking place in an ad hoc manner, as each internal business functional group seeks to optimise its relationship with that stakeholder with which it has the most contact. This will generally be to the partial exclusion, and therefore to the detrimental neglect, of the other stakeholders. Or, alternatively it can lead to the stretching of scarce resources in an attempt to address the needs of all stakeholders, resulting in all stakeholders being poorly satisfied.

In order to identify the company's most critical business processes, it is important that the management identify, agree upon and prioritise their stakeholders.

Expectations

Stakeholders have expectations of the organisation. 'Expectations' is an umbrella term used here to include not only specific requirements, but also their needs, wants, and any legal obligations that the organisation has to address. Stakeholders whose expectations are satisfactorily addressed are more likely either to exert their power in a way that is beneficial to the organisation or to reduce the deleterious use of that power over the organisation's strategy and objectives.

However, once organisations identify their stakeholders' expectations they realise that there are inherent conflicts between them, such that they cannot all be satisfied at the same time and to a satisfactory level. Moreover, while a stakeholder might well have an expectation, the organisation may not actually *want* to satisfy it. Hence, business leaders need to segment the stakeholders' expectations according to whether they wish to 'satisfy' the expectation, 'create' an expectation that the stakeholder does not have currently, 'modify' the expectation in some way, or eliminate the expectation altogether. That last option – elimination – is often the least well managed because this requires the organisation to say 'no' to a stakeholder. Hence, expectations continue to be met even though people in the organisation know that this should cease.

There is also the option for a company to create an expectation that the stakeholder did not know they had, and in recent years the attempt to do this is a characteristic of a number of companies which have chosen innovative ways to bring their product to market, not least through the development of e-business, although internet access is now firmly within the scope of existing stakeholder expectations.

In order fully to understand the stakeholders' expectations, each one must be measured in terms that are relevant to that stakeholder. A variety of measurement units can be used, including time, cost, accuracy and quality, but whatever is chosen, the managers need to understand the metrics attached to each measure and the extent to which their organisation is actually delivering against the expectations.

They also need to understand the extent and nature of conflicts between the expectations of their different stakeholders. The conflicts need to be resolved or, at the very least, it must be recognised that people in the existing functional structure, who are required to deliver against the conflicting expectations, are attempting to meet mutually exclusive goals. Resolution is obviously the better option in terms of efficiency, and the managers have to decide which of the expectations will be met, modified, created or eliminated. Such a decision will then determine the allocation of resources, via identified business process.

Business Processes

Business processes are derived from stakeholder expectations. If this definition is adopted, it precludes any and every activity in the organisation being labelled a process, or a collection of activities such as that in Figure 1.1, where the arbitrary boundary has been drawn according to functional limits. Many companies have defined their processes in this way, and in the short term it allows the management team to avoid messy turf and political battles. Over time, however, each ill-defined 'process' is redesigned in ways that make integration of the functions difficult, as we shall see in later chapters.

One particularly virulent adverse consequence of defining process within functions becomes apparent as the information systems department are asked to develop or enhance applications that meet the requirements of one functional unit but not those of another. Many managers in companies which have seen the 'process' light admit privately that their organisation took several months, if not years, to recover from defining 'functions' or 'silos' as processes.

Another technique often used to define processes begins with a map or flowchart of the current activities performed by people. These maps are often depicted in the form of swim lane diagrams, depicting the inputs to and outputs from different departments. Once the map is completed, current activities are grouped together and labelled as a process. The basis of clustering current activities into a process is often unclear, though. Furthermore, the merits of beginning a change programme with such mapping are increasingly being questioned. The cynic might suggest that 'process' mapping is an excellent way of not actually doing anything at all, and certainly it has been used as a way of diverting attention from the changes that are needed. However, such mapping also tends to restrict the scope of those who are seeking to introduce change by directing the thinking along the lines of current practice and organisation. While non-value-add activities can be identified and removed, and while chronological disconnects, duplications, and so on may be identified, the basic structure is rarely questioned. The lanes in which the staff must swim are seen as immutable. While a suggestion that this is the desired outcome for many of those involved might also be dismissed as cynical, the experience of the case studies described in the following chapters provides quite compelling evidence in support of such a notion.

Whatever the merits and demerits of 'process' mapping as a tool, business leaders need to be in a position to define processes in a manner that is neither arbitrary nor constrained by the company's current organisational structure. The linkage of stakeholders' expectations to processes ensures that the scope of the processes is cross-functional, and this avoids the trap of labelling individual, existing, functions and activities as processes. In this way it also removes the restrictions on the achievable degree of change.

Processes that are linked to stakeholder expectations and, hence, to business objectives, are self-renewing. This means that where an expectation of a stakeholder changes, so the process that meets the expectation needs to adapt accordingly. A significant and rapid shift in expectations may require the process to undergo a radical change. Similarly, where business leaders change the organisation's strategy as a consequence of shifts in the external environment – as in the situation discussed in the introduction and in the next chapter covering the drivers for change – or where they reprioritise the business objectives so, in response, will one or more processes need to be adapted.

Business leaders need to decide and agree the basis upon which they will define business processes, and have this formally agreed. Individuals in each process should be explicitly aware of the particular stakeholders' expectations for which they are responsible. Measures should be attached to each expectation and business objective and should be binding upon the appropriate process. For example, if customers expect deliveries in 3 days, 100% accurate bills and 100% accurate information presented only in graphical format, then these expectations and measures have to be delivered by the process, and should be used to evaluate the success of that process.

For many organisations, managing according to processes – as opposed to functions or to arbitrary process definitions – is still new, and we shall see below how the failure to do so not only creates significant business issues, but presents a formidable barrier to the resolution of those issues.

Such a comment provides an appropriate start point for our investigation of radical process-based change, but to complete the picture of what a process is, we should take the description down one more level to the process constituents – the activities pictured in Figure 1.2 which make it up – and provide a definition of exactly what these are.

Activities

The term 'activity' incorporates the work, roles, responsibilities and tasks that one or more individuals perform as their 'day job'. At a more formal level activities are contained in job descriptions, work profiles or individual work plans. An activity, when considered in isolation of other activities, adds only cost to an organisation.

An example might be 'take customer orders'. Regardless of the high level of efficiency or effectiveness with which this activity is performed, it, of and by itself, is unlikely to lead to financial prosperity. The organisation will have incurred a cost (e.g. paying sales people) and received little benefit if *only* this activity is performed. It is only once the 'take customer orders' activity is combined with other activities such as production, distribution and billing that the organisation adds value. This does not mean that individual activities are unimportant or that they should not be undertaken. However, it becomes apparent that performing any one activity is a cost to the organisation, until it is integrated with other activities to produce or deliver something of value to an external stakeholder. Hence, activities performed in different functions must be co-ordinated and integrated in a business process, which satisfies stakeholder expectations.

This description of activities reinforces the point made in the previous section about the restrictions imposed by so-called 'process' mapping. Where this is based on current activities, it is highly introspective. Organisations that begin to flowchart current activities find that people latch onto the past and the historical evolutionary developments made to their current job. Organisations have also found that people react defensively when having to expose their job to scrutiny. As a consequence, people have difficulty in considering the ways in which the processes 'should be' organised in the future, and little change is proposed, let alone implemented.

To link all our definitions from bottom-up, the activities should be designed such that they provide what is necessary to make up the process of which they form a part. That process delivers against the stakeholder expectations which the business objectives specifically target, according to the overall business strategy. In that way any single activity – each of every person's 'day-job' tasks – can be linked to that element of the business strategy to which it contributes, through the vital medium of the integrated business process.

Summary

This book defines a business 'process' to mean the co-ordination and integration of activities performed in different functions (or departments) to create outputs that are of value to one or more stakeholder. Hence, the characteristics that specify business processes are:

- Processes add value to stakeholders. In the context of this book, the phrase 'adds value' means addressing external and internal stakeholders' expectations.
- Processes co-ordinate those activities that people 'should' undertake to address stakeholders' expectations. The implications are that other activities currently undertaken are superfluous to a business process and a set of activities constitute a process when linked explicitly to stakeholder expectations.
- Processes cross functional boundaries. This means that intra-functional or intradepartmental operations form only part/s of a process rather than being processes in their own right.

Let us go back to consider X department illustrated in Figure 1.1. Within that department a number of activities were being undertaken, and around some of them an arbitrary line had been drawn. It is reproduced in Figure 1.3 without that arbitrary 'process' line.

Given our definitions of processes and the activities which constitute them, it is clear that, assuming the activities have been designed in a sensible business manner, they will all form part of a process, as illustrated when X department becomes the middle of the three departments shown in Figure 1.4.

Here we can see how each process 'travels' through the departments as it takes an original customer requirement – or stakeholder expectation – and satisfies, or hopefully exceeds it. We shall see later

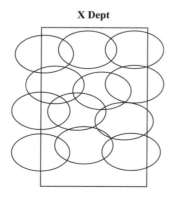

Figure 1.3 *The conglomeration of activities within X department*

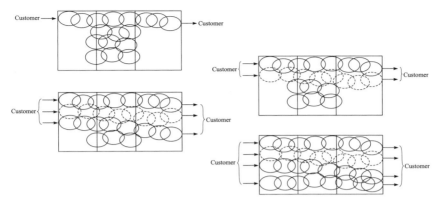

Figure 1.4 *Departmental activities contributing to various processes in a linear depiction*

how this linear description greatly simplifies the actual case, where work items 'travel' back and forth between departments, and are split into several different, sometimes simultaneous, paths through those departments. The point of the diagrams, though, is to provide a backdrop to the fact that the decision to split the activities between the various functions and to enshrine those functions as the building blocks of the company organisation has been an important factor in both the creation of the need for process-based change and in the prevention of its successful achievement. That is not to say that the functional structure should be removed – such a suggestion would be overambitious to the point of being unworkable – but the realisation of the restrictions imposed by that structure is vitally important, as we will see in the following chapters.

The functional organisation is not only enshrined in almost every company's past and present, but it is also firmly ensconced in the staff psyche. People describe 'what they do' in terms of the function in which they work or the activities which they undertake. 'I am a distribution manager'; 'I am an underwriter'; 'I work in finance'. It rarely occurs to these people that in fact their activities form part of one or more processes, and that it is these processes which address the stakeholder expectations rather than just being 'what they do'. The distribution manager, for example, organises those activities which conclude the process of satisfying the customer requirement which started with an order for whatever is being distributed. The underwriter is performing a function within, say, a new business process which culminates in the provision of a life assurance policy. No customer wants simply to be 'underwritten' with no other goal in mind. And for the finance executive: sadly, very few companies have the luxury of being able to send out invoices or receive payments without performing a service or providing goods for which they can charge!

As we shall see in the succeeding chapters, it is this ingrained habit of thinking in terms of function, reinforced by functionally based targets, measurements, bonuses, budgets and even internal competition, which sometimes gets in the way of the desired end-point – the satisfaction of a customer expectation. Only processes can achieve this, and then only if the activities within them are properly designed and aligned. Those working in many companies do not align the activities appropriately because they do not have a definition of a process. They lack the definition because they lack the very notion of a process. In the cases of our example studies below, the realisation that specific processes were required to satisfy their customers came only when any alternative would have been insufficient to stave off financial disaster. Lesson one for a reader of this book might well be to consider your own business processes before a market crisis forces you to do so.

T W O

Why Change?

'We need to be convinced, Parsons,' George Downs told his new Customer Services Director, Alan Parsons, at the board meeting. 'Change is disruptive. We've been doing things the same way in Downs Tools for 27 years. If there was a better way of doing them don't you think we'd have done it 27 years ago?'

He reached for his glass – a carved stone chalice – and sipped water that had fallen as snow on a prehistoric Antarctic.

'Things have changed in the last 27 years,' Parsons pointed out, reasonably.

'Well, yes. You were born for a start,' rejoined June Brown, and sensed Downs's half smile with satisfaction.

'Our customer service badly needs improvement,' Parsons continued, ignoring Brown. 'It's damaging the firm's reputation, business and profits.'

'How do you draw that conclusion? The number of complaints hasn't risen in the last two months.'

'No, but the number of customers available to make complaints has fallen. If you like to do it on statistics, the average number of complaints per customer has risen.'

'To what?'

'Well, the figure doesn't mean much but we get one complaint for every 100 customers now.'

'Sounds good to me: 99% happy.'

'Not necessarily. What about the ones who don't complain, but just leave? What about the new customers who would come here if the word of mouth about our firm wasn't a four-lettered one?'

Downs twisted in his chair, causing a slight squeak to emanate from the white rhino leather which covered it, and pointed to the graph on the mahogany-panelled wall behind him, between the Picasso and the Rembrandt.

'How do you explain that then, Parsons? Those figures never lie.'

The red line rose steadily from the bottom left-hand corner towards the top right. Downs beamed at an upward trend that would have defeated Hillary and Tensing.

'Ah, yes, that.'

Parsons stood up and waded through the deep pile of the carpet to the framed graph. He took the bottom left-hand corner firmly between finger and thumb and lifted it so that it became the top left-hand corner. The peak of the graph suddenly found itself as a nadir, while the downward track towards it was now the sort that a theme park would splash on its advertising to enthuse kids and scare their parents. It clearly terrified Downs, who gripped the carved ivory arms of his chair.

'What are you doing, Parsons? Stop that! My profits!'

'The frame came loose some time ago. Profits have actually been falling sharply and steadily for six months. At this rate we'll go bust in less than a year.'

Downs dragged his gaze back from the ghastly truth and looked around the table, expecting to see his own shocked reaction reflected there. No one met his eye.

'You all knew, didn't you. Why did no one tell me?' He waited while a tumbleweed rolled gently across the far end of the room. 'You all allowed me to believe that we were doing well, and no one had the guts to say any differently. You're all just a bunch of yesmen.' He suddenly turned on Brown. 'Isn't that so, Brown?'

She looked up, while her brain searched for an answer that wasn't … that wasn't … 'Yes, Mr Downs, sir.'

Downs stared at her for a moment, but snapped his glare away before she suffered permanent damage. He laid it instead on the bringer of the tidings, who was retaking his seat. 'Okay, Parsons, I'm convinced. We need to improve Customer Service. You're now my new Change Director. So see to it.'

'Yes sir.'

Parsons reached forwards and lifted his own chalice from the board table. The liquid inside seethed and gave off a poisonous green smoke ...

* * *

Introduction

Why change? The old adage used to be 'If it ain't broke, don't fix it', and in the days when the marketplace was a slow-moving beast that might have been sound advice. Today, a reluctance to change based on favourable internal conditions is akin to standing still in the middle of a race, since any company not seeking constant improvements will quickly see their competition disappearing into the distance. In the fictional scene above something clearly *is* broken and requires fixing. There is a very obvious, convincing driver for change here, and current thinking is that organisations must be presented with such drivers before they will initiate radical change, including that based on processes.[2] The drivers are considered to fall into the category of either threats, as above, or opportunities. Identified threats include increased competitor activity,[3] severe economic downturns,[4] industry changes,[5] and outdated working practices that no longer satisfy stakeholder expectations.[6] Opportunities include the development of new competencies,[7] new product introductions,[8] and improving customer service.[9]

As the fictional managing director George Downs said, though, 'We need to be convinced.' An attempted change will not be successful if the rationale behind it is not supported within the organisation. So in order to create a case that can be used to gain that support, the change drivers must be real and convincing to a broad cross-section of people in the organisation. Current wisdom concludes that people must be satisfied that a threat often referred to as a 'burning platform' or an opportunity exists before the need for radical change is embraced.

That sounds logical, but is it backed up by the facts, and does it oversimplify the case? Let us consider the evidence drawn from the case studies.

CASE STUDIES

CARTON CARRIER

The first is a company we shall call Carton Carrier. Carton Carrier is the distribution and delivery division of one of the UK's largest retailers, which we shall refer to as General Merchandise Retailers plc (GMR). Within GMR there are four divisions: Home Merchandise, Financial Services, Information Services, and Carton Carrier. Each division operates as a business unit, in the form of a limited liability company. GMR's largest division is Home Merchandise, and its main line of business is the direct sale, to end customers, of a wide range of household and clothing products. It is one of the largest companies in its marketplace, and Carton Carrier is the distribution and delivery division that supports the Home Merchandise sales operation.

So what started Carton Carrier's change initiative? Did it identify drivers for change? Were they threats or opportunities? If so, what made them convincing? The situation at the time is described below, largely from the testimony of interviewed staff.

To set the scene: every evening each of Carton Carrier's 36 depots received parcels for delivery in its pre-defined geographical area. Trailers, each carrying between 8000 and 10000 parcels from the GMR warehouse, arrived at the depots where the parcels were off-loaded. The night staff separated the parcels into about 60 separate 'rounds' – one for each of the drivers employed at the depot. Each pile of parcels was placed on what were called the drivers' 'pads', large cages from which the driver would then select parcels for delivery. Records were kept of the total number of parcels which were received on any one night, and also of the number which were booked out by the drivers, so that a tally of those remaining could be maintained. The records were purely 'hash totals' however, recording no more information than the numbers of parcels received, dispatched, and remaining.

Generally, about 200 parcels were chosen by each driver for his next round, and that selection was almost random. The customer might assume that priority would be given to those which had first arrived at the depot, but that was not actually the case. There were some criteria for choosing the parcels, but date was not one of them. Ease of the delivery round certainly played a part, though. As one of the depot managers from the time explained it …

If you (the customer) lived in a tower block on the 23rd floor and you'd ordered a bike, you might have got it in six months time. You might not get it ever because the driver didn't want to go to your flat. So he'd just leave it there (in the depot) because it was a pain in the bum to take it up there (to the customer).

The services manager provides another example of the selection criteria.

Drivers would go to their cages of parcels and say 'Oh Christ not that address – it's got an Alsatian!' (Services Manager)

Any parcels which were chosen but not delivered for any reason were returned to the pile on the driver's 'pad' where they awaited selection once more. That next selection would be based on similar criteria, and if the first attempt at delivery had proved problematic, the second might not be made for some time. This resulted in some fairly spectacular delivery periods. A visit by Carton Carrier's management to the depot in Malham one January discovered a parcel that had been in that depot since the previous May. The services manager who passed on that particular story admitted that the depot manager would not thank him for repeating it, but one imagines that the customer would be even less impressed!

It is clear to the outsider, and with some benefit from hindsight it was evident also to those in Carton Carrier, that the drivers were the ones who controlled the parcel delivery process, and not the depot managers or their superiors.

The combination of the almost random parcel selection procedure and the lack of information on parcel movement (apart from the total numbers) also meant that information which could be made available to enquiring customers was severely limited. The exact location of a particular parcel was unknown, as was the likely date of its delivery. Equally unknown were the chances of it being selected for delivery at any point in the foreseeable future. Those answering the phones would be aware that there might be a driver whose round took him into the vicinity of the caller, but what he was carrying was a mystery. Perhaps a better idea of the potential delivery period could have been ascertained if the enquiring customer was asked if they owned a large dog!

So why was the situation allowed to reach this stage? The answer is that it had grown up over time to be the accepted state of affairs. From an internal view, it was based on a perfectly reasonable premise. Those in the depots – the drivers certainly and their managers tacitly – saw the delivery of a certain number of parcels as being the be-all and end-all of their job. Again, looking from the outside, or looking from the perspective of the customer, it does seem a very parochial point of view, but from inside the depots no other was considered. Besides which, this internal focus was engendered and condoned by the board and senior managers. The driver's job was to deliver parcels, full stop. That delivery was not seen as part of a much wider process which involved not only activities outside of the depot, but outside of Carton Carrier; namely within the Home Merchandise division with which the customer had made the first contact. So long as 200 parcels were collected by each driver, nothing needed to change. In the words of one of the drivers …

> We used to do what we thought was a fair day's work. I'd come in in the morning and I'd sort out maybe 200 parcels for what I thought would be a good area, and which I knew I could cope with.

The personnel manager summed up the mind-set:

> 200 parcels was, to use a well worn GMR (Transport) phrase, 'a good day's work'.

Which particular parcels did not matter, as the depot staff, from management to drivers, did not see their purpose as being the fulfilment of the order which had been placed with the Home Merchandise division. The customers, though, obviously did, since the process which they initiated by placing their order would only be concluded with its delivery.

One would expect that the customers would quickly make their feelings known, and would move their business from Carton Carrier, and that the internal realisation of that would result in steps being rapidly taken to improve service. That did not immediately happen, though, for two reasons. Firstly, although customers were starting to complain about the length of the delivery period and the inconsistency of successive delivery periods, mail order customers were known by Carton Carrier to be very forgiving. The theory within Carton Carrier, to use the words of one regional general manager, was that the customers were largely 'working class', and therefore saw themselves and the drivers as 'kin'. For that reason the complaints stopped short of the point where they might get someone into trouble. Furthermore, to a certain extent, the customers of Home Merchandise – and hence Carton Carrier – had to shop where they could get credit, and therefore had little alternative but to stick with Carton Carrier. 'They had to put up with whatever we dished out to them' was one phrase used which might be considered something less than entirely customer satisfying. But despite that, the pressure for change built only slowly from the end consumers of the parcel delivery process.

The second reason for the lack of internal pressure for change was the perceived relationship between Carton Carrier and Home Merchandise. As far as Carton Carrier was concerned, its main customer was Home Merchandise, and they couldn't 'walk' because they were committed to using the delivery arm of their sister company, that is Carton Carrier.

Since it did not matter what service levels were provided either to Home Merchandise or to the end customer, these were not even considered as benchmarks for a job well done. Instead the only measure of 'a good day's work' was the number of parcels that a driver loaded each morning.

In terms of our discussion in the previous chapter, the priority given to satisfying stakeholder expectations – whether the external customer or the internal 'supplier' – was not high.

Another problem with focusing on 'a good day's work' rather than on satisfying stakeholder expectations was that when more than 200 parcels, per driver, were delivered to the depots, the assumed standard was not sufficient to clear them. The response, though, was not to increase the delivery effort, but to allow a backlog to build up. The visit to Malham depot mentioned above which discovered the antique parcel also discovered that the depot was currently home to 82 000 undelivered items, and that there were another 27 trailers in attendance which had not yet been emptied into the already full drivers' pads. These parcels, as we have seen, would be delivered over time with no particular regard for the end customers' expectations, or the requirements of Home Merchandise, at the rate of 200 a day by a staff who truly believed they were adequately performing their function.

That discovery itself might have been enough to tip the scales in favour of remedial action. But, to add further impetus, the situation at the Malham depot became apparent during a time when competition in the market was becoming significant. This gave the customers more of an alternative when Carton Carrier's service levels failed to meet their expectations.

Industry changes, which affected Home Merchandise's growth, were reflected in press reports at the time. The competitors began to offer an equal or greater range of products. A few years before the process change project was initiated most customers had a catalogue from only one company, and were spoilt for choice as each catalogue often held 1000 pages with 50 000 different items from which to select. By the time of Carton Carrier management's January visit to the Malham depot, 55% of customers with one catalogue were likely to have a competitor's catalogue as well. This, in a stagnating market, led to a limited amount of total customer expenditure being spread ever more thinly across competitors. Home Merchandise, along with those competitors, therefore increased the number of catalogues distributed; some companies nearly doubled the number they circulated. In 3 years the number of catalogues sent out by Home Merchandise rose from 3.7 million to 5.7 million. The average number of customers per agent fell from twelve to less than three over a 10-year period. Modest sales increases were generated only by huge promotional spending.

This was also a time when the economy of the UK was on an upturn. Against that background of improving national economic performance credit was becoming easier to obtain, as banks, credit card companies, and retailers all offered less restrictive terms. The wide range of product choice, coupled with the more ready availability of credit, meant that customers were becoming far less willing to accept poor levels of service.

It is not difficult to see the drivers for change – at least the threats – and perhaps these would have been sufficient to initiate some action within Carton Carrier. But the company's board members and senior managers also identified an opportunity here, and this added to the impetus for a change initiative. The aim was to redefine the customer in the minds of the depot managers and delivery drivers. It is difficult to say who the drivers at the time thought their customer was, if they had any such definition in mind at all. Although it might not have been explicitly stated, the drivers' apparent customer was the depot manager, since the requirement from that quarter – of a 200 per day parcel delivery target – was the one, and only, which the drivers strove to meet. The identified opportunity was to change that mind-set such that the consumer became the end customer of the parcel delivery process; the one who had initiated that process through placing the order with Home Merchandise and within which the ultimate activity was delivery. The drivers should then start to see their 'job' not as delivering a 'good day's work' worth of parcels but of meeting, and exceeding, the expectations of the end customers.

If that mind-set could be changed, then the notion of the parcel delivery process itself would become apparent, and that would allow the senior managers the opportunity of co-ordinating the whole of the order fulfilment process across both Home Merchandise and Carton Carrier. The management wanted to seek improvement of the levels of service offered to end customers by taking control of all

the activities performed to deliver a parcel. One of the most important of those activities in terms of customer satisfaction was the
choice of parcels to be delivered, and management sought to take
control of that in the wider process context. The fact that, ultimately,
they did so is demonstrated in the words of one of the drivers after
the project's completion.

*Decisions about which parcels would be delivered were taken
out of drivers' hands. All our jobs are now planned for us and
we can only take out what they want us to take.*

Without the identification and acceptance of the opportunities – to
redefine the customer, to change the mind-set, to introduce the
notion of process, and to take control of the whole process –
although change might have occurred, it is unlikely that a radical
process-based change initiative would have been undertaken.

The conclusion from this one case study is that we should not
draw a distinction between finding threats *or* opportunities, but
rather look for *both* when considering those drivers for change
which can be used to gain people's support.

FOUNDRY INSURANCE

Foundry Insurance is the engineering insurance subsidiary of
Composite Insurers plc., one of the four largest insurance companies
in the UK. A major part of Foundry Insurance's business is the
inspection and insurance of boiler, mechanical and electrical plant.
Its engineers inspect the plant to ensure that it conforms to health
and safety legislation, and the company insures organisations against
plant breakdown and third party damage. The organisation has a
wide range of customers – from corner garages to nuclear power
stations – and a long heritage. In the mid-nineteenth century
manufacturing industry began using high-pressure boilers which,
due to poor design, neglect, or both, often exploded, resulting in a
loss of life and business. A group of high-pressure boiler users
formed the 'Steam Users Association', and a few members banded

together to offer a service that inspected and ensured the quality, design and safety aspects of the machinery. Foundry Insurance grew out of this service and since then has provided services in response to changes in health and safety legislation.

Prior to the change initiative being undertaken, Foundry Insurance's inspection service operated in a highly paper-intensive and individualistic manner, with each surveyor working in his own way, but none armed with anything more technologically advanced than a portable typewriter. Often, for these and other reasons, the service provided to the customer was well below standard.

The surveyor would typically spend the first half of the working day inspecting a customer's plant and equipment, and would then type a report of that inspection in the afternoon. Since some clients required up to five copies of the report, this involved a large number of sheets and carbon paper, so that if anyone actually wanted to read the bottom copy they would require a pair of corrective glasses and a good imagination! The various surveyors produced reports with different typefaces and different layouts. Mistakes were painted out with correcting fluid on all the copies, and some had added hand-written changes.

For the customers, who paid considerable amounts for the surveys, this report was the only deliverable. It was no secret at the time, and was even more evident in hindsight, that the low standard of the reports was not going to impress those paying customers.

Furthermore, diverse reports from different regions but for the same client would often end up at a central customer location, where the differences in content, style and presentation would be noticed. And due to different procedures in separate regions, the same customer was told that Foundry Insurance could do things in one region, but not in another. Foundry Insurance appeared fragmented, with various parts of the company governed by different corporate standards, and all of those standards pretty low. Customer service did not appear to be high on its list of priorities, and for the most part that appearance was not deceptive.

Regardless of these inherent problems, though, business was very good. In fact, as the engineering manager put it, at that time they had 'more business than they could cope with'. And that of course brought further problems for the already neglected notion of customer service when the administration departments began to get overwhelmed.

To give an example: the surveyors' reports passed through Head Office for 'acceptance' before being issued to the client. That acceptance involved large amounts of data being input onto a basic computer system and the movement of vast quantities of paper. The managing director recalls a tour of the Head Office during which he approached an acceptance engineer at his desk ...

> *Well I think he was at a desk, but all you could see was paper all around him. I said to this chap 'You seem to be struggling a bit here', and he said 'Well it's not as bad as it was, the backlog used to be six months. It's only five months today, it's improving.' That was typical of our organisation at the time.*

So the reports for regionally located plant for the same client might very well take different periods to be completed and delivered, as well as being of disparate and low standards when they did arrive.

Furthermore, in most cases, statutory regulations set out the required frequency of the inspection. Failure to meet the statutory deadlines left customers exposed to censure under law and affected whether or not they could operate their plant. Foundry Insurance's contractual obligation with its customers stipulated plant inspections within the timescales determined by law, and yet there was a growing backlog of late inspections.

The situation was no different in the issuing of new policies, which was also undertaken at Head Office, after passing through several different preparatory functions. One department calculated the number of days cover required, while another calculated the cost of that cover. Another department calculated premium information, and yet another typed the policy. A final department checked the details, and if any errors were found, the embryonic policy went back to the start again. Given the amount of business that was being serviced at the time, it is not surprising that it could take anything from 3 to 12 months actually to issue the policy.

Each department did its own pile of work and had the pressure of volume with which to contend. And of course, when there is a constant struggle to clear the piles of work in a functional department, that department has little time – or incentive – to consider the wider process of which its activities form a part. Already we can see similarities between Foundry Insurance and the earlier case of Carton Carrier: the insular, parochial view of the activity being undertaken in a department being the totality of the job, with no reference to a wider process perspective. The words of the deputy managing director make this point clear.

> *Managers were really just supervisors of functions. 'My job is to do this.' I can quote a guy who was in charge of the policy production department. When somebody wanted a policy as a matter of priority, he was very upset because it upset his scheme of things. 'Here's my pile of priorities, and I work through this pile. Now you want this one instead! That's very upsetting because it's going to put this one back', and so on. The fact that the customer's screaming like mad wasn't his concern. 'I've got my job to do.' I think one of the major failures was that we weren't too worried about providing a service to our customers, and therefore that's why we were going downhill.*

The same disregard for end customer satisfaction as we saw in Carton Carrier eventually manifested itself in the same inevitable result; customers began to leave. In Foundry Insurance this was not an action taken lightly, as clients tended to stay with their insurance company for long periods. It was an action which some very significant clients *were* beginning to take, though, and just before the new managing director joined, Foundry Insurance lost the biggest contract of its type in the UK market to a competitor.

The area where fundamental change was needed was not difficult to see. The realisation began to dawn that the end customers were the life blood of the company and Foundry Insurance had better start looking after them. What really was the last and most significant

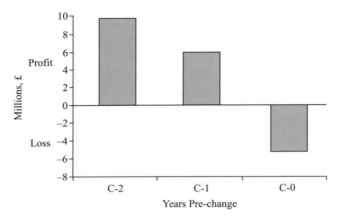

Figure 2.1 *Foundry Insurance profit/loss*

straw for what must have been a sagging camel's back, though, was the effect on the bottom line. Figure 2.1 shows what happened to the profits of Foundry Insurance in the 3 years prior to the change project being initiated.

While the state of customer service within Foundry Insurance might have been something that could be obscured from the view of Composite Insurer, the profit and loss figures were not. The new managing director of Foundry Insurance reckoned that after what he referred to as the 'staggering loss' of almost £7 million, shown above, the company had at best 2 years to turn things round before their parent company terminated the subsidiary.

Once again, the drivers for change which can be classified as threats are quite clear. There were deep flaws in the business process, with a highly fragmented inspection service, involving significant duplication and repetition, while reams of paper passed between Head Office and the engineers. Long-standing customers were beginning to move to competitors as service standards fell and Foundry Insurance had unfulfilled contractual obligations. Finally, and most visibly, the company suffered its first financial loss. They were powerful threats indeed. They were tipped over the edge to crisis proportions by the realisation that in less than 2 years the parent company might well pull the plug. Foundry Insurance would disappear down the resultant hole.

But the board also saw an opportunity here. They had recognised the fragmentation and the different standards of output and service provided. They recognised too that it resulted from the lack of control which they, the management, had over the conduct of inspections, and the administration involved in issuing reports and policies. The management saw the chance to bring all activities which affected customer service under their control, instead of leaving them to the devices of individual engineers and diverse department heads. In that way control of the whole process could be regained and the company set on a better footing to recover to a profit-making position.

The management of Foundry Insurance accepted drivers for change which were both opportunities and threats, and without that acceptance, the radical process-based change initiative would not have happened.

Drivers for Change

The conditions that existed in both Carton Carrier and Foundry Insurance which resulted in the commencement of their radical process-based change initiatives were not, and are not, exceptional. Research has unearthed many examples in diverse market sectors. For example, an administration functionary in a large pension company sent a request for information to one of the salesmen, in order that the installation of a new policy could be completed. The salesman gave the request a low priority because the information was difficult to obtain and did not affect the timing of his commission payment. The unanswered request was therefore followed by duplicates and reminders, until, eventually, the administration manager sent a birthday card to congratulate the original memo on its first anniversary!

A company which we shall call Software Inc. provided a case study in the field of radical process-based change, and, as mentioned in the introductory chapter, we shall call on its evidence when it is apposite. The company implemented systems which enabled customers to receive information from a number of external sources. When business volumes grew by a factor of four in a short period, largely due to deregulation in its marketplace, the weaknesses in Software Inc.'s order process were made clear, largely by customers complaining about lead times, errors, and late and incorrect invoicing. Up to 15 different people in five different functional departments – sales, technical, finance, purchasing, and customer training – were involved in completing an order from sale to installation, and spent much of their time pushing bits of paper from one department to another. Slowly! The engineers, much like Carton Carrier's drivers, chose an order from their in-trays pretty much at random. Certainly there was little notice taken either of the elapsed time to process the order or of the potential income for Software Inc. once the system was installed. Prioritisation and measurement were no more than ideas in the ether. The diversity of departments, each doing their own job, meant that the orders were often found to be incorrect at the installation stage, and the engineers amended them. No one told the invoicing department, however, so they billed the customer on the expected delivery. The customer queried the payment with the invoicing department and refused to pay, by which time the debt control department, in splendid isolation, had initiated proceedings to recover money from a long-standing customer who, only hours beforehand, might have agreed a revised invoice and payment terms with some other part of the company.

Many companies, if they study their service to the end customer, will find that this service has become subservient to internal functions which should contribute to their 'delivery' process. But instead of contributing, the functions hinder the process by becoming more concerned with their own 'job' in isolation, and ignoring its wider responsibilities. Many become protective – precious, perhaps – about the task which they perform. The credit checkers in Software Inc. described their activity as 'an art, really'. This attitude adds more invisible bricks and mortar to the walls within which the functions operate and further isolates them from others which contribute to the customer-serving process. Not only does this fragmentation and isolation create, sooner or later, a change-driving threat, but it also represents an opportunity to bring the different fragments together in some sort of structure which recognises customer service as its prime goal.

People differ in what convinces them that change is necessary. Some will be convinced by threats against the current or recent prosperity or market position – the kind of threats mentioned in the introduction to this chapter. Some will wait until crisis point is reached, as can be argued to have happened in Foundry Insurance when the managing director reckoned that there were less than 2 years left for the company. Others will be convinced by the sort of opportunities also mentioned above – the chance to make improvements which will strengthen the company. It is the acceptance by people within the organisation of those drivers for change – of the need, the imperative, for change – that will allow change to commence. Seeking to identify both the threats *and* the opportunities acting as drivers for change is a strategy which will give the change initiative the greatest chance of getting off the drawing board.

The 'E-' Change Driver

The drivers for change which we have seen in the two case studies arose because an opportunity was seen which, when taken, would stave off a threat. Once the trees were cleared to allow a view of the wood, the threats became obvious, and in identifying the opportunity, so too did the area in which the action had to be taken (if not the action itself, as we shall see). However, drivers for change do not always arise through internal factors such as the organisational structure causing discontinuities in important customer-serving processes. External factors can arise as drivers as well, and as both threats and opportunities. Today, the most obvious change driver is the advent of the internet and its implications for the way business is conducted.

Some will see e-business as a threat in that it brings the possibility for a new company to revolutionise the marketplace. Customers can access information and products from in front of their computer terminal or television screen. Expertise can be made available on-line instantaneously. Comparisons of cost and quality can be made through third party organisations, where before such comparisons were so arduous that they were rarely undertaken and then only half-heartedly. 'If we don't react to this quickly, our business will plummet', is an argument that has been clearly reverberating around many a board room for a few years now. Every company rushed to get a website up and, if not running, at least giving the impression of movement. For the most part, in the early days of the technology, websites were little more than multipage billboards as companies recognised that they had to do something on a tactical basis, but were not quite sure what to do strategically. The most common reaction appeared to be that the threat needed a response.

Some however, see the internet as an opportunity, and this class is not only filled with new companies taking advantage of the low rent of a website when compared to a high street presence. Existing companies see the technology as a new way of accessing their customers, and of accessing those who had not been customers before. A new way of advertising, of getting their brand name known and their message across. The most enlightened see the internet as a possible new way of undertaking processes which had formerly required paper and staff – how might Foundry Insurance's process have been streamlined if they could have got their customers to supply information on-line which fed directly into some policy-producing software?

Whatever type of driver was interpreted, the internet certainly brought, and continues to bring, changes, and it is surprising now to find a company which does not have a web presence. Some, certainly, see the technology as nothing more than a flash-in-the-pan, which will have no longer term impact on the way business is conducted. It is these companies – the ones who simply do not *accept* the driver for change – who either pay no more than lip service by authorising static websites which add nothing to their processes and much to their overheads, or who decline to play the new game at all. It is these who, tomorrow, will perhaps see the error of their early dismissal of this change driver in terms of dwindling market share.

Once again, drivers for change must be recognised as the threats and/or the opportunities they represent. Those drivers must then be accepted before change can happen. This brings us to our first axiom.

Conclusion

> **Axiom for change: 1**
> **Radical process-based change is more likely to be achieved when people accept the organisation's drivers for change, which can be both opportunities and threats.**

Where does your Company stand?

There are bound to be drivers for change within, and without, your company:

- Are they mainly threats?
- Have you tried to identify any opportunities which might also be present?
- In addressing the threats do any opportunities present themselves?
- Are the drivers for change universally recognised in the company?
- Are they recognised at a level high enough to instigate some action?
- Are the drivers for change sufficient to initiate a radical change initiative?
- Once that suggestion is mooted, will the acceptance of the change drivers be strong enough to withstand the initial, probably adverse reaction to proposed change?
- By stressing the opportunities as well as the threats, will that tip the balance in favour of acceptance?

THREE

Why Process-based Change?

Alan Parsons passed the last cup of coffee around the table and addressed the gathering. 'I've called this meeting to discuss what we can do to turn the situation round.'

'Why are *we* all here?' asked June Brown, the Deputy MD, indicating the rest of the directors, most now munching on Danish pastries. 'You're the Change Director. It's your problem.'

'I'm going to need your help. I'm going to need everybody's help come to think of it, but first I want us directors and department heads to throw a few ideas around. The only thing I'd say at the start is that we're looking at big changes, radical ones.'

'We obviously need new computer systems,' said the IT Director.

'To do what?'

'Well, duh! The same as they do now, of course, only faster. And we could use the internet for, um, for, well, stuff. You're the business experts.' He waved a vague hand at the rest and then used it to reach for a Danish pastry, happy with a problem solved.

'We should downsize your Customer Services department, Parsons,' said the Finance Director. 'That would reduce costs.'

'Rightsize,' corrected the Head of Personnel. 'The term is rightsize.'

'"Rightsize?" What does that mean?'

'It means downsize, but it sounds a bit more like a well-thought-out plan rather than a kneejerk reaction.'

'Okay we should "rightsize" the Customer Services department.'

'Is that the answer?' wondered Parsons out loud. 'Customers are leaving because of our overall service. If we're not providing a good service at the moment, how could we provide a better one just by cutting the number of people?'

'Well you wouldn't have so many people making mistakes then, would you. Therefore you get fewer mistakes, and fewer mistakes equals fewer dissatisfied customers. Simple.'

'It's a nice theory. But I think we need something that addresses the root of our poor service quality. We need to look at everything we do. I don't think just concentrating on one department is radical enough.'

'Total Quality is good,' chipped in the new Production Director. 'If we had Total Quality we wouldn't get any complaints. No one would phone up and say that we had done things far too well.'

'Okay, we could try that. How would we go about it?'

'You put up notices. "Quality Comes First" sort of thing.'

'Ye…es.' Parsons tried to encourage some elaboration. 'Then what?'

'Well then everybody does everything well and the customers are happy.'

'But that's all you do?'

'That's what we did in my last company. Loads of posters. Actually ours said "Quality Cones First" by mistake, but the thought was there.'

'Did it work?'

'Not really. People brought in some really nice cones, but it didn't help too much since we sold mortgages. If we'd been an ice-cream company …' He tailed off and took another bite of pastry to indicate a concluded contribution.

'Okay, that's good, but I'm not sure we're addressing the real problem we've got here.' Parsons thought it was about time to make the suggestion that he had hoped might have been forthcoming from someone else. 'The fact is that the left hand of this company doesn't know what the right hand is doing. Each part – each department – may be doing a fine job – a quality job – in their own eyes, but put all the parts together and it simply doesn't add up to what the customer wants. I think we need to do something which crosses the internal boundaries, which brings the teams together in a way that addresses the actual customer requirements. We need to break down the functional silos and address the processes which ultimately serve the customer.'

There was a stunned silence for a moment, then, oh, how they laughed ...

*   *   *

Introduction

The drivers for change have been recognised, and accepted, both as the threats and the opportunities which they may represent. But what change is required? How do we get from the identification that something is needed to the adoption of the type of radical process-based change initiative with which we are concerned? Certainly, the scene above gives one or two insights into why the pursuit of change based on process orientation might not be the next seamless step, after change driver acceptance, on a smooth road towards mercantile nirvana!

Organisations are faced with a number of different options for dealing with their drivers for change. For example, increased competition can be countered through merger or acquisition with that competitor[10] or a third party, or by forming strategic alliances, as has recently been prevalent in the airline industry. Rapidly changing technologies could be addressed by outsourcing to specialist companies.[11] Internal options for change are not limited to addressing process orientation. The most commonly chosen option, sadly, is to build new computer systems. Or worse still, to buy new computer systems from external suppliers and then adapt them beyond recognition to fit in with existing legacy systems and with existing working practices. Both of those approaches are lengthy and often expensive ways of avoiding change altogether, and in later chapters we shall see reasons why such 'frantic inaction' is such a great favourite.

But there are alternatives to process-based change initiatives which are certainly valid. For example, the total quality initiative suggested in the fictional Downs Tools above is perfectly valid under the right circumstances and if undertaken rather more thoroughly than was suggested! In earlier chapters we have already mentioned financial restructuring, reorganisation, downsizing (or rightsizing) and renewal.

Although these options are not the subject of this study, they are certainly valid alternatives which may be considered. Why should a company, having accepted its change drivers, choose a radical process-based change initiative through which to address them?

Some commentators argue that drivers for change lead directly to the need for a radical initiative based on processes, and this is supported by two lines of reasoning. One is that process-based change is the best choice when radical measures are required, since other options are inherently limited.[12] But while the criticisms of those other options may be valid, the argument that, by default, radical process-based change is automatically more appropriate is very weak. Conan Doyle's Sherlock Holmes argued that elimination of the impossible always left only the right answer. In the real world, however, and especially in the realm of business change, not only might there be no one right answer, as we shall see, but new approaches are always being developed, so we cannot be sure that we have eliminated all the 'impossibles' after disregarding other traditional methodologies.

The second line of reasoning is that drivers for change require organisations to achieve radical performance improvements, and that radical process-based change is an effective means of achieving such improvements.[13] Yet initiating such a change project purely on the basis of the performance improvements required can lead to failure,[14,15] as the changes are found to be unacceptable to people within the organisation. People must surely accept the suggested solution and its implications in just the same way as they must accept the drivers which call for that solution. Returning to the case studies, we shall see how the two companies came to adopt change programmes based around their most important – and troublesome – customer-facing processes.

CASE STUDIES

That our two case study companies did eventually choose process-based change is plain – both because we reported the fact in introducing the studies, and because they would not feature here had they not – but it was not inevitable. Both case study companies attempted other change initiatives first.

In Carton Carrier, for example, the first reaction to the identified change drivers had been to initiate a work study, which involved examining the activities performed to deliver a parcel. Such a study had been used already in Home Merchandise, and the chairman of Carton Carrier had moved from that part of the business, bringing the 'recipe' with him. Some viewed the study as 'a first stab' rather than the complete solution, although that view might have been formed with the aid of hindsight since at the time there was no suggestion that it was only a prelude to a more substantial project.

While the work study may not have been the complete solution, it was a valuable first step along the path. Although its terms of reference were restricted to each of the current functions in isolation, rather than as a process-spanning whole, it did provide a degree of control such that the managers could begin to direct the drivers in their daily routes and deliveries. A new notion began to take shape: that the criteria for the parcel delivery activities forming the ultimate parts of the order fulfilment process should concentrate not only on the number of parcels which were delivered, but on which particular parcels they should be.

Foundry Insurance had chosen a different route, upgrading its information systems and carrying out a reorganisation. The upgrading of the systems, unfortunately, was not the result of an in-depth study into what those systems should be doing, largely because of the lack of IT systems knowledge within Foundry Insurance, where such technology had been only sparsely used. Instead, the company relied on the IT services provided by Composite Insurers, the parent organisation, whose knowledge of the needs within Foundry Insurance was not exhaustive. That IT department undertook a project to replace the Foundry Insurance's plant database (which was a central database on which a record of all activities was to be held). The system was developed remotely from the end users, taking 3 years to build and a further year to test. During each of these years the cost to Foundry Insurance for the development was

£2 million. Unfortunately, when the system was delivered, it did not do what the users required. Furthermore, because the system was remotely developed and delivered, the workforce perceived it as having been imposed on them, and, in particular, the surveyors felt that it was a reflection on their inability to do their job. To the surveyors, the message of the new system was: 'We don't trust you'.

Developing and implementing a computer system with hardly any, let alone full, involvement of those who will be using it is a cast iron recipe for failure, the more so if those upon whom it is 'imposed' see it as a direct criticism of their performance. Foundry Insurance were not the first and will not be the last to do just that, though. Nor, as we intimated in the introduction to this chapter, will they be the last company to address a fundamental business problem by throwing money at the IT infrastructure, without first considering changes to the business. However, we have already said that few of us are in a position to cast the first stone.

Foundry Insurance's second attempt at remedial action – the organisational restructure – also failed, because it was concentrated on the functional aspects of the company, and continued to ignore any cross-functional processes. Up to 40 individual work groups were created, of varying sizes. These were distributed such that five or six regional teams serviced one geographical area, and each of these teams performed what was supposedly the same set of tasks in the ways which they deemed to be most efficient, and the ways were all subtly, or not so subtly, different.

So while the intentions might have been good, the reorganisation in fact not only maintained the functional splits within the processes, but further fragmented the business. Minds were concentrated even more on the single job in hand and not the whole chain of those activities which only in total addressed the customers' expectations. The situation was, if anything, worsened by that misdirected reorganisation.

It is clear from both Carton Carrier's and Foundry Insurance's experiences that a radical process-based change initiative was not the inevitable consequence of the initial identification of the drivers for change. So how did the companies move to the adoption of such an initiative? We saw in the previous chapter how the management teams in both organisations identified the opportunity – and the need – to regain management control over several different functions in order to co-ordinate a process which related directly to a vital stakeholder expectation. It was this identification, and the acceptance of it – rather than the recognition of the change drivers – which led to the radical process-based change initiatives being undertaken. The companies realised that departmental activities had to be co-ordinated and directed as a whole at satisfying the customer requirements.

In Carton Carrier it was recognised that the clearly defined parameters of responsibility between departments were in themselves divisive. So long as an individual department's house was in order, there was little incentive to assist any other department. The definition of 'in order' however, was with reference to the departments' internal activities, and did not take into account the wider process content. After the changes were made, the emphasis was on the process and on the contribution made to that process by each of the departments, whether positive or negative. Beforehand, though, it simply did not happen. There were no board meetings at which the directors of the different functions met to discuss the wider implications of their individual actions. They were not working together to satisfy customer expectations. At best they were working in isolation from each other, and, at worst, in competition.

A realisation of the importance of the process, as opposed to the activities, can lead to enormous changes. In Foundry Insurance that realisation is best illustrated by looking at the performance of the revised process. At the conclusion of the project, no more did the surveyors struggle with a manual typewriter and reams of carbon paper. Instead, their reports were typed on a personal computer, transferred electronically to Head Office, printed overnight to a high standard on a laser printer, and issued the following morning, 95% of reports being ready for despatch by 1a.m. The other 5%, where problems were discovered, were reported to engineers at the beginning of the working day. The resolution of those problems was the top priority, and the reports were ready for despatch by 10 a.m.

That is some improvement on the 5-month backlog situation which formed part of the drivers for change.

A further improvement came in dealing with customer queries. Whereas before a customer could talk to half a dozen different people about various aspects of their policy – a problem with a piece of plant, a claim, or a new policy, for example – that changed so that one person would be able to respond to all queries. This epitomised the realisation of the need to satisfy the end customer through acting as one seamless company rather than in a parochial, functional manner. It recognised implicitly what the customer's expectations of the query-answering process were, and it showed acceptance that they must be satisfied. In further appreciation of that, the IT work that was undertaken during the change programme was targeted at the process rather than at the function, and the functional activities of departments such as engineering, boiler, electrical, machinery, administration and customer services were co-ordinated at both management and operational levels.

Why do Processes Go Wrong?

When Carton Carrier and Foundry Insurance, and any other company, were first set up, the processes which were created within them were probably reasonably efficient. The outputs were known and the steps required to produce them were determined and introduced. Over time, given the evidence here and in numerous other examples, they became inefficient, and any emphasis on the customer went missing. Why? What are the contributory factors in the degeneration of processes? Were the seeds of that degeneration sown with the initial creation of the processes? The answers are not only instructive in their contribution to the change drivers and the choice of change initiative, but are vital in the wider context of resolving those degenerative problems and in achieving a radical process-based change. Without identifying why things go wrong, we are unable to target the causes and therefore prevent a repetition of failure once remedial action has been taken.

Since the industrial revolution, companies have been created on the basis of the military structures which stretched back many hundreds of years before them, and which were seen as the only way to organise anything of any size. Someone was in overall command, and beneath him (in those days it was invariably a 'him') there were a number of divisional commanders, or functional managers, each of which had a hierarchy of 'management' beneath him. At the bottom of the pile were the troops themselves. For the most part, everybody did what they were told by those at the next superior level, with strict controls over the amount of initiative which might be shown. One only has to consider that clerical, shopfloor, non-management staff are still frequently referred to as 'the troops' to see how the analogy is as relevant today as it ever was.

Henry Ford's production lines indicate how this structure was used to generate the most internally efficient method of manufacture, given that the activities within that production line – that process – were linear and unchanging. It is this type of process which is depicted by our 'chain of activities' in Figure 1.2. However, this is the simplest form of process, and while it is a useful diagrammatic representation it is rarely mirrored in real companies which do not operate such a production line. The feature most relevant to process 'failure' is present, though, and that is the departmental split, with the hierarchical management structure controlling it.

Boundary activities

That departmental split brings with it one quite unavoidable inefficiency, and that is the very activity of passing work items across the divides between departments. These 'boundary activities', depicted in Figure 3.1, can be any sort of activity, either manual or system. It can be the act of placing a work item in an out-tray, from which it is collected via the internal postal system, and deposited in an in-tray, from where it is eventually chosen and distributed. (In that case of course there are many activities, and Figure 3.1 would need to include a narrow 'postal' department between each of the other departments.) It can be the performance of that type of task by some

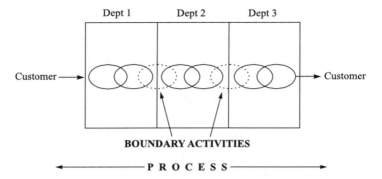

Figure 3.1   *Boundary activities in the process*

'workflow' software. It may be the creation of a computer file which is transferred to a different system or provided on printed output. Whatever it is, the boundary activity represents a break in the flow of activities which are necessary to the completion of the process. Nothing within the process of making and delivering a product – whether a physical good, a financial policy, or whatever the process output might be – requires that the work item be passed between departments, except the organisational structure which has been imposed upon that process. It would not be sensible to suggest that all departments everywhere are merged into one, and that intra-departmental hand-offs are also removed such that one 'super-user' completes all activities in a process. However, the further one moves away from that, the more inefficiencies are introduced into the overall process, to the detriment of the stakeholder who must await their completion.

The departmental improvement

A structure which creates such distinct departments, each under its own management, almost certainly leads to an internal rivalry between those departments. The hierarchical structure of a company inevitably means that the further up the greasy pole one climbs, the fewer opportunities there are for advancement. The pyramid narrows towards the top. The higher a manager goes, the more he or she is in direct competition with the managers at the same level, all trying to be the one in prime position for the next promotion. Not only is there a lack of incentive towards co-operation, there is a distinct disincentive as each departmental manager seeks to outdo his/her perceived rival. That is bad enough, but it inevitably leads to an ever more parochial, functional and introspective view.

Carton Carrier's experience suggests that changes which were made within a department were designed to help that department perform its tasks more efficiently. Little or no thought was given to the effects of the revised activities on departments in other parts of the process chain. Indeed, notification of the changes was rarely given to other departments in sufficient time for them to react, let alone to question the efficacy of the changes on the process as a whole.

But when an organisational structure is defined in such functional, departmental terms, no one is responsible for posing such a question. Management have far more important things to worry about. There is that longer term jockeying for position in readiness for the next promotional opportunity. And in the shorter term there is the target to be more efficient, with an end-of-year bonus depending upon it. What does the overall process matter when weighed against those considerations?

Indeed, not only *do* very few managers pose the question regarding contribution to process efficiency, but very few *can* do so. People's mind-sets have become restricted such that they consider only their own department. Their view of the business – their 'focal length' – generally stretches only as far as the boundaries of their particular function, and often even more narrowly than that, encompassing only their specific activity. Occasionally they will look beyond it to the department which passes work to them – apparently always late and riddled with errors – and occasionally to the department to which they pass work – which is always complaining unfairly. Without some internal change that focal length will rarely stretch to the stakeholder who probably initiated the process of which the departmental activities form a part, and who waits, ever more frustrated, at the end of the chain for the output, however defined, to be delivered. As a result, the effects of any change within the

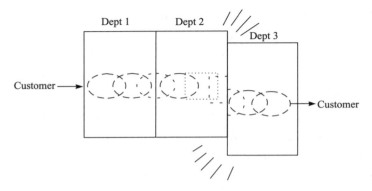

Figure 3.2   *Disruptive departmental improvements*

functional depths of an unrecognised process are only of interest to the people who make them in as much as they affect the one department. Figure 3.2 shows what will happen when unexpected changes are made.

Figure 3.2 depicts the process which was defined in chapter one where each activity was in tune with the preceding and succeeding ones. It shows the effects of an activity improvement introduced by the manager of Department 2 (the rectangular activity). Immediately this impacts the boundary activity which initiates the activities within Department 3. What is that receiving department to do? There is little purpose in them demanding that things be returned to the way they were. The management of Department 2 have been charged with improving their performance according to various measures – cost, resource usage, turnround and so on – and this they have done. Why would they revert to the old methods? If anything, people in Department 3 are advised to change themselves, to be 'proactive to the opportunity for improvement', or at least to be responsive to the initiative shown by Department 2. The management of Department 3 may even be labelled 'dinosaurs' or 'change blockers' if they don't themselves make positive noises about Department 2.

Undoing any changes becomes particularly impossible when the change represented by the rectangular activity in Figure 3.2 is in terms of a newly implemented computer system, which, for example,

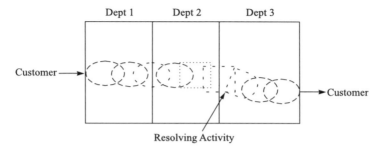

Figure 3.3 *Another link in the process*

does not provide the same information in the same way that it used to, since its design was not co-ordinated across the functional boundaries. It is not feasible to remove such a new system, and impossible to change it in the short term.

Whether through peer or other internal pressure, or through being faced with the fait accompli of a new computer system, Department 3 therefore has little or no alternative but to react to the new boundary activity by amending its own activities, as depicted in Figure 3.3.

The receiving department has had to introduce a new activity to resolve the changes which it has received from Department 2. If this 'resolving activity' is in response to a new computer system then it must stay in place until such times as IT resources can be allocated to amend the system as required. The chances are that by the time such resources are available, the priority of the amendments will have been superseded by other requirements. The resolving activity will eventually become part of the way Department 3 works – it will become part of the fabric of existence – and it will add to the complexity of the process.

Of course, if measurements are taken across the whole of the process, it may prove that the improvement introduced in Department 2 has been beneficial, even given the extra activity within Department 3. However, in such a functionally oriented organisation, such measurements are not taken, because the focal length of those within the departments is simply too short, so the overall effects remain a matter of conjecture.

Then, as a result of Department 3 changing in duly 'proactive and supportive response' to Department 2, the same argument and disruption starts all over again with the departments affected by those new changes. And so ad infinitum. We call this phenomenon 'death by a thousand changes'.

The fabric of existence

That phrase – 'the fabric of existence' – can be used not only in the context of necessary departmental reactions to changes elsewhere, but to any change that, over time, becomes accepted as the way things are done. Changes are introduced into a department's activities for any number of reasons: the new finance director requires a different monthly report; a particular backlog requires some extra managerial activity; a new manager wants to see samples of 10% of the output; accounts want a triplicate record of the day's production; the frequent failure of the computer system means that we keep copies of everything on paper and CD-Rom in a set of filing cabinets which now covers an area roughly the size of Wyoming. Over time, the reasons for those extra activities disappear: the finance director is replaced, the backlog is cleared, accounts no longer do things the same way, and the computer system is replaced. But the activities themselves have by now reached the stage where they are capable of self-preservation – if this were Star Trek they would have become living organisms! Many is the business analyst who has questioned 'Why do you do that (activity)?' and received the answer 'We've always done that'. New staff are introduced and taught the redundant activities without question as though they were ancient monks faithfully reproducing the spelling mistakes when copying even more ancient manuscripts.

It may be that a new and enterprising manager can tackle some of the purely internal redundant activities. But the most insidious ones are those which cross the boundaries. In the list above, for example, the accounts department will still receive their triplicate copies of the day's production – all top copies, no doubt – and will immediately put two of them in the bin. The report which goes to the new finance director will be produced, yet no one knows why. The finance director will receive the report, and likewise will wonder why. He or she will probably assume that he is merely copied on its distribution and that it must mean something to someone. A particular story has been repeated in many companies – but that does not make it apocryphal – wherein the sudden cancellation of the vast numbers of reports which flow around has been proved to elicit a response from the former recipients of quite staggering indifference.

While the internal departmental 'fabric of existence', 'we've always done that', activities may be addressed, it is far less likely that those which cross the departmental boundaries will attract investigation. Over the departmental walls are areas of the unknown – 'there be dragons!' – and we do not question what goes on over there.

Quality

How can quality make a process 'go wrong'? It sounds like a contradiction. Anything which improves quality must be a good thing, surely. And 'yes' that must be the case, but only up to a point.

It is a fact that most people – most of the troops – are keen to do a quality job. They are proud of the output which they produce from their activity. They want to do a good job not only for their own feelings of self-esteem, but because they are loyal to their department and to their departmental managers, regardless of what they may say about them in the bar!

Ask these people why processes go wrong and you will often get the same sort of answer. Processes go wrong because the guys in some other function – marketing / production / finance / administration / actuarial / manufacture / and so on – don't do their job properly. So what is the answer to that if we want to maintain the quality of our output? Well, as soon as the boundary activity has been concluded and we have the work item in our control, we check what the previous department did with it. And in each department down the process line that checking of the previous department's activities adds to the time and resource taken to complete the process.

The stakeholder does not need this to be done. If a stakeholder – say, the customer – was asked if they were willing to pay for each of the individual activities which made up the process as a whole they would not want to pay for multiple checking activities. They would ask, rightly, why the organisation cannot get the activity right the first time it is done and therefore remove the need constantly to check it.

It may well be that the company does get it right first time, or it may be that the first department is performing its tasks according to one specification while succeeding departments have another and therefore need to check and change the output. It is the absence of trust between departments, the poor communication, and the lack of understanding of the contribution of any one activity or set of activities to the final process output, which means that the process cannot be streamlined.

Chronology

The depiction of the process as a linear collection of activities is, as we have said, a diagrammatic simplification. It is likely that the different departments are dealing with a work item simultaneously. It is likely, also, that there are some activities in one department which rely on the completion of other activities in another department.

In Figure 3.4, if activity '3' is dependent upon the completion of activity '2', which in itself is dependent on the completion of activity '1' then the third department is likely to see a backlog of work growing while waiting for the green light to complete it.

If the situation were as simple as that, and if the chronological dependencies were recognised, then perhaps something could be

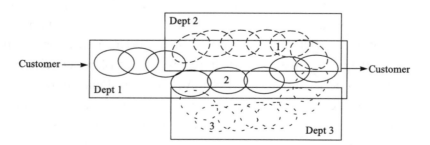

Figure 3.4 *Time dependent activities*

done about it, assuming a basic level of communication between departments. What, though, if the dependency is not realised? What if Department 3 believes it can carry out its task without waiting for the activities '1' and '2' to be completed?

Such a situation is exactly what arose in our Software Inc. case study, and has done so in many other companies. If activity '1' changes the characteristics of the work item – if the engineers installing the software make adjustments on-site according to discovered local conditions or a redefinition of requirements – then those performing activity '3' – the invoicing for the work, let's say – are doing so using the wrong data unless they are informed of the changes. But because people in different departments often do not talk to each other and have no notion of the effects of their activities on other activities, such information is not exchanged. In Software Inc.'s case, one possible answer was that the invoicing for the work should have been delayed until the engineers had actually installed the software and informed invoicing of the work that was actually carried out. But because such a dependency was not recognised, because the departmental barriers were too high, this did not happen and as a result customers received poor service levels.

Duplication

We do not need a diagram to explain duplication of activities. It is something which is perhaps most prevalent in the IT systems field. The more separate departments there are, the more they are likely to have their own computer hardware and software, either bought off a shelf or provided by internal bespoke manufacture, or both. Administration, sales, marketing, finance departments, and many others, want to keep records of customers, intermediaries, sales, and so on. Each may well do so on the computer systems within their own departments. The same data get loaded in many different places onto many different databases.

There are two problems with this. Firstly, it is clearly a waste of time to load the same data in different places onto different systems, if it can be done once and then accessed by all those who need it.

Secondly, and probably more dangerous for customer service as opposed to internal efficiency, the data will quickly get out of alignment. This is not a 'maybe' situation, it is an immutable fact. The data *will* get out of step. Output from one department will have different data on it than that from another. The customer will receive both, just as the customer may receive multiple requests for the same data. Worse still, the customer is likely to provide the correct data to one department – thinking they are dealing with an efficient and integrated company – only to find that the next load of output they receive from (unknown to them) a different department, still has the old erroneous data on it. Customer perception is of great importance, and this internal discontinuity of unnecessarily duplicated activities is a sure way of influencing that perception disadvantageously. In the emergent world where external stakeholders have direct access to the organisation's data, any errors become embarrassingly apparent very quickly.

Silo walls

We have made reference in the above discussion to 'barriers' between departments, both explicitly, and implicitly in numerous cases. It is time to come out and say it. The boundaries between departments are walls. Thick and seemingly impenetrable (see Figure 3.5).

For whatever reason, and we have seen a number of them in the examples above, these walls have grown up between departments over time. Within the walls the managers and staff do the best job they can, for themselves and for their colleagues. Over the walls they lob their items of work prepared in the ways which they believe to be required, and with those work items goes the responsibility for them.

Communication through the walls is limited or non-existent, and the more distant any department is from your own, the more walls there are between you and the less communication occurs. All that comes back appears to be complaints, unreasonable requests, errors and problems.

And remember, as far as some managers are concerned, the other

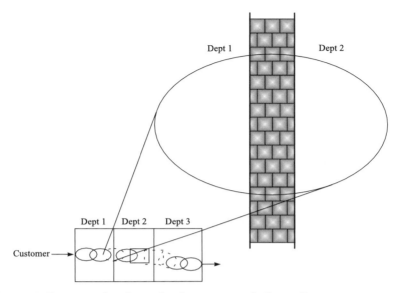

Figure 3.5 *Many bricks in the departmental silo walls*

managers over the walls are their rivals. They are not there to be communicated with; they are there to be defeated.

The walls need not exist in reality. They do not have to be real walls in an office, or an ocean between departments in an international company. They do not have to be flights of stairs between floors. They can be nothing more than the names which are given to different functions, but that is enough. Within the walls each function becomes its own silo. The troops dig in and take occasional potshots over the walls, taking their lead from their superior officers. And we have come full circle to the military analogy which began this discussion.

Summary

As we said in the introduction to this section, the reasons why processes 'go wrong' are not only important to see why the change drivers arose in Carton Carrier and Foundry Insurance. They are vital in determining the solutions. It is only when one recognises both the mentality – hopefully not as extreme as that depicted – which holds sway within the boundary walls, and the enormity of the task involved in removing those boundaries, that one is able to address the root causes of the problems. Or at least address them with a good chance of success. If the symptoms are addressed while leaving the cause untouched, the solution which is designed and implemented will be temporary at best.

Conclusion

We began this chapter by asking whether radical process-based change was an inevitable choice as a result of identifying drivers for change, and we have seen in our case studies that it was not. We have seen in the above discussion why it was not, and why it would not be in practically every other company we care to consider. Such is the deep-seated nature of the functional silos that it is highly likely – some might even say inevitable – that other methods will be mooted and attempted first. When the walls of the silos are assailed, deflection is easier than outright repulsion.

In Software Inc., for example, a quality initiative was introduced as a response to the growing level of customer complaints, but its introduction was within each of the individual departments, with no consideration given to cross-functional quality. The idea was one with which the functional managers could feel comfortable, in that it did not threaten them. Hence, the invoicing department could consider that they were doing a quality job, and based upon the data to which they had access, they probably were. The problem of course was that the data were erroneous by the time the invoice was issued because of changes in other departments which had not been notified. Each department within Software Inc. could strive to achieve an official total quality standard, but so long as they did so in isolation, the customer was still going to experience the same problems. Only when the levels of complaint were seen to be quite unaffected by the isolated functional 'improvements' was it accepted that a multi-cross-functional process-based change was required.

It is a fact that most people in most organisations in most markets are keen to do a good – a quality – job. It is a crying shame that what they perceive as quality is ruined in the eyes of their customers by colleagues in other departments doing their own quality jobs but at some level of contradiction. Poor quality is much less likely to be the result of poor, uncaring staff, and much more the result of the structure, and mind-set, within which they are made to operate. But that structure and that mind-set are what they are comfortable with, and cross-functional changes, while they are likely to be required, will almost invariably be a reluctant, sometimes a last-resort, choice.

Our conclusion then is that, since radical process-based change addresses fundamental organisational – functional – barriers to the satisfaction of stakeholder expectations, it is only when the removal of those barriers is specifically targeted that process-based change becomes the inevitable choice.

Axiom for change: 2
The successful implementation of radical process-based change is only possible when people establish the need for a transformational cross-functional response to change drivers rather than any other type of change initiative.

What the 'correct' choice of any initiative does not guarantee, however, is the success of that initiative. This is especially so in the case of a radical change programme, and particularly one which addresses cross-functional processes, for all the reasons we have considered in this chapter. The next chapter looks at the changes which actually need to happen to ensure success in addressing the drivers for change which require a radical process orientation solution.

Where does your Company stand?

Studying the situation in your own company, consider the following questions:

- Do your company strategy and business objectives give sufficient weight to customer satisfaction, or do they concentrate too heavily on the shareholder as stakeholder, e.g. on cost reduction and profit increase?
- Is customer service suffering because the processes are being disrupted by the internal functional requirements?
- Is there more emphasis placed on people's 'day jobs' rather than satisfying customer expectations?
- Do people see and describe themselves in terms of the departments in which they work or do they include the processes of which they form a part?
- Which are more important to them?
- Are managerial bonuses dependent on departmental performance rather than on process performance?
- Is there sufficient knowledge of what happens across functional boundaries to guarantee that all activities are contributing positively to the process, and in a timely, efficient manner?
- Are all the managers directly responsible for end customer satisfaction, and not just those with direct contact?
- Do you actually know what your processes are, and what activities they should contain (rather than what they *do* contain)?

F O U R

The Process or Function Myth

'Did you know,' Peter Window asked his boss, Alan Parsons, 'that "performance-related pay" is a perfect anagram of "mere end of year claptrap"?'

'Is it?'

'It is. Try it.'

Parsons tried it on a pad in front of him. 'Well I'll be ...' He didn't finish the sentence, but continued the thought. 'The trouble is, if I don't convince people that PRP is almost certainly one of the things we need to look at, then I probably *will* be.'

'Will be what?'

Parsons shrugged. 'Choose a verb. None of them good, and all meaning fired after failing.' He sighed and leant back in his chair. 'Downs has told me that he wants a 40% reduction in rework, a 25% reduction in turn-round time, and a 20% reduction in unit costs.'

'Well that's good. He's recognised the need for radical change.'

'Kind of. He's certainly bought into the drivers and the need for radical *improvement*. The trouble is he hasn't actually bought into the kind of radical change we need to achieve it. He not only wants to have his cake and eat it, but he wants his cake to go further while being sliced exactly the same way it is now.'

'And the staff will follow his lead?' Window asked ruefully.

'In this case, like sheep. They'll see the need for improvement too, but they won't want change.'

'They don't mind some sort of change; I've asked around.'

'What sort of change?'

'Guess. They want new IT systems. They all reckon that they could do their jobs quicker if we updated the computer programs.'

'Yeah, right. They want us to chuck good money after bad and only change things that are inanimate.'

Window nodded. 'It's easier – computers don't worry; they don't have emotions.'

'They do in science fiction – they have special chips for it. If we put one of them in our computers here you know what would be the first thing they'd all say? They'd say "I'm wasted here". All that potential and we cram it into the little functional silos so it couldn't support a process if it tried. Which, if we gave it that chip, it would.'

'Maybe that's the answer. Let intelligent computers take over.'

'Don't denigrate the humans round here,' Parsons advised. 'It's nothing to do with their level of intelligence. No, the answer is to get the people to see that real changes have to happen; real changes linked to the processes we all contribute to.'

'Yes, but you know what reception you got when you suggested process orientation – some of the directors still haven't got the stains out of their underwear.'

'It's not necessarily the orientation that matters. It's the orientation of people's *thinking* that matters. If they *think* process, then we can reinforce the thinking with systems, and even PRP and bonuses targeted on end customer satisfaction. But we don't have to threaten their way of life to do it.'

'That's not in the textbooks, is it?'

'No, it isn't. But then sometimes I think that the textbooks were written for people whose staff have had their emotion chips removed. I reckon it's time we rewrote them a bit.'

'Well, I'm with you, and good luck to us!'

'Aha. That's a very imperfect anagram of "Fat Chance!" is it?'

*   *   *

Introduction

What does the project sponsor have in mind when a radical change is called for? On the surface it seems like a question from the 'extremely obvious' category. The sponsor wants radical change. Maybe as demanded by George Downs above, that radical change could be defined as large improvements in various specified measures as a way of addressing the change drivers. Except that describing change in terms of its 'bottom line' results is not the whole picture. It does not actually describe the changes, but rather the results which the changes bring. The question we must ask is whether the link between the improvements in performance measures and the radical changes required to attain them is specifically recognised by the sponsor. The danger, if this link is not identified and accepted, is that a number of sponsors will, maybe even subconsciously until it is pointed out, want to achieve the perfect omelette whilst leaving the eggs quite unbroken.

That link is not always addressed by those who research the fields of radical change based on processes and those who consider the other alternatives mentioned in earlier chapters. Those in the radical process-based change camp define the attendant changes in terms of significant expected performance improvements. For instance, Dixon et al,[2] assert that their working definition of re-engineering is that it is a revolutionary approach which focuses upon the attainment of significant desired results from a business process, much like those demanded by our mythical George Downs, above. Stoddard et al,[16] drawing on the work of Davenport[17] and Hammer & Champy,[13] assert that radical change refers to the magnitude of the performance improvement:

> *a change that results in incremental improvement (e.g. a* 10% cost reduction*) would not be considered a radical change.*[16]

This view of incremental improvement stands in stark contrast with that of Tushman, Newman, & Romanelli:[18]

> *almost any organisation can tolerate a* 'ten-percent change'. *At any one time only a few changes are being made; but these changes are still compatible with the prevailing structures.*

The stark contrast here is not between the 10% figures mentioned, but in the unit of measurement. A 10% change in an organisation may well result in a 50% reduction in costs. Nowhere is there an accepted definition of what a 10% change might be, except in terms of the improvements it generates.

Two consequences, in particular, stem from defining radical change in terms of performance improvement. One is highlighted in a recent survey,[19] which found a fundamental problem facing organisations embarking on radical process-based change. If people focus on measuring performance improvements rather than changes to organisational elements,[20] then the 'need for managing change is not recognised' by board members and senior managers.

The second is that a radical process-based change programme is deemed to be a strategic initiative simply because organisations set out to achieve order of magnitude improvements.[21] The apparent logic is that a target of 70% cost reduction makes the initiatives strategic. One reason why this logical relationship does not hold is that the organisation might be reducing the wrong cost. For example, one oil company removed a layer of its hierarchy as a cost-cutting measure. The supervisory level were deemed to be adding little value to the company's activities, so were dispensed with, and costs duly fell. Two years later the company were haemorrhaging cash as equipment – significant equipment, like oil rigs – was being ordered at the wrong time. The purchasing activities had, of course, formerly been under the control of those supervisory managers.

The definition that researchers into process orientation ascribe to radical change is at odds with that of those who study radical change itself. These latter consider a radical change to be one that culminates in a significant change to organisational elements such as strategy, structure, people, and systems. They do not consider the measure as being one of performance improvement.

This is not to say that researchers in process orientation overlook the views of the change theorists; indeed, they assert that the radical nature of re-engineering involves the organisation in making a change in direction or challenging the status quo.[2] Nor do change theorists argue for change just for the sake of change, that is, without a corresponding improvement in performance. However, process orientation researchers emphasise radical performance improvements when defining radical change. This has led to those researchers urging implementors to set stretching goals and dramatic performance improvement targets.[22] The organisational change implications, which stem from a quantum leap in performance improvements, are regarded as little more than a contingent effect. This is an inappropriate definition of radical change because 'change' is seen as a subsidiary issue to performance improvement.

Radical change theorists, on the other hand, focus upon changes to organisational elements – namely, strategy, structure, people's responsibilities and appraisal criteria, behaviours and information systems – and treat performance improvements as a result of implementing radical changes to these elements. Those organisational changes are labelled change management issues or change management problems.[23,24] The change management issues frequently highlighted in the literature are summarised in Table 4.1.

Table 4.1 *Content of changes that occur during a radical process orientation initiative*

Change Author	Responsibilities	Organisation structure	Appraisal criteria	Information systems	Behaviours
Hammer & Champy (1993)[13]	✓	✓	✓	✓	✓
Hall et al (1994)[21]	✓	✓	✓	✓	✓
Asamoah & Duncan (1993)[27]	✓		✓		
Caron et al (1994)[26]	✓	✓		✓	✓
Davenport & Nohria (1994)[25]	✓	✓	✓	✓	
Ascari et al (1995)[3]	✓	✓	✓	✓	
Earl & Khan (1994)[29]	✓		✓	✓	✓
Kilmann (1995)[28]		✓	✓		✓

At first glance, Table 4.1 suggests that there is a high degree of consensus about the content of the changes that occur. However, on closer examination, the details of the organisational changes differ widely, as the following detailed analysis reveals.

Detailed changes to people's responsibilities are given as, variously:

- greater empowerment, where people in the process decide how and when work is to be done[13]
- decision-making authority is increased for the person responsible for the process[25]
- defined along the horizontal or process dimension rather than on a vertical or functional basis[24]

Detailed changes to organisation structure are:

- hierarchy flattened in terms of the number of levels[13]
- a decrease in the number of vertical functions[25]
- size and power of the functions decrease[3]
- organise by process rather than function[26]

Detailed changes to appraisal criteria are:

- introduction of performance related pay[27]
- team-based compensation[26]
- compensation linked to profitability of the process[25]
- linked to broader process goals[24]
- linked to the individual's and group's contribution to improving the process[28]
- rewards should be in the form of bonuses linked to value created by the process[13]

Detailed changes to information systems are:

- development of new systems that support the process[26]
- a mix of old and new systems[25]

- tailored IT solutions[3]
- shared databases[29]

Detailed changes to behaviours are:

- employees believe they work for and take ownership of customers[13]
- enhancing trust, communication, information sharing, and willingness to change in the organisation[28]
- demolishing old assumptions[29]
- changing business practices[26]

The above shows that there is little agreement in the literature in terms of detail, and it highlights a lack of clarity in current thinking about the nature of the changes. Some proponents argue that the changes lead to realignment from a functional structure to a predominantly process orientation; others suggest that organisations retain their functional structure. Some are quite silent on this issue.

There is clearly a great disparity of views on the areas where change can be expected, and what specific changes might be expected in those areas. In order to shed some light from the real world on the theoretical deliberations, let us turn once again to our case studies. We will focus specifically on those areas outlined above and on another which was previously mentioned, strategy. From the case studies we are trying to answer the questions:

- What areas will change?
- What are the detailed changes?
- Is the change always the same?
- Which is right – a process *or* function orientation?

CASE STUDIES

We shall consider each area of change mentioned above in relation first to Carton Carrier and then Foundry Insurance.

CARTON CARRIER

Strategy

Prior to any changes being made, the strategic focus of Carton Carrier was easily stated. 'Make profit!' That was the instruction to all of the autonomous companies (of which Carton Carrier was one) within the GMR group. Each pursued the goal to the exclusion of any other of the sister companies. Changes were made to increase profitability with little regard to the effects on other activities further down the process line. For example, Home Merchandise changed its sorting activity even though the change resulted in difficulties in the depots. Each function operated on the basis that as long as it performed its activities it was unconcerned with others' performance. If it saw a way of improving, then the new method would have been implemented in isolation. The personnel manager describes the situation:

> *We'd have just changed, and the warehouse and other departments would have done the same. They would have just changed something, and we would have probably found out about twenty-four hours beforehand.*

By which time, of course, it was too late to stop or react to those changes. No one saw the need to communicate any proposed changes to the next department down the process line. The situation was a perfect example of the short focal length described in the last chapter, of the 'departmental improvement' method of making a process 'go wrong'.

The warehouse was the last port of call before a parcel became the responsibility of Carton Carrier, and that description embodies the problem. Once the warehouse had received its orders to pick, assemble, pack and despatch, those activities would be carried out, the parcels would be loaded on the trailers and the doors closed, literally on the lorry and metaphorically on the warehouse staff's perceived ownership and concerns. As the managing director put it, beyond that point:

It's somebody else's problem, even though it was within the Group, it would be assumed then to be handed over and thereafter it was Carton Carrier's problem to deal with it.

Once the functional mentality was replaced by a process view – once the focal length of those performing those activities was increased – so the strategy in relation to profit also changed. As we described in the previous chapter, the inability to see beyond one's own function meant that any improvement was measured only in terms of the department in which it was introduced. The overall effect on the process was never measured, and may even have been a worsening of the situation. Carton Carrier moved to a situation where the effects of any change could be monitored across the process as a whole. Something which might incur a cost in one activity – and which therefore would have been resisted – may have been seen to introduce a greater benefit elsewhere, and so would be accepted to the overall gain of the process. The strategy of each department within Carton Carrier – indeed within the order fulfilment process spanning Home Merchandise and Carton Carrier – changed so that overall profit was considered as opposed to departmental profit.

And not only was the strategic view of profit altered, but that single-strand strategy was augmented with more process-driven, customer-facing concerns. From being something which, thanks to the short focal length, was only a blurred notion on the horizon, customer service and quality – defined in terms of customer expectations – came into sharp focus and was held to be as important as making a profit. This was a big change in the strategic approach of Carton Carrier's management, and it took a long time to achieve. As we shall see, though, it was central to the successful implementation of the process change initiative.

Roles and responsibilities

Once the process orientation became part of the mind set within Carton Carrier, and quality and service became part of the strategy, it was clear that roles had to change in order to support the new paradigm. One of those changing roles was that of the depot supervisor. Typically there were three supervisors to a depot, working shifts, one covering the night and the other two taking over in the morning. Formerly the supervisor's role was, tautologically, to supervise, but it was not to *manage*. The three supervised a total of about 60 drivers, but in a largely impersonal manner in as much as the drivers were not split into three groups of 20, but were supervised on an ad hoc basis by whoever happened to be in the depot at the time. Furthermore, the supervisors had no real control over the depot, but simply booked people out, dealt with the figures – the various lots of 200 parcels – and checked totals. They had no participation in recruitment, discipline or any of the wider management activities.

With the realisation that the functions formed part of the parcel delivery process, the supervisor role was redefined, and renamed, so that they became 'parcel delivery managers'. The role was still there, but its responsibilities changed so that it became a vital element in support of the overall process. The parcel delivery manager was allocated a team of drivers and was responsible for everything they did, as well as for their training, discipline and counselling. In a wider context, this new type of manager was responsible for the final stage of the parcel delivery process and thereby had a responsibility both to Home Merchandise and to Carton Carrier. That process-wide responsibility was spread across all those working in their various functions by giving them all the same, revised, overall objectives; namely the consistent delivery of parcels and improved quality of service, while at the same time ensuring the achievement of process-wide profitability.

The managing director described it as 'delegating responsibility', but that is not entirely accurate, and it is important to make the distinction. Delegation implies the removal of the responsibility from a higher level of the hierarchy and relocating it downwards, but that was not the case in Carton Carrier. Instead, staff in all levels of the company were made aware of the responsibility and in that way they all came to share it. The responsibility was not repositioned, it was extended.

As well as the supervisors, the depot managers saw their role change significantly, and along the same process-oriented lines.

Previously, the depot managers barely managed the depot at all. They had hands-on, day-to-day operational responsibilities, and reacted to problems, focusing internally and with little time for external customers. They dealt with operational issues from paying cash wages, to disciplinary matters, to dealing with head office. However, they were rarely involved in managerial issues such as improving the depot's financial performance, reducing customer complaints, or improving operations. They had little interaction with their counterparts in other depots – why should they? – which meant that they rarely shared good practice or resolved common difficulties.

Following the changes, the depot managers became responsible for all those activities within the depots which formed part of the parcel delivery process. These included ensuring that their depot achieved agreed levels of customer service, which was defined as the delivery of parcels within 3 days. They took operational decisions that balanced customer service with delivery costs. But they still maintained their functional responsibilities in that they were responsible to the regional general manager for their depot's profitability.

As it did the drivers and the depot managers, so the broadening of responsibility also affected the directors. They were previously responsible only for their function and barely concerned themselves with problems within other functions. This changed to a situation where directors were responsible both for their own function and for the wider parcel delivery process. The warehouse, sort centre and trunking functions became the responsibility of a director in Home Merchandise, and responsibility for the depot operations function became that of a director in Carton Carrier. Furthermore, these functional directors were on the boards of both organisations so their joint responsibility for the parcel delivery process was brought under co-ordinated control at the highest level.

The point to note, though, is that the responsibility was not retained purely at that high level, but was disseminated throughout the organisation, so that everybody was concerned with customer service, and found their roles changing to support the new mind-set. A regional general manager describes the difference:

The responsibilities have broadened out. We are far more consciousness of service. We always said that service was a depot manager's job, and now with the development of the process and the ability to measure performance it has been possible to widen the responsibility for providing good service. There's far more autonomy in the field now than ever there was. For example, when I was depot manager at Liverpool, I wouldn't even work a week-end – you know, turn the drivers out on Saturday – without talking it over with my boss.

Appraisals

The apparent realisation within Carton Carrier that people determined how the service was provided as well as how profitable the organisation would be resulted in a change to the appraisal system to monitor the performance against criteria which now were deemed to matter. Before the change, the yearly appraisal report for the managers was often written out before the appraisal took place. Discussion with the appraisee resulted either in agreement, in which case the appraisal was recorded unchanged, or disagreement, in which case it was still recorded unchanged! While that may seem slightly less than a full and frank bilateral assessment of performance, it was perhaps better than for the drivers, who did not get an appraisal at all.

This changed so that everybody's contribution to the cost and effectiveness of the parcel delivery process could be assessed. Measures were sought which reflected the quality of the service performance under a particular depot manager as well as the depot's profitability. The drivers were brought into the system such that their contribution could also be measured. Any complaints they received, or the percentage of parcels brought back to the depot were recorded, along with more positive achievements.

Reward criteria

Linking rewards to these appraisals was the next step, where appropriate. If there was a clear opportunity to measure individual performance, then part of the remuneration would be based on contribution to the business. Bonus payments were linked to profit achievement and to quality of service. Both depot managers and the more senior regional general managers became subject to such a reward system, with the average senior manager able to earn an extra 15% of salary if performance exceeded a defined standard.

In the case of the drivers, bonuses were linked to performance. Whereas before the payment was simply by the parcel – leading to those which took too long to deliver sitting forlornly in their cages – the new system allocated a fair number of parcels to be delivered in a 10 hour period, with those parcels being chosen according to the service criteria laid down in the order fulfilment process.

Behaviours

The conglomerate of behaviours is identified in the theories as a significant area for change, and perhaps the most important change for Carton Carrier was in the hearts and minds of the people whose 'day job' activities actually made up the parcel delivery process. Although the word was not used specifically by the interviewees, what emerged within Carton Carrier was teamwork. Everyone realised that they had a part to play in a process which was much wider than the function within which they operated. The walls of the silos were broken down, and the tin helmets removed.

It used to be:

A complete and utter dictatorship. You had no input at all into anything that happened in the Depot. You were just told what to do. If you didn't do it, then basically your arse was kicked. And it was all 'You will do', 'You will do'. The only time senior management used to come and see you was if you was in trouble, and it was for a bollocking session… (depot manager)

This was not just the biased view of the put-upon. The old culture was very dictatorial, with a good deal of management by fear. If people did not toe the line then their jobs were in danger. Such an environment is always going to concentrate the minds of staff on their own particular task and no other, and it will suppress initiative. In a blame culture, there is no incentive to risk an innovation which might result in failure.

To change such a situation requires more than just verbal denials at the senior level that the blame culture exists (and a number of organisations would do well to reflect on that). If the staff are still of the opinion that a ton of bricks will follow closely on the heels of a failed innovation, then heads will be withdrawn well below the parapet, ideas will be kept strictly under wraps, and stagnation in the processes will continue. Fortunately for Carton Carrier, the new board and management 'walked the talk'. The managing director installed a feeling of ownership of the business into the organisation. He recognised – and made it plain that he recognised – that the 'people on the ground', as he described them, were the keys to the success of the business. And while many business leaders make the same comment, largely by rote, Carton Carrier's managing director was keen actually to use those keys to unlock the business problems. But in order to tap into the skills and experience which these people had amassed, their trust had first to be gained, and to do that the management by fear had to be consigned to the past.

Depot managers began treating their drivers as real people, appreciating the fact that they could not work within exactly the same specifications for every day of every working week, because occasionally they would have problems both at work and at home. Whereas before a problem which affected performance would be met by a threat – 'if you can't do the job, then you know where the door is' – now the managers sought to identify and resolve the problems. Formal modes of address were removed, and first names used instead. Senior managers learned that not only did they have one mouth, but twice as many ears, and they began to use them. The new approach was noticed all the way down the line. It was not dismissed as a flash in the pan or a false dawn, and therefore had a significant effect on the organisation.

Senior management now are prepared to listen to us. When we had meetings we'd go for lunch. And I know it's a small investment, but it was something that they'd never ever had before. You just didn't do things like that. The environment improved; in the depot, we painted the floors, we cleaned the place a lot better. We employed a cleaner ... We even put flowers in boxes out there. (depot manager)

As another comment (unattributed here to protect the source!) puts it most eloquently, something which would previously have been quite unheard of in Carton Carrier was having the importance of flower arrangements in the depot entrance being discussed by 'hairy-arsed depot managers'.

Information technology

Carton Carrier's computer systems, pre-change, were entirely under its own control, and that control was exercised such that the information technology spend was not too great a strain on the company coffers. The criteria for purchase of a computer centred around cost and had little to do with the capabilities of the hardware, so that often it was not up to the tasks required.

Furthermore, there was no link to the activities within Home Merchandise, and with the mainframes employed there. So the responsibility which was relinquished at the Home Merchandise warehouse gates by the people was also passed on by the computer systems. Once process orientation had been introduced into management thinking, so the use of the information technology was expanded such that it supported the new paradigm encompassing both service and profitability. The purse strings were not loosened to the extent that technology was introduced for its own sake, but decisions included the considerations of whether there were advantages for customer service, for overall costs, or, ideally, for both.

Computer records now tracked a parcel at every stage of its passage through the order fulfilment process. The only point in the process where an assumption was made was where a parcel had been designated for a particular driver's round, and it was assumed that the parcels taken were those which had been allocated. All the information was held on a central mainframe which could be remotely interrogated by all interested parties in both Home Merchandise and Carton Carrier. Delivery information for the enquiring customer could be provided at the touch of a few buttons. Furthermore, with all the people in the process now determined to provide the best service possible that information was almost invariably accurate. That was a dramatic change from the situation where the honest response to a delivery query would have been at best an unsubstantiated guess.

FOUNDRY INSURANCE

Strategy

Studying the strategic view of the Foundry Insurance management prior to the radical change initiative, we get a strange – or perhaps not so strange – feeling of déjà vu. The business plan for the year prior to the change project being initiated was a short document which, basically, stated an intention to keep doing exactly what the company had been doing in years past, and to make a profit doing it. If one had sought evidence of service standards by reference to the business plan one would have concluded that Foundry Insurance did not have any, since there was no mention of them. Given what we have seen of the disparate and fluid-corrected technical reports, that might not be a surprising conclusion.

Everything in Foundry Insurance was under the control of the then general manager, who according to the deputy managing director 'was quite ruthless. Nobody did anything without his say so.' While this led to what the previous management might have considered maintenance of the status quo, it was in fact a stagnation in the company, which certainly contributed to its problems. Illustrating exactly the point which we made above, a 'ruthless' management style is not one which will encourage innovation from below. If the one person who is formally allowed to make changes does not wish to do so, then the maintenance of the status quo is the height of the company's ambition. Such was the case in Foundry Insurance. Nothing was changing; the aim was to make a profit next year the same way they did last year. When people were asked where they thought the company was going, the answer, in the words of the deputy managing director was, 'Well, we're chugging along as ever'.

The changes which occurred in terms of strategy mirror those in Carton Carrier in the same way as did the former concentration on profit. The new managing director encouraged the management team to consider not only cost control and profitability as important, but also service quality to customers. He concentrated people's minds on identifying those various activities within the company which were unnecessary to the processes, with a view to removing them, and of the need to automate or make more efficient those which were necessary. He saw the most important activities, though, as those where the person involved in that activity 'actually adds value for our customer'. In the same way as did Carton Carrier, the management team in Foundry Insurance learned that, of course, they still needed to be profitable, but that servicing the client was equally important.

This recognition of the importance of contributing to the process, rather than merely performing the function – carrying out the 'day job' activity – came as something of a culture shock. Before the change the now familiar short focal length was clearly displayed. People saw themselves as underwriters, or engineers, or surveyors. Those involved actually described it as 'vertically structured', harking back directly to the diagrams we have seen in chapters one and three above. The vertical functional or departmental boundaries cut right across the horizontal process orientation which better described the path between stakeholder expectations and the satisfaction of those expectations. Those working within the vertical functions – within the departmental silos – had their jobs to do and did them to the best of their ability whilst having no idea of their contribution to the process or to the company as a whole.

The change to process orientation, while not a physical change, occurred in the same way as it did in Carton Carrier. Led by the new managing director, the managers had to learn to look at the business process as a whole rather than simply at that one point where their function impinged upon it.

The change in emphasis from functional silo to process-based customer service forced some pretty fundamental changes in a company which had not changed in a long time. The evidence for that is provided vividly by a comment from the managing director, who, shortly after his arrival in Foundry Insurance, spoke to his then deputy:

> *Colin had been with the company 43 years, not a long time actually by our company's standards ... and I said to him, 'When did this process last change?' Colin said 'Well not in my lifetime here'.*

Colin and his like had never been encouraged to change because their job was their job, and they had always done it as instructed from above. One is reminded of the exasperated boss complaining to his employee that the latter never showed any initiative. 'Well,' the worker defends himself, 'you've never told me to!' While that worker did not come from Foundry Insurance or from Carton Carrier, he might well have done.

Roles and responsibilities

Within Foundry Insurance, the freedom to make decisions affecting the wider process made a strait-jacket look spacious. The previous general manager clearly saw the responsibility for making decisions as being his own. While his was a view adopted with the best intentions, it served only to remove responsibility and any feeling of ownership from the lower levels of the company. For example, the manager nominally responsible for underwriting did not actually make any underwriting decisions; they were passed up the line to the top. Two-thirds of the budget was controlled centrally. Employment of any new member of staff was subject to the general manager's approval, so in effect the responsibility for staff numbers was also removed from the operational managers.

> *The code would always be that the general manager makes all the decisions, not just major decisions, all the decisions. (deputy managing director)*

*The general manager had to agree everything. You couldn't
hire, fire, or spend any money without his signature. (implementation team member)*

This state of affairs was shown to be particularly incongruous when
one took a step back and looked at some of the company employees'
indirect responsibility to the general public. A line manager in
Foundry Insurance was trusted to take decisions regarding the
certification of public elevator safety – a matter of life and death – but
he or she was not able to take a decision to purchase a photocopier.

Driven by the change in strategy and the emphasis on the process
rather than the function, all that changed. Although it was a hard task
to change a culture whereby everything was passed up the line, this
was slowly achieved, with people taking ownership of and responsibility for a number of tasks which, before, had always been dele-
gated upwards. People's initiative was reawakened from its enforced
slumber, so that, in the words of a member of the change project
implementation team, 'We work more on the basis, "Let's do it and
argue about it later". Or not argue, hopefully.'

That one sentence encapsulates the change which was sought in
people's roles to support the new mind-set. The new board of
Foundry Insurance wanted all their staff to take responsibility for
what they were individually doing and also for their contribution to
the overall process. And that responsibility was one which was
shared across all the functions which supported the process. In
delivering service to the customer, and doing so profitably, the
responsibility and the ownership were shared across the functions.

Appraisals

As before, with extra responsibility, and with the alignment of
activities towards both the original function and the process in which
it resided, came the logical change to appraising contribution based
on those criteria. And the appraisals were conducted openly, which
was another change. Under the previous management team,
managers were instructed not to talk to people they were appraising.

Typically, managers decided in advance the desired new salary grade for an individual and then wrote the appraisal to justify it. Foundry Insurance were neither the first nor will be the last where the original intention of appraisals becomes corrupted. When this sort of thing happens the appraisals can become full of banal generalisations which bear little relation to improving a specific individual's contribution to the overall process. It is all very well saying that someone needs more experience to fulfil their potential as a useful member of staff, as was often the case in Foundry Insurance, but that says nothing about where the experience is needed, and nor does it tie the 'usefulness' of the person to the process of which their activities form a part.

That approach changed and the appraisals were reinstated as a process-supporting and individual development tool. An individual's specific shortfalls were identified, as well as strengths and specific contributions. Any areas of weakness could then be addressed through targeted training. While the appraisals were impersonal reiterations of much-used salary grade justifications, Foundry Insurance were wasting a valuable tool which could help to support their processes. This refocusing of the procedure allowed the tool to be reinstated into the armoury.

Reward criteria

We saw that the next step in Carton Carrier was to link remuneration to the remoulded appraisal system and in that way directly to link people's performance not only to their functional activity but to their contribution to, in that company's case, the overall parcel delivery process. In Foundry Insurance, however, that step was not taken. The reward structure remained very much on a departmental basis. An overall salary increase was negotiated on a company-wide basis, but then there was some latitude allowed within each department. For the engineering surveyors, the salary increases were still negotiated by the trade union. For all levels of surveyors and supervisory staff up to assistant manager, everyone received the negotiated settlement, with no variation for individual performance, whether better or worse than any average. While the mind-sets and appraisals were changed to support the notion of quality of customer service, further assistance to that via the reward criteria was either seen as not appropriate, or, as long as the union supported the existing arrangement, was seen to be a battle too far.

Behaviours

So not all the changes have been duplicated between the two case study companies. What about behaviours? Will there be flowers in the Foundry Insurance offices where there were none before? Certainly the original situation sounds familiar.

> *When I first came to this company, there's no way that the management of the day would have departed from their offices on the first floor except once a year, perhaps at Christmas, and the second time, during the annual con-ferences, when they told the staff 'the state of the nation'. (engineering manager)*

Information was kept very close to senior manager chests. A 'need to know' basis operated, and it was the view of the senior management that very few people did need to know. They were happy that the staff beneath them performed their designated tasks, without neces-sarily knowing why they were doing them in the wider context of the processes of the company, assuming those processes had even been identified. The responsibility for the broader performance of the company rested entirely with the senior management as they saw it. Therefore, they were the only ones who needed to be aware of the facts and figures which related to it, and how the various individual activities contributed, or detracted.

When that situation changed such that the staff were aware of how their role fitted into the wider whole, so information relating to that became more available. So too did the senior managers. The new management team recognised that the responsibility for the wider performance of the company rested with everybody. It was clear that engendering the much-needed team spirit in Foundry Insurance meant getting out among the staff and providing them with the working environment in which they could maximise their contribution. A departmental team leader noticed the changes in the managers.

> *Far more approachable. I mean, really you never saw your general manager or any of the managers, not on this floor. But now you're quite likely to bump into them anywhere. (departmental team leader)*

The working environment became much more open as the behaviours changed to support the new paradigm. Everyone in the company was responsible, collectively, for performance and customer service. There was no place for 'us' and 'them' because as far as the profitable, high-quality completion of the process was concerned, such a distinction did not – indeed, could not – exist.

Information technology

The situation with regard to computers in Foundry Insurance was largely one where, if the systems architecture had been mapped, the result would have been a large empty space. In the days of the portable typewriters, even the IT department had only one personal computer, and that out of a company total of maybe half a dozen. A little later, out of 500 surveyors, 47 had bought their own PCs to replace the typewriters, but this was through their own initiative – or more likely through their exasperation with carbon paper and correction fluid finally reaching breaking point. Typewriter training was provided by the company, so while all surveyors had some keyboard skills – including, one presumes, knowing through constant irritation how to hit one very hard – few had any computer skills at all.

The new board of Foundry Insurance realised that information systems were needed to provide seamless support to the newly identified process, and they called on the help of parent company Composite Insurers, who already had systems in place. Foundry Insurance developed two new systems to front end Composite Insurance's existing record-keeping system which controlled re-newals and accounting. By so doing Foundry Insurance sought to control their own records, facilitate the process, and remove any of the overdue inspections which epitomised the earlier poor customer service.

Summary

Strategy in both the companies changed, and in each case it was to introduce the notion of customer service as a strategic aim, and a specific concern of all those in the companies from top to bottom. Those buried deep within the functional structure of the companies would have seen customer satisfaction as being the responsibility of those who dealt directly with the customers, but the management teams introduced the notion of collective or joint responsibility for satisfying stakeholder expectations. Without the change in strategy, such collective responsibility would not have been accepted, since concentration would have remained on departmental profitability.

Roles and responsibilities changed in both organisations, as they had to do. Taking a wider view of the process across functions, as people were encouraged to do, was in itself a change of role. Spreading the responsibility for the total process downwards and outwards was a fundamental part of the change.

Appraisals in both companies were amended such that they supported those elements of the jobs which contributed to the process in terms of profitability and customer service. From a start point where predetermined generalisations were used – a situation in which appraisals were no doubt seen as a time-consuming necessity of no great value – they became the means through which could be targeted those specific improvements which would posi-tively impact on the individual's contribution to the new strategy. The best type of appraisal should tie in performance reviews and improvement measures to the targets of each individual. All of those measures, taken collectively, should realise the overall company strategy.

The reward structure was only used to support the new roles and responsibilities, via the appraisals, by Carton Carrier. It was not introduced in Foundry Insurance due to potential resistance from the MSF. The fact that Foundry Insurance was successful in its introduction of the change initiative shows that the reward structure did not need to change, but one could argue that success may have been achieved *despite* that lack of change. Refusing its use did represent a potential hole in the change strategy down which some of the benefits could have slipped. Whether it is used as encouragement for people to adopt the new way of working, or reward for the ones who best do so, the remuneration structure remains a very useful tool. Sometimes it will be an indispensable one. There is no doubt that some people see their job as a way of making money and nothing else; the sort of person for whom job satisfaction is defined solely by the width of the wage packet. For these, some of whom will remain in any new environment, no amount of calls to improve customer service or think along process lines is going to produce the most positive of responses without the promise of hard currency when the new strategy is successfully adopted.

Behaviours have to change. In both cases the senior management teams proved that they were serious about the changes they were encouraging by 'walking the talk'. We will look at that further in chapter six below. They adopted the new culture as well as promoting it. In both cases the unspoken notion of teamwork was prevalent, and teams can only be formed in more than name when all members interact. Staff at lower levels will take their lead from their managers and those further up the line. If it is evident that the senior managers are only paying lip service to the proposed changes then there is no way the staff will do anything differently. And why should anyone reasonably expect more of them?

For both Foundry Insurance and Carton Carrier, the need to extend the **IT systems** in order to support the newly identified process was recognised early in the change programmes, and it was acted upon. It is no surprise that this was the case since IT today is practically always going to be the enabler for change. Sometimes, as we have seen, it can be the driver as well, especially for e-business. It is also something which is extremely easy to change, not in terms of cash or expertise required, but in terms of acceptance of the change, of buy-in to its necessity. Changing computer systems is not something which is perceived to be threatening to people's immediate livelihoods and so it will generally meet with little resistance. As we shall see in the next chapter, gaining acceptance for the people-related changes is not so easy, but is just as, if not more, fundamental.

Conclusion

It is clear that many of the changes associated with radical process-based change are those in the areas described in the radical change literature. The areas and the changes within them are linked together. When strategy changes to consider process as well as function, so must the people working within those functions. To support the process a team ethic must be engendered. We intimated above that with a functionally oriented mind-set customer service is seen to be the province of those who have direct contact with the customers, and so too is the response to customer complaints. Consider the figures in chapters one and three showing the activity chain making up a process through the various functions, and the discussion of a functional worker's focal length, above. Any complaints from the customers can be thought of as being made to the last department in line, which has actually provided the poor service in the customers' eyes. Those working in departments further removed from the customer will either not get to hear of the complaints, or will consider that the failure in service levels is indeed the responsibility of that last 'front-line' department. Any attempt to change the activities – and thereby the overall process – in a department which is not one's own, and which is not the point at which the customer complaints are received, is doomed to failure, regardless of where the blame for the poor service lies. And of course, that blame is usually spread over many of the activities, and stems from them not working together.

As evidence of that, consider this comment from a director of Software Inc., to which we have referred in earlier chapters. The main cause for complaint, and one of the main drivers for change, was the inaccurate invoicing, but:

> *Poor invoicing and, therefore, failure to pay bills was actually the last carriage of the train. Prior to that were confused installations, failure to understand what it was that had gone in, what the client wanted or poor attention to dates and responsiveness and lead times.*

So the causes of the poor invoicing were far more widespread than simply within the invoicing activities, but lack of communication hid this fact.

Here is a further example to illustrate that point. A hi-tech electrical goods manufacturing company recently targeted what it termed the raw materials forecasting 'process' (although it is likely that this was not a complete process). This 'process' was seen to require redesign since the organisation was about to outsource the manufacturing function. During the analysis phase of work a workshop was attended by representatives of each department and activity which made up the process. It transpired during that workshop that this was the very first time that all contributors to the 'process' had been brought together in one place, and that while all had some notion of the activities which impinged upon their own, no one had a 'process'-wide view. Furthermore, it was only through discussion that those who performed early activities in the process appreciated that some of the things they were doing might actually be contributing to the poor results for which everyone was berating the later, customer-facing departments. Those departmental representatives came into the workshop as functional representatives, and left it as embryonic 'process' members.

The team ethic must encompass the organisation. It demands changes in behaviours which would formerly hinder it. The dictatorial management techniques within both Carton Carrier and Foundry Insurance would have prevented the changes from being made had not they undergone a transformation themselves. It is interesting to note a comment from within Software Inc., which suffered exactly the same command and control management style prior to its radical process-based change initiative:

> *I'd put it akin to when the army go into battle, you don't sit about chatting about the best way to do it. There's a man at the top who says what happens, and that's what happens. That's how the old Software Inc. used to work because it was like going into battle. You had all these orders, you have to satisfy them, so you just go and do it. (implementation team member)*

Within such a structure there is no incentive – quite the opposite in fact – for asking why you are doing what you are doing, and this simply reinforces the functional silo effects. You have your orders, and little more information. You carry out those orders by doing your day job, and if you ever think of looking beyond your departmental boundaries to see the wider implications of your activities then it is a thought you do not pursue.

Not only should that team ethic be engendered, but also, to encourage the new mind-set of joint responsibility for the process, people's job performance must be in some way linked to that process orientation.

It is also clear, however, that these changes are not prescriptive. We saw both Carton Carrier and Foundry Insurance changing the appraisal systems but only the former backing that change with a subsequent alteration to the remuneration package. Software Inc. followed the same route as Foundry Insurance, though some people in the change team do feel that the final step is yet to be taken. One comment by the IT manager in Foundry Insurance is interesting.

> *We are starting to change rewards but it is not something we have totally worked out yet. In some of the older, central departments we still have not grasped that one totally. Still working on it.*

It must be remembered that all the changes directly affect real people, even those to the IT systems which people have to use. Those which most closely affect them are the ones which are the most difficult to implement, as we shall see. Any type of change programme, but especially a radical one, will depend in large measure on the people who have to make and accept the changes. We must be wary of saying that such-and-such changes *must* be made, or imposed, to put it a different way. It is the management of those changes which are deemed feasible and which still achieve the desired results which will determine success.

For the past decade many people have advocated the necessity of turning a company's organisational structure through 90 degrees, going from a functional to a process basis. In both the case studies, that change was deemed a step too far by the companies' management, possibly tacitly if the question was never raised. Given the deeply imbedded tradition of functionally based working, and our comment on the difficulty of implementing changes which most affect people, this was almost certainly a sensible stance to adopt.

Radical business-wide change demands that the processes be identified and that the contribution made by the various functions also be identified and made clear to the staff within those functions. Once the board, management and staff have been convinced of the sense of a process-oriented mind-set, one that considers the satisfaction of stakeholders' expectations, and the part which each functional activity plays in that satisfaction, then the need for wholesale structural changes is removed. The requirement is to address, and where relevant exceed, customer – stakeholder – expectations. That comes about not through a forced, and often resisted, reorganisation of the physical structure chart, but more through a realignment of the hearts and minds. Whatever changes are eventually implemented, they should be chosen such that people align both to a functional *and* to a process orientation.

We posed four questions during the introduction to this chapter, and through the case studies we can now answer them. The first three questions are interrelated in as much as the areas within which change takes place and the detailed changes themselves differ between our case studies. Therefore we can conclude that the changes are not always the same, although there is a close correlation between them. Both case studies agree on the matter of process versus function orientation, suggesting that neither is correct in isolation. This conclusion is borne out by many other experiences where companies have either tried and failed to introduce physical process orientation, or have balked at the idea of trying and have then allowed the whole change initiative to wither.

The lessons can be summed up as follows:

Axiom for change: 3
Radical process-based change is more likely to be achieved when people recognise that organisational elements, namely strategy, structure, people's responsibilities and appraisal criteria, collaborative behaviours, and information systems, will change and that these elements should align to a function *and* process orientation.

Where does your Company stand?

If you are undertaking a radical process-based change initiative, consider the following questions:

- Has the company strategy changed to reflect the stakeholders' expectations?
- What are the prevailing behaviours contributed to the current situation and are they required to meet the future strategy?
- Whose behaviours are they and are those people aware of the changes required?
- Are they able to make the changes required?
- Is there a feeling of teamwork being built up along the lines of the processes which ultimately lead to satisfaction of customer expectations?

- Is the internal appraisal system being used to devolve the changes throughout the organisation?
- Should the remuneration package be amended in order to encourage and reinforce the required changes in activity and behaviour?
- Have you tried to shift the organisational structure to a process basis, or is the emphasis going to be on people's mind-sets while leaving the structure as it is? (And if you are trying to change the structural organisation, is that an overambitious step?)
- Do IT developments support the cross-functional process?
- Are IT budgets allocated to functional directors? And do they develop systems in their own silos?

FIVE

Crossing the Rubicon

'The first thing we must do,' Alan Parsons told George Downs, 'is explain to the staff exactly what state the company is in.'

Downs shifted uncomfortably in his leather chair, and at least one of them squeaked. 'We do what?'

'We tell them the truth.'

'The truth?' Downs searched his mental dictionary, and discovered a little-used entry part-way between 'subterfuge' and 'whopper'. 'But if we do that, won't they know what's going on?'

'Yes, sir, they will.'

'Hmm.'

'That's the idea, you see, sir.'

'Well, I don't know, Parsons. I knew you were a bit of a renegade but I didn't expect anything quite as off the wall as this.'

'The idea is that we then make them see where they fit in the wider scheme of things; in the processes which culminate with customer contact, how they contribute to customer service. How what they do contributes directly to the state of the company, whether good or bad.'

Downs looked hard at Parsons and started gradually to nod his head, his brows drawn low as if considering the merits of the idea. Finally he spoke.

'Nope, lost me there, I'm afraid. Why do we do that?'

'We have to bring everybody on board, to use a common cliché. We have to engender teamwork across the different functions.'

'We've got teamwork. This company is one big family. It says so on the adverts.'

The Simpsons floated inexorably into Parsons's mind, but he kept the thought under wraps.

'Yes indeed, sir. But I can't help feeling that the staff would be better oriented towards customer service if they felt that they could contribute to strategy; that their views were being listened to; that they really are the important members of the team which, frankly, they really are!'

Downs shook his head frustratedly.

'Look, you're going too fast for me here, Parsons. We've got a team here, surely. I'm the coach and the rest of the team do what I tell them. That is teamwork, isn't it?'

'A good coach listens as well, sir.'

'I can do that.'

'Excellent. Because one of the things I want you to do throughout this project is to meet the staff and talk to them *and* listen to them.'

'I do that anyway. We have management meetings every Friday afternoon.'

'Not the directors, sir. The staff.'

'Oh *those* staff! Hmm. Not sure about that, Parsons. I suppose I could.' He paused and looked around the board room. 'You will make sure they're all washed, won't you.'

'We could have a disinfectant shower set up outside the door.'

'Good idea.'

'It was a joke, sir.'

'Was it? Pity. First thing you've said since you came in that made sense. You see, Parsons, I think you're making this all a bit complicated. All I want to do is reduce cost and rework, and improve service. They're the changes I want. Can't you just do them without all this other touchy-feely, tell-'em-what's-going-on, bleeding heart liberal stuff?'

'No, sir. No, I can't.'

Downs stared for a moment, nonplussed. No one had ever said 'no' to him before. This was more serious than he thought.

Introduction

It is argued that the concept of 'buy-in' is critical to the achievement of radical business change. A number of empirical studies have identified the loss of board and senior management buy-in to be the major barrier to such change being achieved, [e.g. 30,31,32] and any number of studies cite senior management support as the most important factor determining the success of any major change project. The components of buy-in manifest themselves in three overlapping ways:

- People being convinced that the drivers for change, be they threats or opportunities, really do exist and that the organisation faces potential risks or missed opportunities were it not to proceed with radical process-based change.[12,2,32,33]
- People commit themselves to the organisation's future vision. The vision may be stated in terms of radical performance improvements, better customer service, or the development of innovative products.[34,30,35,36]
- People buy-in to the steps or methodology being taken to implement the redesigned process. Examples include managers being more open with each other, involving employees in the redesign, and increased levels of communication. A survey revealed that insufficient buy-in to the steps by which the changes associated with radical process-based change were to be achieved was one of the major implementation problems encountered by organisations.[31]

The general approach does not appear complicated. First you determine the drivers for change, then you gain the buy-in to those drivers, and then you choose the implementation methods, gain buy-in to them, and implement. The problem comes when the implementation methods – the actual changes that are needed to address the drivers in a radical process-based change initiative – are unacceptable. In the two case studies, the previous management teams were acutely aware of the problems which the companies faced, but they were unable to resolve them. The words of those involved in the changes which were made – presented and interpreted below – suggest that this inability was due to a non-acceptance of the changes required. But we will return to the question after looking at the evidence because it is not as simple as that.

CASE STUDIES

FOUNDRY INSURANCE

As we saw in the previous chapter, the situation in Foundry Insurance prior to the change initiative was one where the general manager led the company from the top, controlling the budget, the purse strings, and taking practically all the decisions of note, and many of little consequence. For whatever reasons, he tried to run the whole company by himself and those beneath him simply carried out functions. Within his office, from which he rarely emerged, he kept much of the company's financial information, and he alone decided who needed to have access to that information. Among that small group were not, apparently, the managers who were trying to run departments on imposed budgets, so they were unable to tell how they were doing at any given moment.

The situation was one which was rarely questioned, not only because the mind-sets of the managers had long been established such that few such questions were considered, but because of the reception those questions generated when someone had the temerity to voice them.

> *I remember when somebody asked him about one of the big taboos – about the investment income – he was nearly banished overseas. You don't talk about investment income. (engineering manager)*

Although we have warned against casting the first stone, it is perhaps tempting when after the end of 'Thatcher's eighties' there were still hierarchical procedures which more reflected the sixties – and those the ones of Charles Dickens! But such appears to have been the case.

The effect of this centralised management approach was, as we have seen, to concentrate the minds of all other staff on their own personal tasks, to the exclusion of any other considerations. It also meant that any areas of influence or responsibility were jealously guarded, and woe betide anything which resembled or could be interpreted as a threat to those areas. For example, while there used to be an O&M division in Foundry Insurance, their attempts to introduce even the most minor of changes were met with great resistance by divisional heads who were loath to share what little control they did have.

The description makes the company sound pretty awful, but in fact it had been operating with no great crisis for many years. For example, there had never been any redundancies. It was not uncommon for staff who joined at the age of 16 to perform much the same job until their retirement nearly 50 years later. The company were proud of that, and it was one of the reasons why there was little internal pressure for change.

When the new managing director came in, the external pressures soon convinced him that changes were needed. He set out his vision, and although it was received initially with some scepticism, it provided a focal point for some of the other changes which actually needed to occur in order to bring about the 'revolution' in customer service. He called for enquiries, correspondence, queries, quotations and policy issue to be completed in 24 hours, and this vision provided a hook onto which the changes could be hung. With that aim on the horizon, people had a target.

It was not quite as simple as that, however, because the vision was contrary to the way things had been done for as long as anyone could remember. For instance, policies were only issued when every internal 't' had been crossed and 'i' dotted. The new managing director was threatening to turn the culture on its head, and with such a fundamental change, buy-in was not going to be achieved easily. When the managing director first outlined his plans and his vision to the management team, they were not met with universal approval. In an initial presentation the managers were told that the aim was to have a person take responsibility for any incoming piece of work, to own it and to see it through to its conclusion in that 24 hours. The MD relates what happened when he had explained his ideas:

At the end of the presentation, you could have heard a pin drop. And from the back of the room someone said 'Hans Christian Andersen – fairy tales'.

There are many different ways of gaining buy-in, but some nuts are too tough to crack. The managing director finishes the above anecdote by saying

He's not with us any more.

The way in which buy-in was sought was originally educational, the theory being that if people understood that what they did was an integral part of the greater whole then they would see the need for change. If they were given the information which allowed them to understand and monitor the contribution they were making both to customer service and to the bottom line profitability of the company, then it would turn their thoughts away from the parochial performance of a specific task as dictated by 'the man at the top'.

However, that wasn't easy, partly because at the start the new managing director was treated in exactly the same way as the old one. The staff waited to hear what was expected of them and then delivered it as best they could. In this case that meant that people tried to adopt the new ways of working because they were told to do so, not because they understood why they were doing it, or agreed with the wider aim of customer service which underpinned it. It was a slow process to change people's mind-sets such that they appreciated that the end customers, and the internal team trying to service them, depended on the activity that they, the individual functional workers, were carrying out.

In order to achieve that realisation, much more information had to be made available, including the financial data which had formerly been so closely guarded. Senior managers accepted the need to allow the information into the domain of the line managers so that they could better appreciate, and thereby manage, the effects of their functional operations on the process and the bottom line.

The new managing director had not made any startling discovery concerning the state of affairs in Foundry Insurance. The drivers for change were present under the leadership of the previous general manager. There was an acceptance that they existed. What were not accepted, however, were the changes that actually needed to occur in order to address those drivers. Process orientation had to be introduced into the culture, and in order to achieve that, those factors which affected the financial performance of the process had to be made known, as did the on-going information to show how the processes and the functions within them were performing against targets. Education was all very well, but without the release of the formerly guarded information the changes would not – indeed *could* not – have been implemented.

Practically all of the people within Foundry Insurance accepted the changes that needed to happen. Those who did not no longer fitted within the new paradigm – the newly forming company culture. The previous general manager was clearly one of those, and so too was the Hans Christian Andersen fan. When the wind of change began blowing, that particular individual's prospects quickly became much less Andersen, and rather more grim!

CARTON CARRIER

In the case of Carton Carrier, two aspects of the business particularly needed to change, but the previous board did not accept that change was necessary. The first concerned the way that the whole operation was pretty much controlled by the volume of parcels delivered. We have learned in previous chapters how 200 parcels per driver per day was seen as 'a good day's work'. Based upon this figure were the depot budgets, the numbers of drivers, the drivers' wages, the length of the working day, and a number of other depot operations. Given that assumption of the standard, a calculation could be made of the number of parcels that should have been delivered, and therefore the numbers which remained or were returned to the depot. If there was more than a 10% discrepancy then, according to one depot manager:

> *You were in for some cack from the bosses, but if you had less than ten per cent, you weren't. All sorts of tricks were played to get rid of that ten per cent.*

The mind boggles when considering what tricks might have been employed to get rid of the parcels, but the implication is that the logical expedient of actually delivering them was not the main one! Nor did it matter which 10% of parcels were left in the depot. They could have been there for 3 months or 6 months or since the company was first created; that didn't matter so long as the numbers added up.

Furthermore, the figure of 200 was in itself spurious, for two reasons. Firstly, it was less than equitable since different drivers had different routes, the characteristics of which varied widely. Some had to deliver in rural areas, where the distances between deliveries were much greater. For these drivers 200 parcels would be a much taller order than for someone on a more concentrated urban route. And secondly, the figure itself was accepted as the norm for no better reason than it had been such for as long as anyone could remember, so no one questioned it any more. The new management team did just that, but no origin of the figure was forthcoming. In the same way as we have described activities being passed on to new recruits because 'we've always done it that way' so this assessment of a good day's work was simply a part of the folklore. Perhaps many decades ago a burly driver said that the best anyone could do was 200 parcels per day, and since no one was willing to argue, the number simply stuck!

The new board and senior managers accepted that these operational assumptions – to give a rather grand epithet to what was hardly more than a finger in the air – were incompatible with increasing service levels to the customers, and they were removed. Instead, the requirement to meet customers' expectations of short delivery times and consistent delivery periods took priority.

The second aspect of the business where the need for urgent change was accepted was in the provision of financial data. Formerly, financial data were rarely made available to anyone beyond the board. The previous board considered that the depot managers did not need to understand what profit they were making. Their role was to manage the operation and ensure that productivity was satisfactory; en route to those ends financial matters were seen as a distraction. 'Satisfactory productivity' meant, of course, that everyone should deliver most of their randomly selected 200 parcels every day, but with no idea as to whether they were doing so profitably or not. The staff fell in with this way of working, and since the amount of profit they did or did not generate had no effect on their function or their remuneration, why would they do anything else? Indeed, although some accounts were issued to the depot managers on a monthly basis, they were mostly discarded unread. Some depot managers did take an interest in the figures, but were not helped in their management task by doing so, since the figures were wrong, and intentionally so. Unknown to the depot managers, the figures were doctored to make it appear that the situation was worse than it really was, presumably as an incentive to the depots to do even better. Of the management behaviours exhibited within Carton Carrier, trust does not seem to have been among the most prominent.

The new board wanted all those involved to be aware of their real contribution not just to the parcel delivery process, but to overall profit and loss. Once that desired change had been accepted, so too, in order to achieve it, was the need to provide accurate financial data to all the managers. If people are going to contribute then they need to be in possession of the facts. The greater the knowledge spread, the more will individual problems be addressed and the greater the pool from which suggestions for improvement can flow. Depot managers were brought right into the heart of management by being provided with full information on such items as fuel cost, insurance, vehicle and driver costs, subcontractors, and so on. The accounts were full and accurate and allowed them to manage effectively

We saw in the previous chapter how Carton Carrier introduced changes to the remuneration and bonus systems in order further to support this drive towards everyone taking responsibility not only for their function's contribution to customer service but also to profitability. That was another step – necessary in the eyes of Carton Carrier's board, if not in those of Foundry Insurance – which combined with the provision of financial information to spread the accountability across the whole of the process. It was just that spread of accountability across a defined process that the board accepted was necessary if radical change was to be achieved.

As with Foundry Insurance, the situation within Carton Carrier did not come as a surprise to anybody. The previous board of Carton

Carrier were well aware of it, but did not accept that the changes described above were those which needed to be made. That was largely as a result of protecting their own position with regard to Home Merchandise, whom they wanted to keep, according to the service manager, 'at arm's length'. But why? The service manager provides a view which in hindsight appears to have been the right one.

For their own personal reasons I think, because they liked the power. They knew that when they got closer to Home Merchandise, they would lose a lot of the power they had as individuals.

This refusal to accept any change with regard to their relationship with Home Merchandise meant that Carton Carrier's board were unable to put into effect the changes required to achieve a process perspective and the benefits for customer and company alike that would stem from it. Without the fundamental acceptance that Carton Carrier's activities formed an integral part of the parcel delivery process which began within Home Merchandise, nothing else could change. The drivers for change were very much in evidence when the old board was replaced by the new, but the refusal to accept the changes which actually needed to happen in order to address those drivers made the situation practically insoluble.

The new board accepted that process-oriented change was what was needed to address the drivers. Having made that leap, other changes necessarily stemmed from the decision in order to bring about that orientation, and these changes had to be accepted as well.

Conclusion

In both the case studies, we have seen in earlier chapters that the more enlightened boards and management wanted to introduce a process orientation to their functional structures, and along with it the notion of customer service, with joint accountability across all contributing activities. They also wanted more individual functional responsibility for the contribution to profit and loss. Once those responses to the drivers for change had been accepted, they necessarily led to other changes which had to be made in order to achieve the aims. It is only if all those changes are accepted and enacted that the drivers can be successfully addressed. There is little purpose in deciding what the ends are to be and then refusing to accept the means required to achieve them. It is no good having buy-in to the approach without accepting the changes which that approach demands. Buy-in is not acceptance.

Nor is acceptance as straightforward as the one-word description implies. There are different levels of acceptance, and it is important for anyone managing a radical process-based change initiative (or indeed any radical change initiative) to be able to distinguish between them.

The new boards of Foundry Insurance and Carton Carrier accepted the changes that were necessary with a belief that they were the only way to achieve their aims. They instigated the changes and were committed to them. But they were coming into the organisations with no historical baggage. To call on Dickens again: Marley's ghost in *A Christmas Carol* dragged a chain behind him, the links of which were forged by every shady deal he concluded while he was alive. Those who had worked in Carton Carrier and Foundry Insurance for many years had forged their own chains each time they performed their functional tasks in the same way they had always done. The more they concentrated on their own departmental goals the more substantial they made the invisible walls between the departments. While the new brooms at the top of the organisation could easily adopt a new strategy, it was not as easy for the long-term staff to shrug off their chains and accept that the walls should be broken down.

Their acceptance was generally gained, though, however much it might have gone against the grain. But that does not matter; acceptance can be grudging, so long as it is acceptance. It is not terminal if, privately, those who have to implement the changes are not wholly convinced so long as the acceptance is achieved. In this instance buy-in to the approach may not have been achieved, but acceptance was.

Some people – not necessarily a small minority – will monitor the potential impact of change upon them and will set a new course for their career accordingly. Certainly willing acceptance is better than grudging acceptance, because the implementation might be undertaken with more enthusiasm. But by the same argument as above, those who know which side their bread is buttered will adopt the appropriate approach when it comes to implementation, so the type of acceptance achieved may not matter at all.

There must *be* acceptance, though. What those running the change initiative must be wary of is the superficial acceptance. The weasel words which suggest that the changes which actually need to happen have been accepted, while in fact they have not. Some people – usually those who are, or consider themselves to be, political animals – will welcome the proposed changes in public and will then work behind the scenes to undermine or delay them or even damage the credibility of the people promoting the change. These people have neither bought-in to the approach nor accepted the changes which actually need to happen.

The ones who can neither buy-in to the approach nor accept the changes and who make their feelings known are more easily dealt with; like the person who considered the new vision to be a fairy tale.

Figure 5.1 shows what is needed to give the greatest chance of success, and is a diagrammatic representation of what we have discussed above. The chances of success centre largely around acceptance of the changes which actually need to occur. While some success can be achieved without buy-in to the approach, significantly more can be achieved with acceptance, and the more willing that acceptance is, the easier it will be to implement the changes.

In the case study companies, the changes which were actually required might well have been identified while the previous management teams were in control of Foundry Insurance and Carton Carrier. But while there might have been buy-in to the need for change, there was no acceptance of those actual changes. We mentioned above that metaphorical walls were built between the

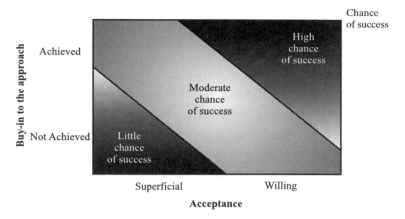

Figure 5.1 *Success is related to buy-in to and acceptance of changes*

departments. In Carton Carrier a real wall became symbolic of the reluctance to change. A depot had an entrance, and the delivery vehicles went through that to off-load the parcels. Once off-loaded, drivers had to reverse articulated lorries out through the same entrance, where accidents occurred as other vehicles entered. The depot manager requested a hole to be knocked in the wall at the far end of the depot to allow egress, at a minuscule cost. The request was repeatedly refused. When the new management arrived, so too, overnight, did the hole. In knocking down that physical wall, so the new managers took a significant step in removing the mental barriers between departments and organisations.

The mind-sets in which the old management operated were constrained by history, experience, personal beliefs, values, and so on and it is quite feasible that the required changes simply could not be visualised. Innovation, off-the-wall thinking; call it what you like, but radical new ideas were needed to identify those changes which were actually required to get the companies out of their respective messes, and this was not – could not have been – done. The residue from that is shown in the reaction of the manager who considered the proposed new vision as being 'fairy tales'. If they were fairy tales then they were of the rare variety that come true. More likely, though, is that the reaction was that of someone who simply could not envisage the possibility of such radical change, whose mind-set made them incapable even of identifying the changes required, let alone accepting them.

A comment from within Software Inc. bears out that argument. Exactly the same situation held sway in that company as in our main case studies, with the problems evident to anyone who cared to look. But the solution, the bringing together of different functions to support a customer-facing process, that was something different again. The functional heads in Software Inc. were described by the deputy managing director as 'barons with their own fiefdoms'. They had not become that way without some calcification of the parts of the brain able to generate and accept new ideas, as the following quote suggests.

> *Over the last 10 years the functional heads rose to their positions on the back of creating their own little empires. I don't believe they saw the new reformed business process as anything more radical than just a different way of doing things. I don't believe they viewed it as being something about cultural and people change; they saw it purely just as titillating the mechanism of working and that they didn't realise that the whole emphasis of the company would shift from the vertical to the horizontal. They just didn't see it. It was alien to think in that way. (IT manager)*

Alien, maybe, but very human.

Our conclusion is that before the actual changes can be accepted – which itself is the major prerequisite for successful change – they have to be identified, and that is not as simple as it may seem to the outsider.

Finally the previous boards' lack of action, and it has already been mentioned in the Carton Carrier case study, where their reluctance to give up any of their autonomy was mentioned. Whether the required changes had been identified or not, they would very probably not have been accepted because they threatened the positions of the board members. This not only illustrates the axiom above, but also leads us to the subject of the next chapter, the willingness of the staff – all staff – to be affected by the changes which have to be made in such a radical change initiative.

> **Axiom for change: 4**
> **Radical process-based change is more likely to be achieved when people identify and accept all the changes that actually need to occur in the organisation.**

Where does your Company stand?

In your company's radical change project:

- Are the changes which are required supported by the chairman, CEO and / or managing director?
- Do the senior managers support the changes?
- Is that support genuine? Is it from the heart, from the head, or is it only skin deep?
- Has your company attempted radical change before and failed or given up on it? If so, do the managers expect anything different this time around?
- Are there some changes which (some of) the managers simply will not or cannot accept?
- Will all of the managers make it into the 'new world'?
- Are you shying away from some of the required changes because they would 'never be accepted', or because they are 'too difficult'?
- Have you really identified all of the changes that need to take place, or has your own thinking been constrained by its historical perspective?
- Are people starting negative rumours about the change team?

S I X

Not in My Back Yard

A lan Parsons, Change Director for Downs Tools Ltd, looked up as Peter Window, his second in command, approached his desk.

'Good news, boss,' Window told him. 'Mac, our esteemed Head of Marketing, is not going to stand in the way of the change programme. He said he'd support us in this afternoon's meeting.'

Parsons sighed. 'He told you that, did he?'

'Yes. Straight out.' Window perched himself on the corner of the desk. 'He said he was all in favour of change which benefited the company. I called that particular bluff by saying we could demonstrate categorically how this project would revolutionise customer service, and he still said he'd support it. Even if it affected Marketing, he said.'

Parsons shook his head and a tired smile spread across his face. 'Peter, my boy, you are an excellent project manager, but I've told you about Mac Yavelli before. If you watch very carefully when he speaks you can see the fork at the tip of his tongue. Of course, that's a prerequisite for getting into Marketing, but Mac was made Head after winning a competition to sell an ice-maker to a family of Eskimos.'

Window raised a quizzical eyebrow, so Parsons explained.

'He told them it was for small repairs around the home. The point is, just because he *says* something, that's no guarantee there's any truth in it.'

'He's fond of the status quo.'

'*Fond* of it! If he could, he'd marry it. As it is, his wife's name is Constance.' Parsons toyed with a pencil, idly doodling heavily bordered enclosed shapes, which he had been doing a lot lately. Ever since he was made Change Director, in fact. 'Let's go over it again. How long has it taken him to get to Head of Marketing?'

'Twelve years, isn't it?' Window did not seem unduly disconcerted.

'Twelve years. And how many colleagues has he clambered over to get there?'

'Thirty-seven?'

'Thirty-six. The incident when Grace Stone was found drained of blood with two puncture marks in her neck is now thought to have been an aborted senior management experiment into increased productivity.'

'Ah. Thirty-six, then.'

'Which is enough. And knowing how much effort he's put into getting there, you think Yavelli won't either flatly oppose us at the Steering Committee meeting, or, far more likely, raise a few terribly important points which have to be analysed in great detail and in that way undermine the whole change initiative? You actually believe he's going to behave this afternoon, after what you knew?'

'Oh, no, I didn't believe him.'

'But you said he wouldn't stand in the way of change.'

'That's right.'

'How can you be sure, then?'

'Well, right at the end of the interview, remembering what you'd told me about him before, just to make certain, like, I put this long document in front of him which I said summed up everything we were proposing to do, and I told him I needed his signature there and then.'

'Uh-huh.'

'Then, after he'd signed it, I said we were counting on him this afternoon.'

'Yes …'

'Then, as I left his office …'

'Yes?'

'I locked him in.'

Parsons nodded slowly, and the smile returned. 'Peter, you're learning.'

Introduction

Organisational changes affect board members and senior managers less than middle managers and employees during the implementation of a radical process-based change initiative. That is the accepted wisdom and indeed the logical conclusion. The major impact on board members and senior managers is seen to be that of a role change to one of leadership.[13,37] This new role requires them to create conditions conducive to implementation,[36,32] and convince and persuade people to undertake the radical change,[2,31] which will then alter their working conditions for ever. Such a role change for the senior managers, though, is expected in itself to be only temporary, lasting for the lifetime of the change project but not extending beyond it. The assumption is that board members and senior managers are unlikely to be recipients of organisational changes, whereas middle managers and employees are significantly, directly, and permanently affected by the changes.[13,31]

Research confirms the natural conclusion that not everyone affected by radical process-based change is going to be happy to allow change to touch them.[23,38] It may be that people inherently resist change,[39] at least when it affects them, although they may welcome it for others. It is not unusual for a manager being interviewed about prospective alterations in business processes to suggest other departments which might benefit from change, but to remain mute on their own department's candidacy.

Some people publicly express their resistance to change, while others remain silent, which makes it difficult to distinguish in advance where that resistance may manifest itself. The characteristics of how this resistance is manifested include uncertainty, fear, anxiety, scepticism, and anger.[40,28,16,39]

Since middle managers and employees are thought to be the ones most affected by organisational change, they are singled out as the most likely culprits for resistance to it.[14,48] By the same logic, board members and senior managers are rarely identified as resistors to change. Yet empirical evidence suggests that board members do exhibit some characteristics of resistance, which infers that they are likely to be affected by radical process-based change.[41]

It is useful to consider the concept of the 'willingness' of people to allow changes to affect them, as opposed to people's resistance to change. The two may form two sides of the same coin but they are different in the sense that resistance is reactive. In order for there to be resistance to change, there must first be change. Willingness to accept change can be produced proactively, before the change itself is imminent. Many researchers advocate that resistance to change should be dealt with proactively, but most of the proposed methods of dealing with resistance are reactive. What these advocates are really saying in their use of the word 'proactive' is that change project leaders should wait until the resistance manifests itself, and then deal with it head on rather than either ignoring or dismissing it. However, the concept of 'willingness' suggests that each individual affected by the content and nature of the changes considers whether he or she is willing to allow organisation elements such as their behaviour, responsibilities, appraisal criteria, and organisational structure to move to a function *and* process orientation. This concept requires individuals, from board members to employees, to assess their own position in relation to the proposed changes that need to occur. That way, determinants of resistance can be brought to the surface early in the change, and, proactively, addressed and managed.

Let us see what our case studies tell us about the willingness or otherwise of the various levels of staff to allow the changes in Carton Carrier and Foundry Insurance to affect them, and what levels were potentially affected by those changes.

CASE STUDIES

FOUNDRY INSURANCE

We have seen in passing how changes affected the managers in Foundry Insurance, but let us look at these changes explicitly.

They had to learn the skills of genuinely managing their departments, rather than simply ensuring that a functional task was carried out, and of doing so within budgets and within stretching service level requirements. They had to manage their people to maximise their potential and thereby their contribution to the process and the company. They had to change their behaviours not only in their dealings with their staff but also with other senior managers in the organisation.

Reporting lines altered. One implementation team leader found himself reporting directly to the managing director, which, for some-one at his level – assistant manager – was previously quite unheard of. And such a change affects not only the one giving the report but the one receiving it, and while the managing director was new to the organisation, he was not the only one who saw the reporting structure change.

Areas of responsibility were altered such that customer service was centralised under one director instead of being fragmented among many. It was absorbed, in fact, into the IT function, as was the support services area. A marketing function was created. The number of people reporting to the engineering director fell from 754 to 589 in a four year period. In the same time period, the number of people reporting to the director formerly responsible for sales and customer service fell from 274 to 102, while the numbers reporting to the IT director, with those increased responsibilities, increased from 29 to 190. A depiction of the changes is shown in Figures 6.1 and 6.2.

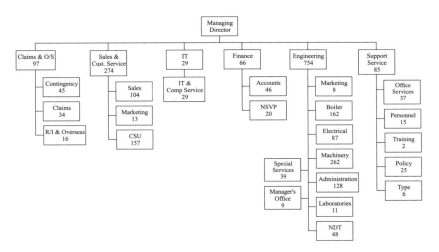

Figure 6.1   *Foundry Insurance structure chart pre-change (nos = staff nos)*

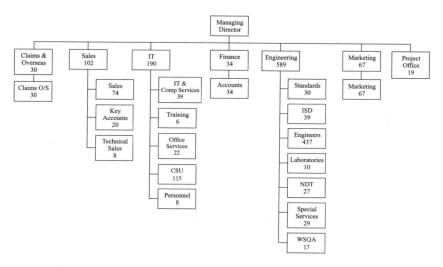

Figure 6.2   *Foundry Insurance structure chart post-change (nos = staff nos)*

   The bald figures on the charts look straightforward, but they did equate to real people, and in several areas the numbers were falling. To the lower level staff, the implication was seemingly obvious, and they were right. Redundancies were required. The board were very quick to say that any redundancies would not be compulsory, but they did encourage voluntary departures where people felt unable to fit into the newly designed company. That such people would exist was likely, given the fundamental changes which were taking place within Foundry Insurance, but it was also acknowledged that the new company needed less people, so a voluntary redundancy scheme was the easiest solution. As a result staff numbers fell by 20% over the period of the change initiative, from 1303 to 1031. Whilst that was a significant departure from the situation where a job at Foundry Insurance was one for life, the majority of staff at least were happy that the choice was theirs.

   It should be noted here though that the people who left would not, as a rule, have done so because they were unwilling to allow 'change', per se, to affect them. The alternative – accepting redundancy and seeking alternative employment – is itself a massive change, and an upheaval compared even with the significant changes within Foundry Insurance. There were some who found the specific changes within the company unacceptable, and who therefore left; some saw the changes as being the first steps on a path which would leave them without a job in any case and whose future redundancy prospects were not as good as the ones currently on offer. But a number would have seen the opportunity of a redundancy payment as their own individual, and clearly sufficient, driver for change, and left because this was a chance for change, not because they were unable to face the changes that were occurring. While it is true that in the majority of cases the characteristics of the reaction to approaching change suggest that resistance is more natural, it is also true that some people will welcome change – those who are bored, 'in a rut', 'in need of a change' – and they would have taken the chance to leave the company while it was offered.

Whatever the reasons for the numbers of staff who left, there were plenty of changes which affected the ones who remained, and many of those were in management positions. Not least was the change brought about by giving the managers a greater responsibility for budgetary matters. Originally the budgets were controlled centrally, but that responsibility was devolved. Financial information was made available to allow each manager to monitor the budgetary situation. Overspends were spotted at an early stage. Adjustments were made to ensure that end-year targets were hit. The review of expenditure became a constant activity. 'As a result,' says the deputy managing director, 'managers have become aware of the role of expenses.' A significant step forward indeed! And a welcome one within the organisation. The managers wanted to be involved in setting their own budget and wanted the responsibility of managing according to it. According to the customer services manager, it was 'just how the job should be'.

This financial accountability went along with the new overall responsibility for customer satisfaction and service which we have already discussed. So the senior managers in Foundry Insurance were most definitely subject to far-reaching changes.

CARTON CARRIER

In Carton Carrier the story was very much the same. By the end of the change initiative, the seven separately managed regions of the company had been reduced to three, and some of the responsibilities which had rested with the central management team were devolved to the managers within the regions. The aim was to move away from a head office autocracy and to give the management of the company a more regional feel.

That the managing director was willing to allow changes to affect him is not surprising, since he instigated those changes. The regional general managers also saw big changes, not least in the fact that the number of such managers was reduced by more than half. Amongst the original regional managers there were obviously winners and losers, but among the three who remained, some were perhaps bigger winners than others.

They used to have Carton Carrier's operations managed by seven regional managers ... now I have the three regional general managers, two of them are now associate directors. (managing director)

It is interesting to note the third regional general manager's comment which confirms that restructure.

My two regional general manager colleagues are both in fact associate directors of the company, because they've been around a lot more years than I have.

For the time being we will leave that comment as simply another piece of evidence showing that the senior management and board members were indeed affected, quite fundamentally, by the changes. We shall return to the comment later, though.

Senior managers below the level of the regional general managers were also affected by the changes; for example the depot managers, whose appraisals were redesigned to reinforce the process orientation and the overall contribution to the bottom line. The depot

managers were made directly responsible for the profitable operation of their unit, and that responsibility was recorded and monitored in the appraisals. Far more than used to be the case, the
success or failure of a particular depot was now seen as a direct
reflection on the manager.

It is instructive to see that, not surprisingly since it was the real
world in which these changes were made, things were not quite
perfect. The words of one of the depot managers illustrate this.

*In fairness we have no control over a lot of the criteria that we
are measured against. We can't control the profitability of the
depots because the profitability's governed by what comes in to
us, what our sales are, and we are told as managers what that
is going to be twelve months in advance. If that isn't achieved,
then your costs go out of the window. Against a fixed budget,
they don't reduce, but against the profitability of the company
they do, because you're governed purely and simply by sales.
Now I know that there are fixes being put in to try and rectify
that, but at the moment depot management feel that the way
we're judged is unfair, to be truthful.*

Of course, those suffering appraisals always do say that sort of thing,
don't they. But in this case, the complaint was given credence by
the regional general manager who accepted that some of the
information used in the process was suspect. And yet the depot
managers' response to this was to get on with the job as best they
could. They recognised that things were not perfect but they still
accepted the changes and appreciated that things were being done
to rectify those areas where imperfections remained.

It is clear that the changes in Foundry Insurance and in Carton
Carrier affected people at all levels right up to those of senior
management and the board. It is also equally clear that the people
were willing to accept those changes, and were willing to be personally affected by them. Indeed, so willing were they that they even
accepted some imperfections in the changes which manifested
themselves in 'unfair' appraisals. It would have been very easy, and

understandable, for such imperfect changes to be resisted. Clearly, the proactive, preparatory work which had been undertaken to engender that willingness to change had been successful.

Conclusion

The importance of having staff at all levels willing to accept changes cannot be overstated. Whatever new manual systems are put in place – and those 'systems' include not only ways of working but ways of thinking and of behaving – it is people who have to adopt them, and most computer systems require human interaction if they are to operate.

In the case of the IT systems, staff who are not comfortable with the changes they face will find ways of increasing their comfort zone at the system planners' expense. For example, mistrusted systems may have their results checked manually, negating any time savings which may have been assumed in the new process or activity. Short cuts will be found – Pentagon security system hackers cannot hold a candle to a group of managers and administration staff who want to bypass unpopular system restrictions! Manual records may still be kept when the use of the new IT system is deemed 'too much hassle' so that the eagerly anticipated benefits of centrally held data are lost at a stroke.

By definition it is people who must adopt manual systems, and a refusal to do so is difficult to counter. Compromise is often reached which waters down or negates the benefits of the new system. A more draconian approach – 'you will adopt these methods or else!' – is, as Foundry Insurance discovered, unlikely to engender a good and efficient working environment, or the essential teamwork which we have discussed in earlier chapters.

These situations are prime candidates for proactively engendering *willingness* to change as opposed to seeking a solution reactively when one encounters *resistance* to change. If changes have been, or are about to be, made and resistance is encountered, then it may already be too late to salvage the situation, unless the reaction is such that the resistance can be mutually and actually removed. 'Mutually' as opposed to the unilateral wielding of line management power. 'Actually' as opposed to the surface acceptance of change which will be followed in very short order by a covert return to the good old days and ways.

If that resistance can be pre-empted early in the project – generally by involving staff, explaining, communicating and encouraging input; in other words achieving buy-in and acceptance – then a situation can be reached where the staff become willing to change and the implementation of that change is greatly facilitated.

Naturally there will still be people who will feel unable to accept the changes, but identifying these early will allow steps to be taken which can remove potential obstacles while they are still small. Some methods for doing this will be discussed in later chapters, but one is the voluntary redundancy which formed a part of the Foundry Insurance implementation.

The above discussion is probably more applicable to the larger numbers of staff at the levels below that of senior managers and board members, and for whom, often, the major factor which influences change resistance, or willingness to be affected, is fear. It is, usually, natural for a change in the 'way that things are done' to engender disquiet amongst those who are doing them. People become happy doing what they do – they may even be happy complaining about doing what they do! – and change is by nature disruptive.

Among the lower level staff (though not exclusively there) the fear of change is largely engendered by a disruption to the status quo. Only part of that disruption is 'What will it do to my job? Will I still have a job?' It is as much the new and the unknown which is scary in its own right. This, again, makes the early addressing of the willingness to change vitally important. The less communication and the more imposition there is, and the more the apparent cloak and dagger method of change implementation, the greater will be the fear factor. Consequently the greater will be the resistance to change when it finally appears over the horizon like a juggernaut heading straight for one's job.

Change, though, as we have seen in the case studies, does indeed affect senior managers and board members when that change is radical enough. The reactions of this group are more complex than those of their subordinates. With this group, not only will the change implementors have to be aware of resistance due to fear, in exactly the same way as above, but they will also have to take into account the added element of a threat to status, power, position and perks.

For the most part, the lower echelon are content with their position in the middle of the office 'tribe' – leaving aside those who are keen to rise through the ranks. The senior managers and board members are those who have sought to rise to positions of power and influence, and have succeeded. Their 'ranking' is often of the utmost importance to them. Successful management of the issues involved includes the acceptance that any change which threatens the position of a high-ranking manager must contend with a fundamental part of these people's make-up. It is not simply a question of fear, but of basic ambition.

To illustrate that point let us return briefly to Carton Carrier, as it was, and replay the comment reported in the previous chapter.

Carton Carrier's old board of directors were very closely knit and they wanted to keep Home Merchandise at arm's length, for their own personal reasons I think, because they liked the power. They knew that when they got closer to Home Merchandise, they would lose a lot of the power they had as individuals. (services manager)

The biggest threat to an embryonic change project is that it is these senior managers and board members who are the ones who must initiate such a project and control its early stages. If they think that the actual changes will adversely affect their own positions of power then the majority of turkeys must vote for Christmas if those changes are going to happen.

Furthermore, the change project manager looking for success should be aware that it is people at the level of senior management who are likely to be responsible for the acceptance and implemen-

Figure 6.3 *Project remission techniques*

tation of the recommendations, or at least the initiation of that implementation. The longer it is left to address the issue of willingness to change, the more dangerous that will be for the project. It may possibly be halted in its tracks by recalcitrant managers, or machiavellian methods will be found to lengthen it until it peters out, to dilute it until it is practically transparent, or any number of other self-protecting approaches. Figure 6.3 illustrates just a few of the signs from senior managers for which the project manager should be on the lookout. While at first sight these may appear slightly flippant, they paraphrase well-used strategies for deflecting a proposed change project, and there are many others besides.

That person (the sponsor, the change director, the implementation team leader) seeking to deal with such unwillingness to change has to recognise that a proposition which weakens the position of a powerful senior manager cannot simply be communicated away. It is not a fear of change which can be removed through education. It is a perceived (and possibly actual) loss of status of which willing acceptance is sought from someone fundamentally – genetically, in fact – incapable of providing it.

For those who gain from the change, there is little problem from this origin. As far as those who stand to lose are concerned, though, either their acceptance must be sought and gained, or they will need to be replaced (and usually by other like-minded individuals who are happy to gain through such replacement).

Gaining that acceptance is not impossible, but it is difficult. In Carton Carrier the number of regional general managers fell from seven to three, not necessarily because four could not accept change, since that may be simply how the restructure was thought to work best. The three left certainly experienced change, and it must be assumed that the acceptance of this change was facilitated by the change representing an increase in status. That the importance of this remained the case even for those three is suggested by the comments of one of those regional general managers, which we mentioned above.

> My two regional general manager colleagues are both in fact associate directors of the company, because they've been around a lot more years than I have.

Promotion of someone because of nothing more than their longevity is no reflection on the ability of one who has not been promoted, and claiming that as the reason allows the one overlooked to retain his perceived 'ranking' despite not getting the title. It may even do so only in his own mind, but that is far from the least important place. We are not saying that this particular manager was making purely an ego-protecting statement, and we are certainly not casting aspersions on his relative abilities. However, rarely would you hear that two colleagues have been made associate directors 'because they're a bit better than me'.

We have seen that teamwork is an important factor in achieving the successful implementation of radical change, especially when that change is based upon a process orientation which has formerly been missing. We have also seen though, in chapter three when discussing why processes 'go wrong' that the normal situation in a senior manager's mind – although probably not stated overtly – is that the other managers are not 'team-mates', they are competitors. This mind-set is even more deeply entrenched than the functional orientation of our case study companies, and many others.

We must make the point here that change is very often welcomed by senior managers and those who aspire to those positions. For these people the path through a company's hierarchy involves the acquisition of new roles and responsibilities, and the repeated chance to prove oneself by making a positive difference in various different departments. For an upwardly mobile manager, staying in one job for any length of time is stagnation, and stagnation is failure. These managers will not only welcome change, but will actively seek it. Furthermore, we should not get too carried away by the driver of personal gain in these individuals, because simple boredom will be a factor. Although it could be argued that the impatience to face and overcome a new challenge is the other side of the same personal advancement coin, it is an important side, and one which is recognised and used to great effect by most companies.

However, we should draw a distinction here between the types of change that are possible. Remember that we are discussing radical change based on processes. Both those terms suggest a movement away from a company's current structure. Someone who has planned a route of ascension based on travel through different departments and different grades may see that route severely disrupted by the proposed radical change inherent in a process-based change initiative. The loss of control over destiny may in itself be a spur to change resistance. And change within a known environment is more comfortable than change which involves an upheaval of that environment, no matter how change oriented an individual might be.

There is no magic formula which one can apply in these cases. We cannot take a 'degree of change', plot it against an individual's numerical 'change seeking' factor, and in that way determine if we are likely to encounter resistance or support. Every person is different, and if a project manager or leader has the tacit knowledge of how to cater for those differences then he or she is fortunate indeed!

Current literature on this topic generally does not consider senior managers and board members to be subject to change. Therefore this group is ignored as a potential source of resistance. This is a significant oversight, even when taking into account the fact that some, at least, will welcome change for its results and even sometimes for its own sake. For a sponsor or change team to make the same error is a recipe for project failure, because resistance at that level will be harder to counteract than at the levels below. The option of excluding senior managers and board members from the change is rarely a real option at all. Changes which are confined to those below a certain level may not be far-reaching enough to address sufficiently the change drivers, and the refusal of the senior managers to countenance change will certainly be reflected in their staff. If the senior managers don't 'walk the talk' neither will the staff. 'Why should they?' is a reasonable question, especially if the only available answer is 'Because we say so'.

All levels of staff must be included in the change project, as it is likely that the change will affect them all. Unless they are willing to allow the changes to affect them personally, the project as a whole will be watered down at best and, at worst, will fail.

Axiom for change: 5
Radical process orientation is more likely to be achieved when people, including board members, senior managers, middle managers and employees, are willing to allow the changes to affect them.

Where does your Company stand?

If you are implementing a radical change in your company, consider the following questions:

- Is the company one where change is frequent (and therefore causes less disruption to comfort zones), or rare (and therefore causes more)?
- Are people willing to allow the changes to affect them?
- How much communication and explanation has taken and is taking place?
- Are jobs at risk, and is this known?
- Is there a swell of opinion that 'what we need is a new / updated computer system' from people who are seeking to deflect the changes that affect people, especially themselves?
- Is the sponsorship of the change project at a high enough level to ensure that willingness to change can be engendered in all those who need to do so?
- Are managerial power bases being affected in such a way as to create 'losers', and therefore resistance?
- Are some managers using tactics to delay or deflect the impact of the required changes?
- Are the managers displaying the behaviours which they are requiring of their staff?
- Have individuals made any change in their: behaviours, job, skills, role, responsibility or assessment criteria?

Confronting the Barriers

Jester Harrold usually arrived at work with an attaché case containing some pens, a pad of paper, and the packed lunch prepared by his mother. That packed lunch, Alan Parsons knew, consisted invariably of a cheese and ham sandwich, an apple, and a small bar of chocolate. As such it was nutritional, although slightly heavy on the fat content. Not heavy on the weight content though, which was why Parsons took an interest in Harrold's arrival that morning. He entered the office which had been allocated to the project team, and heaved his case onto his desk with both hands, swinging it up like a novice hammer-thrower. Either Jester's mother had concluded that her son was in dire need of a growing spurt, and had decided to instigate that through feeding him several hundred thousand extra calories, or …

'What have you got in that case, Jester?'

Harrold turned with as much as of a smile as he could manage through the pain of a newly induced hernia. 'It's for the project, sir. I've got 200 packets of sticky notes and four rolls of brown paper.'

'O … K. What are they for?'

'Stage one. Modelling the current processes. You have to write down everything that you do and stick it to the brown paper which will be pinned to the wall.'

'I … C. Then what?'

'Stage two. Then you call in your free-thinkers and innovators.'

'To suggest different ways of doing it?'

'Sort of, yes. First, after the free thinkers have come in, you have to do stage one point five.'

'And that is?'

'Pick up all the notes that blew off when the free thinkers came in and stick them back on the wall ...'

The look on Parsons's face started to take on a somewhat dubious aspect. Harrold removed a slim volume from the case.

'It's true. It says so in the book I got.'

'And that would be?'

'It's the book on how to do process change. *Re-engineering Made Easy*, it's called.'

'Sounds like a work of fiction. But I'm nothing if not open minded. What are the next easy stages?'

'Stage three is identifying those bits and pieces that don't add value. And stage four is identifying the people who are doing the bits and pieces that don't add value. And stage five is getting rid of them. The bits and pieces and the people. Then apparently stage six is having some sort of celebratory lunch to congratulate all involved and use up the remainder of the project budget.'

'I see. Doesn't the book say that you have to keep some of the budget to fight the unfair dismissal court cases?'

'Not specifically, no.'

'And does it mention the fact that Mr Downs's son, who, even after an intensive training course, would struggle to qualify as a village idiot, would be the first out of the door were we to follow those stages to the letter?'

'I don't think it knows about Mr Downs's son.'

'Nor, presumably, does it know about Mad Evans?'

'You mean Madeline Evans? The shop steward?'

'The very same. And, let me warn you, we don't shorten her name as a sign of endearment.' Harrold looked forlornly at the book in his hand. Parsons spoke quietly but with finality. 'I think not, for that book, Jester.'

'But you said you were open minded.'

'I am, my boy. But one of the tricks is not to become so open minded that your brains fall out. We have to think for ourselves on this one. No book is going to do it for us.'

'But all these notes?' Harrold said plaintively, holding up one of the myriad packets. 'Where shall I stick them?'

Alan Parsons took a deep breath. 'Oh, Jester, you do walk straight into them don't you ...'

* * *

Introduction

When one undertakes a journey for the first time from a known geographical location to a destination, it will often involve the use of a map. These days, travel by car is facilitated by road maps which are printed in great detail in books or on the internet. The person or company at the destination may provide a more detailed local map to guide a visitor over the final stages. International travel is facilitated by similar devices, and often by intermediaries who will accompany us through certain parts of the trip, such as airport-to-hotel transfers. Before we set off on any journey with a fixed destination, we know where we are going, and we have a predetermined route and instructions.

Radical change initiatives can sometimes appear to be like that. There are many printed works purporting to describe how to get from the original position to one where radical process-based change has been achieved. They describe what must be done in various stages to initiate the process-based change, and they offer a number of discrete steps which should be followed. It is true that these steps usually coincide with the proprietary methodology of the company which has produced the guide, but saying that is not to condemn the approach. Other guides give warnings of the pitfalls to be avoided, and the areas which must be addressed to give the greatest chance of success, and these are very often provided in no order of priority or probability of encounter. Since such guides are usually a generic description of what to look for, that seems a reasonable approach.

A number of years ago, travel between destinations was more likely than today to fall under the heading of exploration, or expedition. There were no maps, or if there were, they were incomplete. Usually a compass was the main tool for guidance, and anything that was encountered along the way had to be dealt with as it was met. Pitfalls in those days were a rather more literal possibility than in the business world, and sometimes they were just as terminal to an expedition as they can be to a project. In order to mitigate some of the risks, one could seek the advice of people who had undertaken similar treks on what to do when encountering wild animals, bogs, poisonous flora, and so forth. But where the expedition was across virgin territory no one could state definitively what to expect.

No two companies are the same. No start point is the same, and every destination is different. At risk of putting the conclusion of this chapter into its introduction; there cannot be a detailed map between the two points until each unique route has been trodden. A project which sets out to introduce radical process-based change can use what literature and guidance there may be, but it will be of help only as a compass, or as generic advice on what to do when faced with similar, but not identical, situations that might have been encountered before. For the most part, the company which takes the first step on the road to radical change is entering an unknown and uncharted territory, unique to itself. In order to reach the desired destination, it must deal with whatever it finds along the way.

Let us return to the case studies to see what they experienced, and how those experiences provide an insight for future companies following similar routes. What were the issues which they identified and specifically addressed?

CASE STUDIES

CARTON CARRIER

The new chairman of the Carton Carrier board was well aware that changes had to be made within the company – indeed, that was the major reason why he was the new chairman. One of his first actions was to appoint to Carton Carrier's board a director from Home Merchandise, and one who had worked with the chairman in other areas of GMR plc. He was initially appointed as services director, with responsibility for the non-operational aspects of the business, while operational responsibilities lay with the incumbent joint managing directors. The two men – chairman and director – had a close working relationship, they knew each other's styles of management, and they shared a similar outlook for the business. The future direction of Carton Carrier was not, therefore, going to be a source of dispute between them. They knew, however, that it almost certainly was going to run contrary to the ideas of the existing board.

So the first issue in the change project had been identified and resolved by the new chairman, in that he recognised the need to have support within Carton Carrier's management team in order to get the change project off the ground at all. Without that identification and resolution nothing else could happen.

By looking at other specific actions, we can trace these back to determine what were the identified issues. They have been implicitly mentioned in earlier chapters, but it is the very explicitness of their identification which allowed them to be addressed and resolved. If they remain somehow in the background of a change initiative then their resolution is unlikely.

The second issue, then, was that the corporate objective of Carton Carrier was too restrictive. It did not include any notion of customer service and the objective which was present – make profit – was not adopted through the organisation as a whole. That objective was restated as being the provision of high levels of service on a cost efficient basis, and everyone was encouraged to participate in contributing to it.

Another way of restating the issue was that each individual's own objectives were too insular, and were not aligned to the provision of a service which began with the initiation of the order fulfilment process within Home Merchandise. There was insufficient information being made available through the organisation to allow people to contribute fully to the new corporate objective, especially as far as the profitability element was concerned. That this was identified as an issue can be seen from the steps taken to address it.

The first step was a behavioural one on the part of the board. Previously, financial information was kept very much within Head Office.

It was like a Head Office rule. You could never tell a depot manager what his profit was. (services manager)

This had to be changed to enable the devolution of responsibility, and it duly was. Information was made available to line managers, and it was accurate information, where before it had been doctored to hide what the board deemed should remain hidden. Regional general managers were given far more responsibility for their region's financial performance. They shared that responsibility down the management line, along with the information required to make the new responsibility tenable. Depot managers met with their regional general manager on a monthly basis to analyse depot performance in terms of financial achievement and service quality. At first this involved a considerable amount of education, since most depot managers had no more idea of budget management and accounting than they did of depot entrance flower arranging. But a situation was reached where full information – fuel, vehicle, driver, insurance, claims and subcontractor costs and so on – was passed to the managers in a complete set of accounts. The day-to-day logistical running of the depots was left more to the assistant managers.

The next issue – one down the hierarchical line as it were – centred around the drivers themselves, and their work targets. Whereas before there was a random element of round choice, combined with the spurious 200 parcels per day figure, after the changes were introduced the responsibilities were far more explicit. Drivers were made responsible for a specific geographical area and for the delivery of parcels allocated to them while ensuring that customers were satisfied with each delivery. To reinforce the change in responsibilities, the board redefined the drivers' working day and changed the basis of calculating their bonus. A working day was equated to a standard 10-hour day, which included 'drive time' to and from the round, plus 'drop time', that is the number of minutes to deliver a parcel, plus the 'depot constant', that is the daily check the driver had to make on his vehicle to ensure good working order and appearance.

Identification of that issue and of its potential resolution threw up another issue, however, and that came in the shape of the trade union of which the drivers were all members. It was an important issue, as we can see from the comments of the IT co-ordinator:

The workforce in some depots will only ever do things that are agreed by the union. So it was very important that the union should be aware of and agree to what was happening. What we weren't going to do was put a system in and then have the union say 'Oh we didn't agree to this. Failure to agree, take it out'.

Such a situation would have been a fast-track back to square one. To ensure acceptance, a number of negotiation meetings were held and an official document was produced in which a unanimous recommendation was made by the Drivers' Committee for the introduction of the new way of working. Once this agreement had been published, depot line managers and union representatives informed drivers that their overall performance would be measured on the basis of service quality criteria as well as the number of parcels delivered in a standard day. Those service quality criteria required the drivers to minimise the number of complaints, the volume of claims, the number of late deliveries, and poor delivery service.

This last consideration raised yet another issue – that of the mind-sets of the drivers. Whereas previously they had been concerned solely with the mystical 200 parcels per day figure, they were now being asked – or, rather, required – to think in terms of service quality, and of how their actions influenced that quality. The change in mind-set was not a radical new approach for all of the drivers, since some of them would have seen service to their customers as important in any case; their natural propensity led them that way. But not all:

Other drivers we've actually had to encourage and coax into being able to be polite to customers, actually knocking on the door and waiting for Mrs Jones to answer it, so that they can physically hand her the parcel. (personnel manager)

As opposed to lobbing it onto the front porch and chasing back to the delivery van in an effort to reach that day's 200 before the big match started on television!

Training was arranged to emphasise the need to concentrate on the customer – how to deal with them, what was expected of the driver, how the customer was the most important person in the whole process. Individual complaints were noted and passed back to the drivers, not immediately as a prelude to disciplinary action or as a warning, but rather as an opportunity to learn. Positive comments that had been received were also passed back to encourage the improvements.

The issue of how to reinforce the customer-centric message was the next that needed resolution, and that came through the appraisal system. But here it was not simply the drivers who needed to understand the changes, but the managers who were carrying out those appraisals. Whereas before they had been largely based on gut-feel – unless the number of complaints had reached a level where they could not be overlooked – now they were to be based on a number of set criteria, all of which contributed to the overall objectives of profitability within a culture of good customer service. These criteria included minimal claims due to missing parcels, customer complaints, and delivery volumes. Standard appraisal documentation was introduced – with the agreement once again of the union – and the managers were trained in its use, as were the drivers who were being assessed.

We can see how, from the initial identification of a new statement of corporate objectives, there stemmed a number of issues, all of which had to be specifically addressed in order to support those objectives through all levels of the company. The Carton Carrier board could conceivably have stopped at this point, where they had introduced the notions of customer service and of financial respon-sibility, both reinforced through appraisal criteria. But they wanted to go further. The issues already addressed would certainly lead to improved support for the objectives, but they would not go far enough to change fundamentally the behavioural culture of the company. The board wanted everything, and everyone, within

Carton Carrier to be oriented towards improving the process and the overall service, and not concentrating solely on their own functional contribution to it. They wanted to instil the teamwork we have talked about. A network of meetings was set up whereby functional experts and depot line managers met their counterparts in other depots to share regional experiences, information on cost and depot performance, and to discuss mutual ideas for improvement. The notion extended across more than simply the order fulfilment process, such that, for example, meetings between the three regional personnel managers began to take place, integrating the strategy across the whole company, and bringing the structure closer together.

This allowed the issue of functional orientation and responsibility to be addressed further. When the mind-set is such that your particular function or activity is what is deemed all-important, then not only do you not take an interest in what other areas of the company are doing, but you tend to perform your own task without asking whether there is a better way of doing it in that wider context. Being part of a broader team means being able to question what is happening, and being able to question any changes that are being introduced to see if further improvements can be made. To quote the IT co-ordinator again:

> We'd find in the depots that people would be rigidly trying to fit in with something that didn't really quite work. Now, if there's a teething problem with a system, we get gyp about it, or we'll give gyp about it, depending which side of the coin you're on. But people are much more understanding and they also know that the suggestions are going to be taken on board. It's changed quite radically in the time I've been here.

The managing director is rightly proud of the fact that people will now challenge procedures and practices, that they have the opportunity to input constructively into the change process, and that their comments will be listened to.

That last point leads onto another of the identified issues. It is all very well encouraging people to have some input into the way things are done, but that input is wasted unless some note is taken of it. Previously, the management were not even prepared to give out information, let alone listen to suggestions coming the other way.

We have seen how management behaviour changed, but it was this issue, supporting the overall objectives as all the issues did, which sparked that change. And when senior management became more open to suggestions, and more prepared to listen, so that attitude cascaded downwards. Depot managers behaved in a much less aggressive manner towards those below them in the hierarchy. New drivers in the past, for example, were often simply thrown a set of keys and a piece of paper with delivery addresses on it, and were then pointed to a van and expected to make 200 deliveries per day. If they could not cope, they left the organisation. After the changes, not only would sufficient training be provided to give the drivers the best chance of succeeding, but if a situation arose where one was struggling, the reasons would be addressed and, if at all possible, resolved. The door to the manager's office was the open one, rather than the one underneath the 'Exit' sign.

A further issue stemmed from that former treatment of the drivers, in that these people were treated very much as a non-expert resource. They were drivers. Drivers drove, and that was all there was to them; or so the previous assumption had it. But the drivers were also those people who were in possession of the first-hand knowledge of the final activities of the order fulfilment process, and as such held valuable information for the company. That knowledge could help improve the efficiency of the delivery activities, and it was used to do so, with the drivers sitting down with their managers and working out the best route around that region in which they were the expert. Furthermore, the drivers were the ones who had direct contact with the customers – at least now that they waited for the door to be answered before leaving – and who therefore directly affected service quality. Their input was recognised as a further way of improving that quality.

Two more issues were specifically identified and addressed. The first concerned job rotation. In order to support the objectives of quality service and profitability, people were encouraged to understand and contribute more to the process as a whole, as we have seen. In order to do that most effectively, they had to have knowledge of the other activities within the process, housed in other functional departments, as well as gaining knowledge of the same functions across different regions, (which was another issue addressed through the regional meetings). Such movement was previously very rare – once someone entered a department, that was where he or she stayed for the rest of what might be a long career.

Once the issue was addressed, managers were encouraged to gain experience of line management as well as operational management, and their technical knowledge was improved. Several training programmes were developed, including eight or nine core courses on the basics of sound management, computer courses which covered basic computer literacy and systems design skills, and counselling and coaching programmes for line managers. Graduates who joined the organisation on a 'fast path' to the management levels were given a thorough introduction and the opportunity to visit different locations as well as performing different jobs for a period. Such visits included the parts of Home Merchandise which housed the earlier activities in the order fulfilment process. They also included activities such as those housed largely in the marketing department which formed part of different, but equally vital, processes, (though it is unlikely that this department actually performed all of the activities which made up a process).

By increasing the 'focal length' of these people such that they could take a wider process view, they were able to understand the implications that a decision, made in one activity, had upon other activities across the order fulfilment process. They would also see how this would contribute to or detract from the overall objectives of cost effectiveness and customer service which the previously disconnected process was historically hindering.

The final issue was a relatively simple enabling one. With all the changes being made such that the people were aligned behind and supporting the objectives, new IT systems were needed to facilitate the fresh ways of working. Carton Carrier invested substantial sums of money in the development of new systems; substantial enough that the amounts warranted a mention in the GMR Group's annual accounts. According to press reports, Carton Carrier invested over £80 million over 5 years in state-of-the-art sorting, routing, tracing and tracking technology. IT specialists in Home Merchandise and the service department in Carton Carrier installed local area networks in 36 depots and about 400 personal computers across all depots, ensuring that people in the order fulfilment process had electronic access to information. They also developed bespoke applications to support the parcel delivery manager's ability to plan rounds, with the input from their drivers. The system was sophisticated enough to reflect the time difference between delivering a parcel to, say, a tower block as opposed to a house on the street. In this and many other ways the IT supported many of the required issue resolutions that had already been identified. The 'relatively simple' tag given above does not mean that the IT developments were not complicated and requiring of high-class technical and project management skills. But it cannot be repeated too often that changing computer systems presents fewer problems than changing people and the way they think and behave. That is why so many companies ignore the real people issues in a radical change initiative in favour of the easy route of pouring money into new IT developments. The development of new computer systems is often an excellent substitute for real change!

FOUNDRY INSURANCE

The first issue facing the new managing director of Foundry Insurance was quickly identified: each of the functional managers had their teams dug in to their own particular departmental trenches like World War I infantry divisions. So busy were they performing their own tasks that the contribution to the overall inspection process was lost somewhere in the mass of activities. The 'repel all boarders' mind-set did not allow for any improvement in terms of responding to the voice of the customers – already much muffled by the departmental walls through which it had to travel. Managers optimised their function's activities but without considering that such optimisation might actually be to the detriment of the supposedly customer-serving inspection process. The departmental managers were not pulling together, and, in terms of Foundry Insurance, that meant they were pulling apart.

The managing director looked at departmental activity in terms of value add to the customer, and found that the contribution was usually 'minuscule'. What was more, the issue was not one which was going to be resolved any time soon, because there was no vision of where the company was going, and no plan for improving anything. Least of all in regard to a process orientation; an orientation not in terms of changing the organisational structure, but in terms of looking at the problems from a process perspective.

The issue was addressed by setting out a vision and making sure that all of the management team – who were the functional owners – bought into and accepted it. Only with a common goal could the direction of the company begin to be changed. Only then could the message in terms of value add for the customer be taken down into the trenches and used to remove them. The managing director had identified very early on the tremendous potential which existed in the company and its staff, but he knew that this potential could only be realised if their energies could be directed towards the right ends. Getting the management team pulling together was the first prerequisite to realising that potential.

The vision was centred around what the managing director termed the 'valuable difference', and the value was defined in terms of customer satisfaction. As we have seen in earlier chapters, the notion of 24-hour turn-round was introduced, and the developing vision became the bedrock on which the changes could be built. With the vision there as a common goal, everyone in the company could at last begin to align their efforts.

In order to achieve the improvements which were evidently possible, many historical characteristics of Foundry Insurance had to be addressed, and one of these was the hierarchical structure. Beneath the level of manager there were differently graded jobs from 'clerk (basic)' through 'clerk (semi-skilled)', 'clerk (skilled)' and 'senior clerk' then up to the heady heights of 'assistant supervisor', 'supervisor', 'assistant superintendent' and 'superintendent'.

As a rule, if someone is intent on moving up their clearly defined functional ladder to reach second assistant to the assistant chief bottlewasher, and if such a move is largely dependent on longevity of service rather than excellence of performance, then the chances for company growth and for the spread of a process orientation into that functional hierarchy are remote indeed.

That issue was addressed along with another one – the belief within the company that change was not likely to happen. Things had been the way they were within the company for so long that the status quo was not only accepted but deeply entrenched. The hierarchical structure was a prime example of that, so to address that structure and fundamentally to change it was also to address the other issue of change itself. The change team did just that, reducing the number of 'levels' beneath the management structure. One idea which was mooted was to have just one level below group managers, but that quickly ran into problems in union negotiations, and eventually they settled on three grades. That such a resultant change was against the expectations of the staff is shown in the comments of the deputy managing director, whose expectation of achievable change was higher than most.

I actually thought that we might finish up with five grades, and [before the changes took place] I thought somebody might even then have argued 'That's too few' – and then we finish up with three!

Once some of the functional hierarchies had been broken down, it was possible to spread the responsibilities of the newly created jobs wider than the departmental silos in which they formerly resided. In that way, the grander aim of process orientation could be furthered. To state it explicitly in terms we have used before: an issue which was interlinked with the above was that the restricted nature of the functionally based hierarchy prevented the ambitious staff-member's focal length from stretching beyond his or her departmental boundaries. The changes increased that focal length, some evidence of which comes from the comments of an engineering manager:

Now I'm in the position of being responsible for not just the lifting and crane men, but all the men, lifting, crane, boiler and the electrical surveyors from the contractual point of view.

The customer services manager sums it up:

We've moved activities round, put tasks together, to break down the barriers between different divisions and departments. We've never been able to do that in the past ... having similar service functions together, or people servicing the same customer base put together into the operations environment ... things that formerly were separate and which reported to the different executive members in the old columnar type structure.

It was not only the jobs which were changed to take on a wider perspective within the company. Another issue was the lack of personal responsibility for company performance and for customer service levels, but that in part had its roots in another issue – the lack of financial and operational information made available below board level. Without that information, without the means to determine what effects the component activities had on profit and customer service, it was no wonder that the responsibility was neither sought nor accepted.

Once identified, that causal issue could be addressed, and it demanded major changes in behaviour and operational procedures. 'Financial and operational information' is a wide-ranging catch-all, and all its components had to be addressed.

On the finance side, the senior managers were given actual profit and loss figures and managers were made responsible for their budgets. Line managers developed plans and justified these through discussions with board members and peers. They were educated to understand the effects of poor service levels upon profitability, and that any improvement in service levels depended upon their actions.

For the first time people did start to realise that what they did – their day job activities – contributed to customer service and hence to company profits. Conversely, they realised that without customer service there would be no profits and without profits there would be no job. As with the majority of managers in any company, though, it was not the potential downside which appealed to them, but rather the chance to make a positive difference now that the difference could be identified. People did want to take on the joint responsibility of contributing to the company's successful future. Once more, the words of the customer services manager make the point plainly:

> *If they're involved, if they feel part of it, then it's their business, their process, their company, their profit. They feel part of it and they can contribute; they're not just sat there in the dark.*

On the operational side, the communication had to be spread much wider, with the aim of getting everybody to understand exactly where their particular task fitted in the wider processes of the company. Previously this had just not been done. People were assigned tasks from 'on high' and they performed them, with any responsibility for that performance being directly and solely through a vertical line management structure. The previous board and senior management team considered that they knew best how to run a successful company, and that therefore there was no need to ask the staff; they 'knew' there was nothing to be gained by doing so. That left the company suboptimal and the staff feeling subjugated. One implementation team member gave the opinion that it is a basic human need to feel involved, to know what is going on and where your own individual contribution fits. The issue that was being addressed had arisen as a direct consequence of that lack of involvement. If you don't feel involved, then why should the wider scheme of things matter to you at all? If you are judged and paid according to performing a strictly prescribed task within a solid functional silo, what possible incentive is there to look beyond the walls and question what happens in the rest of the company?

'People need to understand why', was the simple but accurate conclusion of the new managing director, and behaviours among the senior management team and the board changed in order to give the staff that understanding. They began to get out and about and talk to the staff in small group meetings where feedback was not going to be stifled by sheer numbers. The operational information – the reason why Foundry Insurance did certain things, the overall business objectives, the relative importance of customers, small versus large, the vital contribution of customer service – was all disseminated in such a way that it was not just preaching to a large gathering, but was as much a discussion as an education. It was a 'warts and all' education, rather than a sanitised version, since that was the only way truly to involve everyone. And involvement was the key. The staff had experience and insight that was valuable to the board and they were encouraged to pass it up the line, not simply through their own immediate superior, but straight to the heart of the senior management team.

The issue was addressed in such a way that the staff felt involved and, as a direct result, they felt valued, and, as a further direct result, they became keen to contribute in action and suggestion to the overall objectives which had now been revealed to them. The words of an implementation team leader précis the changes which came about:

In a less dictatorial organisation, individuals who are doing the work, who are closest to the customer, who probably have an awful lot to offer in terms of ideas and suggestions, feel more able to contribute. So I think it aided the flow of information with suggestions and ideas. I think also it helped individuals in the organisation as well; you don't get the same positive result if you are dictating to people. If people feel they've been involved in the change process then they're going to make sure it works. They've had the opportunity to contribute and shape their future effectively. If you have someone on high saying 'We're going to be doing this', then with poor communication as well, you might get compliance but you will lose great opportunities for the development of the organisation.

And of course, the bottom line of the communicated message was that the customer was the one who mattered. The managing director recognised a major issue in the fact that Foundry Insurance had lost the confidence of the customer, as evidenced by some major customers leaving altogether, and that confidence had to be restored. The message was given a commercial edge simply because it was the truth. If the customers continued to lose faith in the abilities of Foundry Insurance efficiently to carry out the processes which were expected of them, then the customers would leave, and the jobs within the company would disappear. By communicating that message, and by providing the information to show exactly how everybody's individual tasks contributed to those processes, no one within Foundry Insurance was left in any doubt as to how his or her contribution was vital to a successful personal and collective future.

Before we leave the broad issue of communication and operational information, there was one further issue within that group which required addressing. We have seen how the information from the centre – from senior management and the board – was unforthcoming, but there was also a problem with information being passed between departments. Or, more often, *not* being passed between departments. It is not a surprise that such was the case from what we have seen of the silo structure and the example given by senior management, but each department was almost secretive about its activities, and used unassailable claims of pressure of work to refuse the request for any 'rush' jobs or any increase in throughput. Engineering managers were unaware of the sites engineers visited on a particular day, and as a result the true state of overdue inspections in their district was obscured, which is a euphemism for deliberately withheld! But once the behaviours of the senior managers changed, and once everyone understood their part in the inspection process and its importance to the company, so the secretive nature of the departments was broken down along with the silo walls. The issue of interdepartmental communication and freedom of information was resolved as a consequence of addressing the same issue where it began; in the ranks of the board and senior managers. And perhaps after that sentence, a number of readers might be quietly replacing that 'first stone' they were aiming to cast!

We can see many similarities between the Foundry Insurance and Carton Carrier experiences, and in the latter, the issue which followed on from engendering a feeling of responsibility for customer service and a process orientation was to reinforce the new mind-set with some meaningful appraisal system. Foundry Insurance were no different. The issue which had to be addressed next was how to nurture the embryonic company-wide team, and how to develop each individual within it. Appraisals and reviews were the simple answer, and that led directly to the 'subissue' that while appraisals existed, they were not much use as a developmental dialogue.

Foundry's management duly addressed this issue. The appraisal was changed to become a more discursive exercise wherein individuals discussed their contribution to the inspection process, their potential strengths and weaknesses, their training needs and successes. Line managers and individuals attended the meetings furnished with information relevant to each individual's contribution to the process. For example, previously, line managers had little information on engineers' performance, and engineers had no criteria against which they could expect their performance to be measured. After the changes were introduced, line managers and engineers agreed the assessment criteria at the appraisals, and those criteria were aligned to the requirements of the inspection process.

Foundry Insurance introduced a personal development system called 'Route Map'. Each employee had his or her own Route Map, which was completed and signed as an integral part of the appraisal meeting. Route Map recorded the individual's assessment criteria, responsibilities and activities, and duties to be carried out. All of these were related to the department's objectives as part of the inspection process and key personal, operational and performance objectives including actions, performance measures, training needs and completion dates. Not only did individuals then know the basis upon which they would be assessed the following year, but all of their actions during that year were then designed to support the departmental objectives, which in turn supported the processes and the overall Foundry Insurance business objectives.

The next issue did not arise as a result of the other changes which had been made, but it became apparent only after their implementation. Foundry Insurance had formerly been a company where a job was a job for life and where progression through the innumerable hierarchical levels was achieved largely through having joined the company before the other contenders, and not yet being dead. That latter qualification was in some ways literal, since the only way to reach the very highest ranks – where automatic progression through length of service was not the norm – was to step into dead men's shoes. While there can be some arguments in favour of such a system, like a sense of fair play, it is hardly a meritocracy, and that was what was needed in Foundry Insurance if the rewards were to be given to those who were most capable and who contributed most to the company. The appraisal system which was amended to reflect the new mind-set, and the new objectives, were created with the express purpose of evaluating contribution and identifying development needs. The rewards which were to spring from that evaluation had to be more than a chronological progression through the ranks or even a monetary recognition of the contribution made. From an individual's point of view the rewards had to come through elevation on merit. From the company's point of view, such elevation ensured that the right people – the most capable people – were in the right jobs, thus maximising the contribution to the wider processes and the overall business objectives.

As we are seeing regularly throughout these case studies, the resolution of one issue reveals another, and the conscious decision to get the 'right people in the right jobs' immediately hit a barrier. Since there was no great upheaval of the organisational structure, and thereby the creation of new jobs, the 'right jobs' were already taken, and of course by people who had arrived there by being long-serving pillars of the old regime. A related issue was that, further down the ranks of the company, there were more people than were needed efficiently to carry out the activities within the revised processes.

The clear but unpalatable answer was redundancy. But Foundry Insurance did not make people compulsorily redundant – it was not done. The bullet was, perhaps only partly, bitten through the introduction of a voluntary scheme. It is interesting to note that what can be argued as only a partial addressing of the issue led to some suboptimal results, in that good people who were valued by the company and identified as among those who would shape the future, took their opportunity to shape a future elsewhere. Tacit knowledge and know-how were lost as well as other expertise which would have been valuable to the company.

It is very easy to look in from the outside, especially with the 20/20 vision which hindsight provides, and suggest that compulsory redundancies might have been better. But in order to make that assertion one has to consider both the union negotiations, which would have been much harder, and also the effects on the remaining staff. Once a company has made compulsory redundancies, it is no longer a company which does not do so. And that engenders fear for one's job wherever one is in the company. Fear for one's job is one of those consequences of proposed change, and the corollary then is that anyone fearing for their job is certainly not going to propose changes. Foundry Insurance had successfully engendered a culture where two-way communication and the spread of ideas and suggestions were becoming the norm. Compulsory redundancies might well have stymied that development, to the detriment of the company.

Whether they would have lost more in that way than through the use of a voluntary scheme which saw some good people and some valuable potential leaving is a moot point.

The final issue we shall address in this chapter's look at Foundry Insurance is one which these days is probably among the most common faced by companies aiming to improve their processes: it was that the IT support within the company was simply not up to the task. Processes were complicated by the need to accommodate and work around the inadequate systems, which as a result were as much of a hindrance as a help. This became especially evident when a process review was being taken internally and the wider, cross-functional role of the IT systems could be assessed. The resolution of the issue was straightforward enough; money had to be invested in developing the information technology. But there was a catch. The Composite Insurance Group which owned Foundry Insurance was about to announce the biggest ever annual loss by a private company in the UK. It was against this background that the managing director entered the Composite Insurance boardroom with begging bowl in hand and asked not just for more, but for twice as much and then some. To their great credit, the parent company granted the request, and this had a two-fold effect. The first was obvious; it enabled Foundry Insurance to upgrade their systems and build something which supported the processes. But the second held a greater symbolic value. The staff saw that in this situation the leader of their company was not only prepared to ask for more than double the existing IT budget, but was able to secure it. The message which this gave the staff about the intentions of their board and the chances of success within their company was significant. The feeling which this development engendered was 'They mean it, and they are able to deliver it'.

Conclusion

'We'd find in the depots that people would be rigidly trying to fit in with something that didn't really quite work,' said the IT co-ordinator of Carton Carrier. Sticking to methods that prescribe how things must be done is rarely appropriate because the situations in which those methods are being applied are almost always different from the one in which they were devised.

The same goes for methodologies, as for expeditions in uncharted territory. The guide which includes 'Step seven: climbing the mountain', followed by detailed instructions, is no use if one is facing a wide lake. As we postulated in the introduction, there is, and can be, no prescribed methodology for the required steps to achieve a radical process-based change to a company because every company is different, every starting point is different in terms of the issues which need to be addressed, and every destination is different.

What we have seen from our case studies is that, yes, there will be similarities, so guides and warnings about pitfalls can be of some use; we do not decry the knowledge to be gained from *similar* experience. But each company will face specific and distinct issues. Those issues fall into two broad categories. Firstly there are the issues which have created the current situation – such as the desire of the previous managing director in Foundry Insurance to control all aspects of business decisions. The second contains those issues which will then prevent the easy resolution of the causal issues – the staff have become entrenched in their functional tasks because they were given no decision-making responsibility; such that now merely saying 'okay, folks, over to you' is not going to be sufficient. While there is a great overlap in the categories, broadly speaking the first will be the ones that are in plain view, and the second will be those that only come to light when solutions are being sought for the first tranche. On the route, once one obstacle has been overcome, it may only be to reveal another; once a peak has been reached, it might only give a view of the next even higher peak.

The situation in Software Inc. provides more supporting evidence. For example, the first issue faced by the managing director and deputy managing director was to determine what changes were required. When they decided that process-based change was the way to go they were then faced with the issue that the senior managers, who would otherwise support them, were unconvinced that what they were hearing were not 'weasel words' since they had heard similar utterances before from different company chiefs which turned out to be just that. Having successfully dealt with that issue, the next was that the company was too big to change to a process-oriented mind-set in one leap. So the company was split into four regional parts which were then manageable units. Even those units were too set in their functional structures thanks largely to the structure which had seven rungs on the departmental hierarchical ladder from support staff to the board. With such focus on the vertical it would prove impossible to shift the view to the process-based 'horizontal', so the management structure was developed to support the process such that there were just four levels from board to the 'shop floor'.

Once the issue of change had been addressed, another issue was identified in that people did not see the need for change, so measures were put in place to demonstrate how bad things really were. As an implementation team member said:

> *Within the installation group, we started to take a few measures and people suddenly realised how awful they were at things. They thought that maybe they could start to think about some of these numbers and do a little bit better.*

Managing the change projects in Software Inc., Carton Carrier and Foundry Insurance appears to be akin to peeling an onion. Stripping off successive layers – or issues – led to further layers underneath which each had to be addressed in turn in order to reach the goal.

There is reason to believe that this characteristic will be a generic one within radical change projects. All the issues, the ones which created the initial drivers for change and the ones which then prevented the changes being made, must be specifically identified and then individually addressed in the way which the change team decides is most appropriate. Of course, that decision is dependent on any number of considerations. Unions have to be taken into account, company history has to be taken into account – how deeply entrenched is the current culture? – personnel have to be considered, internal mechanisms, reward structures, mind-sets, behaviours and a host of other factors. But if an issue is left unaddressed for whatever reason – maybe it is deemed too difficult; maybe it is too uncomfortable – it can threaten the overall achievement of the objectives.

From the above discussion, and from the case studies, it is evident that identification of the issues which need to be resolved is an iterative exercise; it is not something which can be completed at the first change project planning meeting, and that is an important point to remember. If a change sponsor wants to know how long the project is going to take and how much it will cost in terms of IT spend, resource input, and so on, then he or she is being unrealistic in expecting an early and completely accurate answer.

For example, in Software Inc., once radical process-based change was identified as the desired route, and once, further down the line, the process itself and the activities within it had been defined, it was realised that the majority of staff required training in order to complete their newly defined activities.

> *In line with the redesign of the process and the restructuring of the groups, we had to train them up, for example, on how to bill, most of the administrators had no idea how to bill the clients, we had to train them. We had to train them to manage all aspects of the order process ... training up 700 staff in the new process and the use of the systems. (deputy managing director)*

While some estimate could have been made at the start of the change initiative of the degree of change that would be required (though that would hardly have been an empirical conclusion), it would have been impossible to say what the training requirements might have been.

Such issue resolution activities will not be unusual, but they will be unpredictable. A commitment to a change project must be such that it allows for issues, large and small, to arise throughout the full term of the project. Earlier chapters have discussed the need for gaining buy-in and commitment to the changes required, and, in turn, neither is this something which is a one-off exercise. As new issues arise, and as new solutions are proposed, so buy-in must be sought once more, and commitment reaffirmed. If that is not understood right at the start of the project then it can easily cause its demise. While a sponsor or steering committee might be genuinely enthusiastic at the beginning, that mood will be sorely tested with each newly identified issue – for which read 'problem' in some minds. Eventually the next step can become one step too far because the number of further steps is unknown. If a project steering committee has been presented with a regular stream of new issues to be resolved and has no guarantee of when that stream might end, they will be tempted to end it artificially.

But what if we are looking from the point of view of the sponsor, steering committee or senior managers involved in the administration of the change project? Surely we cannot expect them to sign a carte blanche resource cheque at the beginning of the initiative and be happy to see it roll on for ever. Well, no, but they must appreciate that this type of project is slightly different. Any stand-alone IT project, for example, will have specific objectives, each with a benefits case attached to it. The costs of the project should be available in broad terms at the planning stage, using the experience of those analysts who have been talking to the business about their requirements. But even for something as well bounded as a new computer system development, it should be recognised that this initial estimate will inevitably involve what some IT professionals rather grandly call the delphic method of estimation. They stick a finger in the air and then add a percentage to the number they first thought of! Only when the development moves through the phases of business requirements analysis, systems analysis and design, and the time and effort needed by people in the business become apparent, should the sponsor and steering committee begin to trust the estimate which is being presented to them, and then only depending on the track record of the project manager and the development team. Only then can the 'go' decision be made with any confidence that the returns are indeed going to outweigh the expenditure in a reasonable timescale, and that the company would not be better served putting its money in a savings account for the duration. After that stage, it should be the case that there are no nasty surprises lying in wait for the sponsor, though that will almost invariably depend on the thoroughness of the communication between IT professionals and business users, who often use a different language, or more often the same language to mean quite different things. For an IT project the sponsor should have information at the start which tells him or her if the development is going to be small, medium or large, within very wide boundaries. He or she will also have estimates of the benefits along the same lines, with those intangibles such as the effect of improvement in service levels, say, taken into due account. Before the bulk of the development budget is committed, those initial estimates should be tied down to a position where the project manager is as confident of coming in under budget as he or she is of overshooting.

A radical change programme is not going to be that empirical. At its start there are also likely to be available some estimates of its duration and its resource requirements, though it is likely that these latter will initially be very much underestimated. Discussion of the various evident issues and those secondary issues which might prevent the achievement of the original objectives will give some further notion of the size of the undertaking being considered. The problem is that there is not, as we have seen, a defined set of steps which have to be taken through the project, after each of which the estimate can be refined such that it approaches certainty at an early stage.

For an IT development, such a situation would be untenable, and the project might well fail on the drawing board for that reason. A radical process-based change project, though, is likely to have benefits – drivers for change – which deny such early dismissal as an option. The drivers for change are often such, as we have seen, that they *have* to be addressed. They cannot be put in the too difficult or too uncertain pile. The road must be trod and the first steps may well be taken without complete knowledge of overall length of the track. If the objectives are all important, and must be reached, then each additional issue along the way must be resolved, and this must be recognised explicitly by the sponsor and steering committee at the start. If a radical process-based change project is going to be brought to a successful conclusion, then the significant issues must be identified and individually addressed.

> **Axiom for change: 6**
> **Radical process-based change is more likely to be achieved when people identify the specific issues which need to be managed and link those to the actual changes that need to occur.**

Where does your Company stand?

- Are you attempting to follow what may be a restrictive, perhaps proprietary, methodology?
- Have you identified all the issues which require resolution in order to address the drivers for change?
- Have you identified all the secondary issues which then prevent the required resolutions of the primary issues?
- Does the steering committee (however it is designated) still support the project?
- Is that steering body aware that further issues may arise before the completion of the project?
- Are mutterings against the changes beginning?
- Can you link the changes to people's day jobs?
- Do people understand 'why' specific changes to their day job need to be implemented?
- Are individuals aware of the contribution of their activity to the company's strategy?

EIGHT

Revolution vs Evolution

'*How* we implement?' George Downs frowned at Alan Parsons. 'I thought we were going to try that new method of yours. What was the word you used? Combinations?'

'Communication.'

'Oh yes, that was the one. Telling everybody in advance, wasn't it?' He shook his head in a 'you youngsters today' kind of way.

'Yes, we are going to do that, but I was wondering more … how do we actually make the changes.'

Downs nodded enthusiastically, but then stopped when it was clear that Parsons was not just pausing for breath before supplying the answer. 'Well, I've already contributed to that debate haven't I?'

'You have?'

'Of course. I appointed you.'

'Ah yes,' Parsons nodded; problem solved, at least for one of them.

By the time he had reached his own office down the corridor, the answer was no nearer. Within the office, Peter Window was in conversation with Arnold Tomb, whose contribution to the change programme would be his last task before retirement. They appeared to be discussing track and field athletics.

'This is a long distance race,' Window insisted. 'Each step we take is one more on the way to the end goal. That's the only way to reach it. It's a marathon.'

'Ah but if you do that you'll find that the people you try to take with you are so tired by the time they've got half way that they give up. They'll hit the Business Change Wall – or the BCW as I like to call it.'

'The BCW?' Window sounded as though he would need a lot more persuasion to be convinced.

'BCW. It's in all the literature.'

'Must be true then.' The words were heavy enough to bounce on their way between the two.

'The point is that this isn't a marathon, it's more like a long jump. We want to take a leap into the future. A leap of faith in our new processes.'

'You take a leap of faith and you never know what you might land in. The company might find itself in the soft and smelly.'

'It already *is* in the soft and smelly. Has been for years. Trust me. These last few months it's just been wading deeper.'

'Okay, okay.' Window held his hands up to stem the flow, then thought for a moment. 'Let me ask you something. How would you eat an elephant?'

'I wouldn't,' Tomb said immediately. 'Can't abide elephant. Was served it once in Mbozo. Tough as old boots it was. In the end I sneaked it out in my napkin and made these old boots out of it.' He lifted a foot to show a grey wrinkled boot.

'Well let's say you *had* to eat an elephant – how would you do it?'

'With a very sharp knife and a big bottle of red wine.'

'No, no, you misunderstand.' On purpose, he knew. 'You'd eat it one bite at a time, wouldn't you. That's how we want to approach the implementation here. Easy does it.'

'Little steps, you mean.'

'Precisely.'

'Hmm. The trouble with little steps is that you end up not very far away from where you started.'

'But the trouble with a big leap is that you leave everybody else behind.'

Both looked round, startled out of their discussion, as Parsons cleared his throat.

'You know the strangest thing?' he began. Window and Tomb glanced at each other, passing an unspoken thought that with that particular poser they were spoilt for choice. Parsons didn't press them. 'The strangest thing is that in amongst all that metaphorical gibberish lurks the right answer.'

The others spoke as one. 'And what's that?'

'Well, it's a bit like a herd of gazelle in a forest fire …'

*   *   *

Introduction

Once the issues have been identified, and the changes required for their resolution have been determined, actions need to be taken to effect those changes. But in what manner should the actions be taken? The title of this chapter encapsulates the argument over the way in which the radical process-based change should be introduced into the organisation. Revolution versus evolution? Should there be a clean break with the current situation, or a gradual move towards the identified 'new world'? There are persuasive arguments on both sides. Consider …

Revolution

A leading golfer from the USA tells the story of how he visited Scotland for the first time to play the Old Course at St Andrews, home of the game. His plane landed on the west coast, the opposite side to where the great links is situated, and he and his caddie determined to drive across the country, a distance of little more than 100 miles. The roads of Scotland, however, are not renowned for ease of negotiation, and before too long they were completely lost. They stopped to ask directions from a local man. 'St Andrews,' he mused, gazing into the misty distance and apparently running through the various possibilities in his mind. Then he shook his head. 'No,' he told them, 'ye cannae get there from here.'

To interpret that in terms of what we are discussing in this chapter, the local man could think of no way in which small steps could be taken from their current location in order to reach somewhere a long way away. Clearly a giant leap was required from that position to put the destination on a viable route, and that leap could not be made given the roads they were on. In terms of business transformation, radical change calls for radical changes, according to one, apparently tautological, school of thought. Once the identification of the issues has been made, those issues should be addressed in a manner in keeping with the revolutionary changes required. A clean break should be made with the past, and the new world immediately ushered in. If the change-over is designed as a drawn-out affair with overlapping procedures and processes, then the chance to stick to the old ways will be taken and the impact of the proposed new ones will be watered down. To put it another way – it is little use trying to adapt the current situation in small steps and hope to reach anything which is too far removed from it.

Evolution

The Channel Tunnel enables transit from the UK to France, and vice versa, in much less than half the time it takes by 'traditional' ferry. Egress at either end and access to the motorways is much easier. During the crossing, no matter what the weather, there is little chance of making the fish a present of one's partly digested breakfast. It is a revolutionary method of travel, and it is shunned by large numbers of people. They cannot get used to the idea of having the weight of the English Channel – or La Manche for the return journey – pressing down on a couple of feet of soggy rock just above the train's roof. A number of ways can be used to overcome people's reluctance to use the new methods. Firstly, education; the rock is some 45 yards thick – 40 metres for the return journey – and is not soggy at all. Secondly, experience; look at the number of trains which have passed under the Channel without being swamped. And thirdly, piloting; taking people through various tunnels under rivers before venturing under the sea. You won't get people to make such a big change in one go, they have to be led step by step.

Radical change in business can only be achieved through evolutionary change, according to another school of thought. People are used to working and behaving in certain ways, and in many cases they have grown used to their current practices over a number of years. They cannot be expected suddenly to adopt new methods, to make radical changes. Comfort zones need to be gently stretched into a new shape; trying to jerk them will only result in breakage. People will find it impossible to adopt the new methods or they may consciously rebel against them. Little by little is the answer. To put it another way – the only way to reach something far removed from the current situation is to move in small adaptive steps until you get there.

So there you have it! Both approaches seem to have their merits, both seem to call on logic. And the advice given to an implementation team will probably depend upon the proprietary methodology in favour at its source. Among those who have studied radical process-based change, the arguments are not resolved. Hammer and Champy argued for the radical method of implementation,[13] but a number of researchers disagreed with their view,[42,43] arguing that while organisations should design radical changes to process, their implementation should be evolutionary in nature, that is to say initially conforming and then only gradually moving away from the organisation's current situation.[33] The argument goes that a radical implementation – revolution – will be perceived by people as being too challenging or overcostly and hence they resist all the changes.[44,45] The counter argument is that an evolutionary mode of implementation leads to 'adaptive' radical process-based change, watering down the intended objectives.[14]

But which, if either, is right?

CASE STUDIES

CARTON CARRIER

Carton Carrier had a computer system prior to the change initiative. Or, more accurately, they had several computers – to call the association of those computers a 'system' might be considered exaggeration. All they did was to record the number of parcels that came into the depot, the number of parcels that went out, and to perform a less than stretching calculation to determine the number that were left. The information was collated by a head office main-frame. It may not have been sophisticated, but the system was there, and there was an IT department which developed and serviced it. That the system was inadequate in terms of process support, parcel tracking and information provision was not a revelation on the part of the new board; the previous board and senior management were well aware of the fact. But the previous board were not prepared to spend the requisite money to develop new, more capable systems. Nor, sadly, were they prepared to invest in the technical training of their IT staff. There again, if those staff were not required to develop anything new, why spend money furnishing them with the knowledge of how to do so?

The change introduced by the new board was not to take the current situation and improve it, through the injection of money into hardware, software, and staff training. Instead they got rid of Carton Carrier's IT department completely. The IT staff within the company were transferred into the IT department of Home Merchandise, as was responsibility for the development and upkeep of Carton Carrier's new systems. Existing mainframe capacity was shared between the two companies, and new systems were developed to support the order fulfilment process which began at customer contact with Home Merchandise and ended with the delivery of the parcel.

Those IT developments required to support the activities within Carton Carrier were purchased from Home Merchandise on a customer / supplier basis. An IT presence remained within Carton Carrier, but it bought in the resources on behalf of the depots and other departments. That presence was important, because it allowed Carton Carrier to retain control over its IT budget, and it specified, prioritised, monitored and controlled each system development being carried out by Home Merchandise. Without it, the company would have faced the prospect of receiving systems into which they had contributed little and for which the staff were unprepared. Given that this sometimes happens even when the IT developments are performed by in-house teams, the chances of its occurrence through third party developers is greatly increased.

The decision taken by the new board did not represent the only option available to them. They could have trained their own development staff and built their own systems to support the new processes. They could have linked those systems to the Home Merchandise IT network without having to go down the route which they chose. But they did not. They determined to make a revolutionary change rather than to evolve. One up to the supporters of the radical method of change implementation.

Fans of the evolutionary method draw level with the evidence that Carton Carrier sought to find out what was wrong with their current service levels with a view to amending them. Change was required, but they were not looking to revolutionise the service they were providing, to change it so that it was unrecognisable from what went before, but rather to improve what was already there in order to satisfy customer expectations. The first step towards doing that was to find out what those customer expectations actually were, which they did through a comprehensive customer survey. They found, interestingly, that while 'next day' delivery of the parcels would have been ideal, what the customers valued above all else was a consistent delivery period. Knowing that every delivery would be made within the week was better than having one parcel delivered the next day and another not delivered for a month.

It was this survey of customer satisfaction which gave the impetus to the notion of the order fulfilment process, in that the customers were talking about the period between their placement of the order and the delivery of the parcel. For the customer, of course, anything that happened between those two customer-touching events was completely irrelevant. They had ordered their merchandise, and they wanted to receive it. They had no interest in the designated intervening steps. It was that which led to the measurement of the various different activities which took place within Home Merchandise and Carton Carrier. The survey prompted the board to ask evolutionary questions – how can we improve what we do now? how can we improve the various current components of the process in order to satisfy customer expectations? – but these evolutionary questions sometimes gave rise to revolutionary answers and approaches.

One of those was the creation of an internal cross-functional team to study the order fulfilment process, and although it may not sound so on first hearing, in the context of Carton Carrier it was revolutionary in more ways than one. Firstly, it was made up of people from operational, systems and services areas and, in the tradition of Carton Carrier, while ostensibly people from different functions were equal, there was no question that some were more equal than others. In designating a member of the services function to be the leader of the team the board were not only challenging the tradition of the company, but showing that the tradition was there to be challenged. It was not a development of the way things used to be, but something well removed from it.

Secondly, the team were given the brief, and used it, to bring a sea change to the way things were done in the company; not yet from the point of view of implementing those changes, but in stipulating the procedures. The team's mandate was to find ways of controlling consistency across the parcel delivery process, and it placed the customers' expectations at the centre of the redesign. The mandate was followed by the team with scant regard for the way the company had traditionally been controlled, with board members and senior managers telling people what to do. The team – known by then as the Magnificent Seven, which gives an insight into the way in which the changes were beginning to be viewed internally – challenged board members' assumptions about the business and recommended a new set of principles by which the organisation would be managed in the future.

The most fundamental change recommended was the one which took the parcel selection decision from the drivers and placed it with the managers. The areas which depots served were split into a number of sectors, within which the managers stipulated the parcels to be delivered during each day, taking into account the nature of the sector – a concentrated city area or a widespread rural one, for example. Any driver returning with undelivered parcels required a better reason for failure than the delivery location's distance above the ground! To someone taking a fresh look at Carton Carrier from the outside, these might have seemed very obvious moves, but for those within the company, who had been working with the old system for so long that even the suggestion of small changes would have been near to heretical, it was nothing short of revolutionary. The following quote from the services manager makes the point vividly:

That's such a fundamental change. That wasn't just tinkering. That was saying to the drivers 'Look, you have decided what you were going to do long enough. Now we're going to decide, in the interest of the company, what you should be doing'.

And the interests of the company mirrored those of the customers. It is a testament to how deeply rooted some internal company traditions become that such a blindingly obvious strategy was seen as being, and for Carton Carrier *was*, quite so revolutionary.

But while the idea was revolutionary, its implementation took a more evolutionary route. It would have been possible to design the new system from scratch and simply introduce it, but to have risked such wholesale disruption to the current methods would have been a bold business risk to say the least (ignoring the cynical view that any disruption at that time could surely only have been an improvement!). There was also a lack of knowledge about how to introduce such changes, and the board determined that the route forwards which gave the greatest chance of reaching the desired end-point was to select a sample depot, study what had to change, implement those changes, and then introduce the new methods into the other depots when they had proved successful. A cross-functional team – more revolution! – was duly appointed to see in the changes, and the new parcel delivery process was defined and documented in detail before being rolled out to the other depots.

A big part of the new system required the support of information technology. Every parcel was to be given a unique identifier which could be tracked throughout the activities which made up the new process. Such a company-wide system had not been used in Carton Carrier before, however, and its development in one go would have been a massive undertaking. The system was therefore introduced gradually. Furthermore, given the limited experience which the company staff had with computers, this evolutionary manner of implementation was easier for the people who had to use it. Systems were introduced and then upgraded over a period of time. As they were rolled out to new depots, the latest versions were implemented. And those versions also 'evolved' thanks to the other changes which had been made, notably the behavioural ones whereby cross-functional teams had been engendered, and the command and control methods of the previous board had been broken down. This 'cultural revolution' meant that people were now willing to question the new systems they were given, and suggest improvements. From the revolutionary change in behaviour stemmed the evolutionary changes to the management of the order fulfilment process.

FOUNDRY INSURANCE

As within Carton Carrier, a customer survey also proved the catalyst for change within Foundry Insurance. To instil the idea that the current situation was not good enough and had to evolve into something better, the company commissioned an external consultancy to undertake the survey and present a report. The report ran to 500 pages, providing feedback on all aspects of customer service, and giving the customers' views of Foundry Insurance's performance. The customers said that the technical excellence of the engineers was of the highest quality. And in the other 16 major areas within which views were sought, they were absolutely appalling. 'Utterly dismal. Dreadful,' according to the managing director. The technically proficient engineers were drowning in a sea not of incompetence, but of misdirected endeavour, and the company was going down with them.

We have seen in an earlier chapter how the head of the policy issue department was averse to any disruption in his order of priorities, regardless of how many clumps of hair the customer had already ripped out. But the attitude was one that seemed, to him, perfectly reasonable until its consequences were forcefully made clear by the survey results. People thought they were trying their best to provide what was wanted in a pressurised, overworked situation, and were totally unaware that what they were actually doing was contributing to the problem by rigidly sticking to internal procedures to the exclusion of customer concerns. The deputy managing director saw the effects of the survey results being made known.

> *When you actually play this back to people – 'This is how we deal with our customers' – people go 'Gosh, it's us'. Nobody fully realised, even managers didn't realise that this was happening.*

The managing director adopted the view of the local Scot in this chapter's introduction, realising that the local roads were not going to lead them to the destination he had in mind; that, in other words, radical change was needed. The process which was in place – or rather the collection of activities which almost inadvertently constituted the process – could not simply be refined, but needed 'a total revamp'. That revamp started with the question 'What stops one person from carrying out the whole inspection process?' And while there were technical reasons that prevented the ideal 'one-stop shop' vision, significant steps could be taken towards it. One intention along the way was to make the managers feel that they were not simply 'paper-pushers', but were adding value within the process, that their job was a worthwhile part of the whole. The more the disparate activities within the process could be reduced in number and performed by one person, the more valuable that person would feel, and, indeed, would be.

More revolutionary change was to happen in the IT function, but this time in the mirror image of the Carton Carrier changes. Foundry Insurance received its IT service from the Composite Insurers group computer development and support department, and the main company database was located on hardware housed in Bristol. Foundry Insurance wanted ownership of their own database, and of its output. While it was not under their control they had no say over the formats of reports, nor over the schedule for their production.

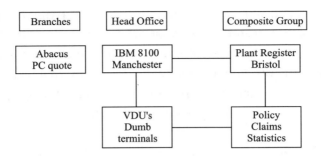

Figure 8.1 *Systems configuration prior to the inspection process*

The data were moved to Foundry's own head offices and stored on their own database. Subsequent to that, the whole IT infrastructure was considered, but in the light of the processes which it was intended to support. In exactly the right way – and in a way adopted by disturbingly few companies – the board looked at the business objectives first, the processes second, and the IT support only third. Figures 8.1 and 8.2 show the systems configuration prior to and after redesign of the inspection process.

IT systems also needed to be built, and Foundry Insurance were revolutionary in this area as well. Although the database had been relocated to the head office, the provision of information system developments was still the responsibility of the Composite Insurer group's computer department. The department was asked to provide three major systems, quickly, and with speed not being bought by employing large numbers of development staff. Such requests were not new to the IT professionals, and provoked the usual indulgent smile to those overoptimistic users who simply didn't understand. But what the IT people didn't understand was

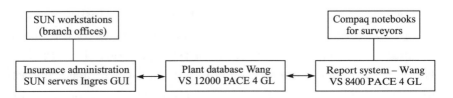

Figure 8.2:   *Systems configuration to support the inspection process*

that Foundry Insurance's board were looking for ways in which their requirements could be met, and not reasons why they couldn't. In the words of the managing director:

The problem I found is, it's not really legacy systems, it's the legacy of the systems. It's the legacy of the people that inhabit these data centres. And they said 'No, we think about 75 man years, we think about 3 years to deliver', and there were too many noughts on the end for our liking. We said 'Well, no thank you and goodbye'. And we decided to do it from scratch.

Having taken the decision to develop the systems in-house, the decision then had to be put into practice, and the usual problems with IT system developments were duly encountered. Timescales started to expand, largely due to problems being encountered with certain elements of the system. A time-box approach was adopted in which a threat to the end date initiated a review of the scope rather than an extension to the project timescale. The board took the view that if 80% of the functionality could be introduced in the time available, then that was a success. The remaining 20%, if it was still required, could be developed in later phases. This also was the approach to the overall cost of the development; indeed cost and timescale were usually directly linked. Where the new process demanded something which simply could not be delivered in the time available, the process itself was considered to see if amendments might be made. This was not to make the process subservient to the system, but rather to ensure – again according to that 80/20 rule – that something was delivered which helped the overall situation. It may not have been perfect – many people in many functions would have liked small changes to what was provided – but it supported a new process which itself supported the expectations and requirements of the customers. Satisfying those in turn supported the business objectives and newly stated strategy of Foundry Insurance.

One of the great banes of an IT system development is the

inexorable expansion of the requirements made of it as it gets under way. The Foundry Insurance board prevented that expansion until after something had been delivered. Get something in place first and then gradually amend it afterwards was the approach adopted. Revolution first, followed by justified evolution. Time could have been taken to move gradually from the start-point to develop a 'Rolls Royce' solution which would satisfy all internal and external demands, but by the time it was delivered, there would not have *been* any external demands. They would have gone elsewhere.

The success of the IT developments – three major systems being delivered in parallel in a 9-month period – had another internal revolution to thank. The board and senior management team were far more visible and supportive than the previous hierarchy used to be, and in times when the system developers were encountering problems, or when the inevitable mistakes were made, visible and public support was vital. The teamwork that the board wanted in the inspection process was nowhere better illustrated than in the development and implementation of the systems which allowed that process to become the success it was.

Conclusion

Companies with proprietary methodologies, which support radical change initiatives on client sites will generally choose a wholly radical or a wholly evolutionary mode of implementation. Once the position has been adopted, evidence can be produced to show where one type of implementation method was proven to be inappropriate. But that evidence will refer to one particular issue in a particular change project where the wrong mode of implementation was chosen. It does not prove – or even suggest in any logical fashion – that the same conclusion can be drawn for any other issue in any other project. Nor, more to the point, for any other issue in the same project. There seems to be a need to support one method or the other, but the truth of the matter is that some issues lend them-selves to revolutionary implementations and some to evolutionary. Whether giving an 'it depends' answer somehow suggests uncertainty, and is therefore avoided is hard to say. But the evidence from the case studies is clear. Evolutionary implementation steps do not inevitably lead to watered-down changes, and nor are revolutionary changes impossible. Both are feasible, and which one to use depends on a number of non-prescribed factors.

When a company's problems are in part caused by deeply rooted assumptions and behaviours, they are going to be very hard to shift gradually. We have seen in earlier chapters how the inability of the old management teams to change the way they acted led to some of the problems, and we have also seen how the new and markedly different behaviours of the new teams gave a new lease of life to the rest of the staff. But trying to move a company culture by tiny steps is very difficult, even if a plan could be devised to do so. The only way is to change radically, completely, and leave the old ways behind.

Software Inc., perhaps even more so than Carton Carrier and Foundry Insurance, had, and suffered from, a strong functional structure. The tendency to identify with one's own function as opposed to the process of which its activities formed a part presented a significant barrier to the achievement of a process-oriented mind-set. The order process most affected the sales, technical and finance functions, which were large, monolithic and internally focused. The change required to move the staff within these functions to a cross-process orientation was a radical one, and to that end the functions were divided into four, and about a quarter of each function was placed in each of the newly created divisions. People from each function were split further into account teams, and that made the previous functional structure superfluous. In this case the functional structure itself was the biggest and most immovable resistor to change, so it was removed. It was not as painless as the bald words here intimate. Getting lions to lie down peacefully with lambs would be a task on a par with getting the engineers to sit with the sales people – except neither knew which was the lion – and it was achieved only through utilising the persuasive powers of the managing director and his deputy. The words chosen by the IT manager indicate how real were the invisible walls that presented the barriers to a process orientation:

> *We put in place multi-disciplinary teams that would support the customer base. ... I think the key was breaking down the functions.*

It is also worth mentioning that radical changes to the functional mind-set are almost invariably led by those at the top of the company who actually control the functions, and that trying to change things further down while leaving one's own behaviours unchanged is a short road to nowhere. The staff generally take their behavioural lead from above, and 'Do what I say, not what I do' simply will not work. If the functional structure remains completely unchanged, then those with managerial responsibility for the functional activities must re-align their thoughts and actions to a process orientation. If they do not lead, no one will follow.

When changing what people do – their day jobs – as we have seen before, their comfort zone is being stretched. A sudden jerk is likely to meet with a lot of resistance – and in some cases the 'zone' will 'snap' – the fear factor will rise, morale will fall, motivation will go with it, some people will leave, and many others will greatly resist the changes. The implementation of the new world under such conditions is going to be much more difficult if not impossible. Incremental changes should be favoured in this situation – either by piloting the new methods, or by introducing the changes through a number of stepping stones, if these can be identified. It is a little like the introduction of the Channel Tunnel to the nervous traveller which we mentioned above; people can come to accept the new methods, but it takes time and maybe a variety of different interim approaches.

When there are 'accepted' current methods of doing things – like the development of new systems – but those methods do not provide the results that you want, then revolution has to be the answer. If something is conventionally impossible, then the successful project manager, whatever the type of project, will just go ahead and do something unconventional instead.

The reverse of that coin is the acceptance that computer systems are not things which appear overnight, no matter how revolutionary your development methodology. In Software Inc., the need was to introduce the newly designed order process, and in doing so to overcome the strong functional barriers which stood in the way of customer service. IT systems were needed to support the new process, but these would not be available in the required timescale. As a result, the existing systems were 'tweaked', and so slightly was the newly designed process, in order to achieve the major benefits of the process orientation. Only in evolutionary steps thereafter were the new systems developed and the new process restored to its intended form.

All of the above situations, and others, are likely to be encountered through a radical change initiative. The response to each depends on the particular circumstances. Sometimes small steps are required, and sometimes giant leaps. It could even be likened to a gazelle running through a forest fire ...

Axiom for change: 7
Radical process-based change is more likely to be achieved when both radical and evolutionary implementation methods are adopted depending on the individual issue being managed.

Where does your Company stand?

- Are you trying to employ either solely Revolutionary *or* Evolutionary implementation methods when a mixture is more appropriate?
- Do the behaviours of a significant part of the organisation need to change as part of the change programme?
- Is there sufficient resistance to indicate that a clean break is the only way of inducing movement?

- Are new computer systems needed, or can current ones be used or easily amended?
- Are there interim steps which can profitably be taken without providing an opportunity for the programme to be halted early?
- Are the current methods of development or change *capable* of taking the company to the 'new world'?
- Have you identified which changes require revolutionary methods?
- Is the senior management team willing to support these revolutionary methods?

NINE

Making the Changes

George Downs knew that his expression was slipping from the happy smile which he had worn after telling Alan Parsons to 'Enter' to one which betrayed the disappointment he felt at Parsons's reaction, but there was nothing he could do to stop it. Normally he would, because the staff were only to see the façade which Downs showed to that part of his world inhabited by staff, but this was one of those moments when the almost automatic role-playing deserted him, and his vulnerability was exposed.

He had made the effort, just as Parsons had suggested, and what was the reception? Laughter. Parsons had tried to turn the guffaw into a sneeze, and very nearly burst his sinuses in doing so, but when you sneeze you only put a hand over the nose, you don't clutch your stomach as well.

Parsons, meanwhile, tried to regain his equilibrium. Given the sight which had met him, it wasn't easy.

'You have to show the staff that you are leading the change, and that you are part of the team,' he had advised the boss the day before.

'I don't give that impression anyway?' Downs had asked. Parsons had shaken his head.

'To them you're stern, aloof, and scary. They'll do what you tell them, but only because you tell them. And it's the same all the way down the line, really. We could all loosen up a little.' He had indicated with his hand. 'Like with clothes, for example.'

That had been where he had made his mistake. He had been expecting maybe a weekly dress-down day. He had definitely not expected this.

George Downs wore his usual black suit with fine pinstripes, a crisp white shirt with starched collar, and a tie which you could only buy in a funeral parlour. Today, though, the ensemble was topped off by a cardboard bowler hat, painted in white and red vertical stripes, with the words 'Kiss Me Quick!' where the band might otherwise be. Above that was some sort of crest device and the words 'Coronation of Her Majesty Queen Elizabeth II'.

'You said the board could do something to kick start things,' Downs said; rather plaintively, Parsons thought.

'It does that all right,' Parsons agreed, feeling that a compliment was in order. 'The hat's in very good condition.'

Downs fingered the bowler gently. 'Yes. There haven't been too many occasions when …' he tailed off, and Parsons just nodded in agreement.

'I was thinking more of a dress-down day for the whole staff. Just to start things off, you know?'

'Oh, right. But you said you wanted the board to make a mark. Something symbolic.'

'I did indeed, you're right. And this is certainly doing that. Don't get me wrong. If the rest of the board …' No, he thought. Perhaps not.

'Black from Corporate Strategy refused, you know. Said the whole idea was ludicrous and that the way to change was for each department head to get his own house in order by cracking the whip a bit. We had a bit of a row.'

'It is a bit of an insular and short-term approach if I may say so.'

Downs shrugged. 'Well, he can try it in his new job if he wants.'

'What job's that?'

'I have no idea. I expect he'll find one.'

Downs continued fiddling with the hat, and a smile slowly spread across his face. Parsons decided to tell him later that the smile said more than the hat ever could, as Downs spoke through the grin. 'And Pixton isn't going to be much use kick starting anything today.'

'Why is that sir?' asked Parsons, wondering what had happened to the head of IT. 'Did she disagree as well?'

'No, not at all. Most enthusiastic. It's just that it's hard to kick start something when you're wearing flippers.'

*   *   *

Introduction

The last chapter discussed the methods for implementing the changes, in terms of a radical or evolutionary approach, and in this chapter we take implementation to a more micro level, to the people themselves. How were changes actually made, and why did people implement them? In the fictional Downs Tools, Alan Parsons clearly thinks that change starts at the top of the organisation, and as we shall see, he is not wrong. While that start-point can itself cause problems, they are not the only ones to be overcome in order to achieve success in a radical process-based change initiative.

We have seen in earlier chapters how the fear of change affects people's acceptance of it, and this has long been mooted as probably the most significant barrier to the implementation of radical change. Clearly, poor communication is a major factor both in failing to address the fear problem and in creating it in the first place,[46] as is an insensitivity to the political aspects of the proposed changes.[31] People who see their power bases or positions being threatened will naturally feel a lack of commitment to the proposals, especially those with the most to lose, such as functional directors.[41] Problems are identified with the lack of know-how of such radical change and its attendant management techniques, for example project management, project planning and information systems implementation expertise.[19]

Broad swathes of tactics have been proposed to overcome the problems. They include articulating a new work contract between the organisation and its employees;[39] extensive communication;[34,17] making the implementation team personally accountable for the change;[46] using persuasion to encourage people to change;[47] enrolling people through appeals to their heart and mind;[31] and involving people in the design of the changes.[5] Some adopt a more direct approach, such as: 'on this journey we shoot dissenters'.[31]

But what is not examined is what such tactics achieve in those 'hearts and minds' – although in the case of the above example it is not difficult to guess! The answer may at first sight be thought to be implied in the tactic – we are adopting these tactics to ensure successful implementation – but there is a missing step here. The *tactics* themselves do not ensure success, it is the *people* who ensure success. What we will look at in this chapter is the effect of some of those tactics on the people at which they are aimed. Once we understand that, and can see what effect we should be striving for, then we can make a judgement as to what approach might be appropriate in our own case.

CASE STUDIES

CARTON CARRIER

In studying the way that the changes in Carton Carrier were actually made, we must make reference to earlier discussions, and the first of these surrounds buy-in and commitment. We have seen how the idea of linking Carton Carrier's operations with those of Home Merchandise was one that threatened the power base of the existing board and senior managers. We have concluded that the presence of such a threat made it impossible for the required changes to be adopted. The management did in fact try to address the evident problems, but they did so by attacking full-on the symptoms of the problems without addressing the underlying causes. The management team sought to resolve the issue of poor service delivery standards by imposing a 'next day' delivery target on the time-critical parcels which arrived in the depots. That target might have been feasible had not every parcel which arrived then been deemed as time-critical. With no cross-functional or cross-divisional links between Home Merchandise and Carton Carrier, and hence no opportunity to negotiate some flexibility – or common sense – into the requirements, there was simply no chance of implementing the new policy, quite apart from the fact that all the underlying causes of the problems were still there and working against any possibility of success. We have already seen the results: the Malham depot's backlog of 82 000 parcels and 27 fully laden trailers.

The newly appointed chairman of Carton Carrier (whose arrival from elsewhere in the group meant that he was not restricted by the prevailing isolationist mind-set) visited Malham and asked why the backlog was quite so high. When he was told that it was due to the inflexibility of the new management orders his response, according to the depot manager, was simple.

> He said 'Well, we're not going to do it any more'. And I nearly fell off my chair. Because it had altered. There was the chairman of the company telling me that we're not going to do what I've been told by the managing directors that 'you will do'. And his view was higher than the managing directors, so I believed him. (depot manager)

Two things became apparent with the chairman's comment. Firstly, the fact that change was going to occur was brought home to the depots and the staff as a whole. Secondly, the battle lines were drawn. In order to carry out his promise, the chairman had to get the support of the board and the senior managers. Some of them, namely the joint managing directors at the time, who were on the far side of those battle lines, were unlikely to give that support.

The first thing that the chairman did was to introduce some support for his position by drafting in as services director the person who would eventually become the new managing director. He was someone with whom the chairman had worked before within the group, being on the board of Home Merchandise, and their business visions were closely aligned. Initially the services director was to take charge of the non-operational parts of the business such as management services, engineering plant, and IT systems, while the operational aspects remained under the control of the incumbent joint managing directors.

What was happening at the company's highest management levels soon became clear, as reported, for example, by one of the project implementation team members, who was not far up the hierarchy, but to whom the situation was evident.

> Certainly, one got the impression that there was a power struggle at the top.

The joint managing directors and the chairman had different views of the organisation's future, with the former wanting to maintain Carton Carrier's autonomy, and the latter wanting to align the company's operations with those of Home Merchandise. The chairman's view eventually prevailed, and managerial and operational control over the depots was split in two: those in the north of the country and those in the south. The existing joint managing director responsible for operations continued to control depots in the northern half of the country, while the still newly appointed services director took control of depots in the south. This was the first time the organisation had been split in such a way, and was the first indication that the expected change had now arrived, and that it was being led from the top. A further, less subtle indication, was that the second joint managing director left the company.

Such a geographical split then meant that the services director could take direct control of the whole of the southern half of the country in terms of day-to-day operations. He could therefore get to grips with the problems being experienced within the depots, unencumbered by a single company-spanning policy. It was decided that the Malham depot – the worst of the lot – would be used as a pilot to show how the integration of activities across the functional boundaries within Carton Carrier and the divisional boundaries between them and Home Merchandise could work in practice. If that depot could be made a success, then rolling the new process out to the other 35 depots would be made much easier. As the then services director put it:

Rather than pick on a soft target, pick on a hard target.

Because that way no one could dismiss the results as a one-off in a depot which was easy to change.

The power struggle at the top of the company was almost won, and when the Malham depot began successfully to adopt the new process, it was over. The remaining managing director left Carton Carrier, purportedly to set up his own business. The services director was appointed as the new managing director and took over responsibility for all the depots country-wide. If anyone was in any doubt that the changes were going to affect them, then they were in a very small minority. As we have said before, staff take their lead from the higher echelons of their company, and this was a clear message from the Carton Carrier board. In some instances, it is easy to buy-in superficially to a proposed change knowing that it is not going to happen, but that was no longer a sensible option. This change was not going to blow over as soon as the wind veered.

While changes were being made in the Malham depot, and while computer systems were being built to support the new process, it was important that the rest of the Carton Carrier staff were not left in a vacuum. The board therefore took the opportunity to make small symbolic alterations to reinforce the fact that the company was indeed changing. These had the effect of beginning a cultural shift as well as calming fears of impending change, generating that willingness to change which we have discussed, and introducing an element of teamwork throughout the organisation. We have seen one of these changes in an earlier chapter – the hole in the depot wall. For years the depot manager had been refused an exit which was different from the entrance, even though such an alteration would only have cost the company £4000. When the same recommendation was made to the new managing director, it was immediately approved and implemented. Other changes cost less or little more; black Bakelite phones were replaced with more modern equipment, managers and their staff occasionally went out for lunch together, parcel delivery managers were provided with a desk and chair, old photocopiers were replaced, and other furniture and fittings were improved. The depot's physical environment was being changed and renewed, and this paved the way for – and made the staff more conducive to – changed and renewed processes.

We have also discussed the reaction to impending change, especially at the lower levels of the company hierarchy. If there is insufficient preparation, generally in terms of communication, then fear will be engendered and resistance to change will start to build up. That fear and resistance will not be alleviated if the changes are introduced by 'outside' elements. Although the changes to the process had already been implemented successfully in the Malham depot, the staff and management of that depot were still 'outsiders' from the point of view of the other depots – the teamwork and process orientation had not extended far enough to cross the UK's north–south divide! Implementation managers – almost missionaries – were chosen from the Malham depot in order to use the experience they had gained and so avoid reinventing any wheels. Those 'external' managers were then supported by the appointment of local teams to roll out the new process and IT systems into the other depots across the country. These teams were cross-functional, with representatives from, for example, operational and service areas, fleet management and the IT departments. The effect was two-fold.

Firstly, the new systems and process were more readily accepted. There was not the feeling that 'men in suits' had arrived from elsewhere to impose a new regime. That lowered the level of anxiety and increased the willingness to change, as we can see from the views of a services manager:

The drivers trust their manager, so changes are easier to implement. They don't necessarily trust us, strangers (people from head office) that turn up at depots, saying 'We'd like you to take this computer out every day with your parcels'.

Secondly, it allowed the responsibility for the changes to be passed to the individual depots. If 'outsiders' impose the changes and then walk away, they leave behind them an open door through which those changes can subsequently be ejected by the supposed recipients. Where changes are owned by the individual depots that cannot so easily be done, since the 'implementors' then own the new process. Carton Carrier required that each depot's implementation team signed off the changes, stating that they had been made to the team's satisfaction, in order to engender that feeling of ownership, and that inescapable responsibility.

The implementation was not simply a matter of giving local teams the new systems and instructions and letting them get on with it. Further preparation was required to ensure that the new methods were successfully introduced into depots. We have already seen how small, symbolic, changes paved the way, but more was required. The management team determined that changes would be more readily accepted into depots where people:

- Did not feel they were being criticised for their current performance and actions
- Did not feel indifference towards the parcel delivery process
- Did not feel alienated from the parcel delivery process
- Were supported in ways that suited them: (for example, some required training, while others required less demanding jobs)
- Were confident while making the transition to the redesigned parcel delivery process
- Felt secure about their future with the company when they achieved what was required of them

To achieve that background, where the staff felt comfortable about the changes, a programme of communication was undertaken between people at each level in the parcel delivery process. Regional general managers reassured depot managers; depot managers spoke to assistant depot managers and parcel delivery managers; they in turn reassured drivers; and functional managers discussed difficulties with all the line managers and drivers.

It was also recognised that the changes required preparation in the form of training. If the depot managers were to be responsible for the financial performance of their location then they had to be provided with the capability of controlling that performance. Training was provided, not to the extent of turning the managers into accountants, but supplying the grounding needed for them to take on their new responsibilities in the revised process and culture. Budgeting, accounting skills, and financial analysis techniques such as ratio analysis were taught to coincide with the new flow of financial information coming out from the centre.

With the best intentions, however, some people are not going to welcome the changes, and others are not going to be able to cope with them. We have already seen how the power struggle at the top of Carton Carrier resulted in the departure of the joint managing directors and in the reduction of the regional managers from seven to three. There had always been a high turnover of drivers, especially in the London and southern depots, and this did not change significantly, but some who were close to retirement or who had been long-serving staff left because of difficulties with the new system. Some managers, now required to take responsibility for people rather than hide in an office, could not come to terms with the new culture, and were either found less demanding jobs, or left the organisation. In the wider scheme of things, the number of people who left because they could not adapt to the changes was small, but it was not zero.

FOUNDRY INSURANCE

The newly appointed chairman of Foundry Insurance was not steeped in the current processes of the company, and was therefore able to take a view of the wood that was not obscured by the trees. It was clear that there were significant problems and that they were not being addressed. In the same way as occurred within Carton Carrier, the chairman needed someone of similar mind in charge who would address the problems, and that person was obviously not one of those who had managed the company while the problems arose. The newly appointed head of the IT department, who had also been drafted in from outside the company, was appointed to be the new general manager (or managing director as that role became) after the rapid retirement of the incumbent. This in itself was a significant move away from tradition, since the higher positions in the company had always been filled from within, by people with vast experience in insurance, and in the way 'things were done' within Foundry Insurance. But the chairman wanted precisely someone who would radically change the way 'things were done' so experience was less an advantage than unwanted baggage.

The new managing director soon discovered the size of the challenge with which he had been presented. One graphic example came from a requested walkthrough of the activities involved in producing the simplest of the company's policies. The policy was worth about £75 to Foundry Insurance, that being what the customer was charged for its production, and the walkthrough took all morning to complete. It meandered through 10 different departments and involved 30 different people performing 43 specific activities.

The managing director started asking questions, such as the deceptively simple 'Why do we do that?' In an organisation which has grown to its current state over a long period of time, and in which the activities within a process are divided by the huge, invisible, functional walls which we have discussed in earlier chapters, the answer to that is often the one which the managing director was given – 'We've always done that'. No one previously questioned why certain activities took so long because no one considered it to be a problem. The industry average for delivery of some policies was 3 months, so why should Foundry Insurance aim to produce them any quicker?

While the problems were evident, so too was the enormous effort required to resolve them. Foundry Insurance was an organisation moving the way it always had and with a collective momentum that one man would find impossible to arrest and redirect. That momentum had to come from the top management team, and the new managing director had to address that problem first, which he duly did. Of the top ten managers, eight left, mostly taking retirement, though there were other reasons, one of which was a stated inability to go along with the ideas of the new regime.

The average age of our management team fell about fifteen years in the space of about twelve months. An awful lot of people left who had been with us an awfully long time. (managing director)

And, without making them sound like obstructive dinosaurs, those people took with them their fixed ideas of working methods and the cultural paradigm which had grown up with and around them. The way was cleared for changes to be made, more people were brought in from outside the organisation, and a very clear signal was passed down to the staff.

Another signal was passed by the more open management style of the new managing director. His 'walkabout' certainly served to uncover problems and allowed him to gain an insight into what solutions might be required, but it also showed the staff that a fresh wind was blowing. The old management team did not undertake walkabouts, but remained in their offices. They did not talk to people; they most certainly did not, as the new managing director did, instruct people to call them by their first names.

As we saw with Carton Carrier, this type of behaviour starts to break down the barriers and induce the first notion of teamwork; the idea that the whole company is in this together. In Foundry Insurance, the previous 'us and them' situation was reinforced by, among other things, 'class' distinctions in the three staff restaurants. There was the staff canteen, then the managers' restaurant, and then the one for the executives. Such obvious anachronisms simply cannot remain when the management are trying to introduce the feeling of cohesiveness, and very quickly the distinctions were removed and a single restaurant was introduced, with, furthermore, upgraded facilities.

The old command and control paradigm was also addressed, initially in small ways, like, for example, a relaxation of the death grip which the managers kept on the number of pencils in the company. An implementation team member recalls what the situation used to be:

If you wanted a new pencil you had to hand your old one in, because everything had to be accounted for, and there were only so many pencils allocated.

The new, more personal style of management engendered by the managing director quickly spread through the new management team, who all walked the floors talking to their staff, and, more to the point, hearing their problems and suggestions. And not only hearing them, but actually listening to them and acting upon them, and in ways that, even in the very early days of the metamorphosis, were not merely symbolic. The reports from the staff highlighted some urgent problems which had to be addressed immediately.

Although the major shortfall was seen to be the inability of the IT infrastructure to support the inspection process, the solution from that source would not come overnight – even the simplest IT systems take time to build. But other short-term changes could be adopted as a way not only of addressing the immediate problems but of furthering the culture change. Overdue inspections were more of a problem in London than elsewhere because engineers could not be housed there, on account of the cost involved. The new management team introduced a temporary solution whereby people on direct commuter lines from other parts of the country – particularly Liverpool, Manchester and the north-east – were seconded to London and put up in hotels for a week or a month at a time. There was early resistance to this change – the old mind-set was still very much to the fore – but the new managers made sure the accommodation was comfortable, and tried to second more than one person at a time, so that the task became more enjoyable, and took on a more challenging aspect. People saw that not only were the problems being heard and addressed, but the needs and feelings of staff were actually being taken into account.

The longer term solution to the problems did require significant IT work, though, alongside the cultural changes and the reorientation of the mind-sets to a focus on the whole process. We have already seen how the computer literacy within Foundry Insurance was at a low level, but there had been efforts to introduce new systems, and these had not met with great success. As with many companies, one of the highest and thickest of the invisible walls is that between the IT department and pretty much all the others. There are a number of reasons for this. Firstly, IT is an easy target when looking for reasons for poor operational performance. Rather than addressing the process as a whole and the activities within it, many people will focus on the technical support for the activities which they currently perform. In some cases, of course, this may be perfectly reasonable. Secondly, though, the development of a new system is viewed very differently by the two 'sides'. Those in IT know, as we discussed in the last chapter, that until all the requirements have been gathered, analysed, designed and specified to a very detailed level, it is virtually impossible to say exactly how long a complete project will take. The business users of the system always consider that their initial statement of requirements is full and simple, and that the tentative timescale put forward by the IT department constitutes a guaranteed delivery date. Pressure on that date inevitably comes as the more detailed requirements are unearthed, and in order to meet the time targets, the quality of the system is often compromised – the last stage of a development is testing, and this is all too often squeezed into a quite inadequate period. The system which is then delivered does not perform in the way the business users expected or required. Blame is then placed yet again, and another invisible brick is cemented into the wall. This situation certainly existed in Foundry Insurance.

One of the problems was that we were very good at creating user expectation, and our user workforce was very good at nailing the IT department to the ground in terms of delivery dates. So the management of expectations could have been better. 'How long is it going to take you to develop this system?' 'Three months.' 'Right, so on the thirtieth of July, we'll have it, will we?' And if it's not there, it's a case of 'Why haven't we got it?' That was the type of attitude. (customer services manager)

I think there was a lack of realism concerning what IT systems are about. Perfection doesn't exist. That's all. And people in the organisation were expecting perfection. One of the things we've got to constantly relearn is to manage expectations. (deputy managing director)

Those expectations were managed, and the relationship problems addressed in the best possible way for anyone developing an IT system – the creation of cross-functional teams to complete the project. User involvement from an early stage, and throughout the development, is key to success, and in Foundry Insurance it also helped to build that cross-functional teamwork. Furthermore, the new IT systems were required quickly. In order to achieve their targets, Foundry Insurance adopted a number of hitherto untried methods, including, as we have seen, the use of in-house teams rather than the parent company, Composite Insurer's, IT department. Those in-house teams included IT contractors as well as bought-in permanent staff, and the reward structure within the company was adjusted to suit that particular labour market. Each team, although it was kept small, contained representatives from different business areas, and each was led by a business representative. That leader, especially, but also the other business team members, were those within the company who would see the most benefits from the successful implementation of the systems. The board showed their support for what the teams were doing by removing the business representatives from their normal 'day jobs' and placing them full time on the projects. And that was not the only way in which support was offered. The managing director describes another, absolutely vital one:

> As a top management team, we made an undying commitment to those people (implementing the change). We said 'We are with you one hundred and ten per cent. Whatever you need to do to make this work, you will get it from us', and we involved ourselves fully in that process.

That support proved to the team members that what they were doing was valued by the organisation. It added to the impetus needed to deliver on time, as did the feeling that they were being given the responsibility, and that senior management were not looking critically over their shoulders at every stage of their work, as might have been the case under the previous management structure. The involvement of the users gave them a greater understanding of the difficulties involved in producing a new IT system, and there was a much greater tolerance of the initial capabilities of the delivered product. Timescale was everything, and if there were teething troubles, then so be it – what was delivered would still be a significant improvement on what was there before and would allow the new inspection process to be implemented. With this added responsibility, the support from the senior managers and the board, and the greater teamwork created by the cross-functional teams, the developers produced their three systems in record time.

Once delivered, those systems had to be used, and a significant training effort was required for people with very limited experience of computer technology. Training was given to all staff from directors to clerks, and was tailored to fit what each needed; so that, for example, the engineers learned how to upload and download data remotely. Pass and fail criteria were set, which made the training challenging and dispelled any lingering idea that, perhaps, this was another transient fad initiative that did not have to be taken seriously. Help was available throughout the iterative training sessions to ensure the highest possible pass rate.

For most, the new systems were welcome and did not pose great problems, but for some the new ways of working proved more difficult, and they did not pass the tests. There were others who simply did not like the changes which had been made in the organisation, and others who could not cope with such a fundamental change in the working methods. There was, to quote the managing director, 'a pretty high attrition rate'.

That the stress of the change was significant was tragically brought home when one staff member suffered a nervous breakdown. Whether there were other factors involved is open to question, but there was a feeling among the senior managers that not enough had been done to prepare people for the changes. Given their fundamental nature, and the speed with which they needed to be introduced, such a feeling might be thought to be overly self-critical. However, the board and senior managers decided that greater support was needed. Although they had changed the behaviours of the previous regime by talking and listening, those behaviours needed even more change to help the staff through the transition, and reassure them that any problems they were having would be addressed.

It is often the case that those who are champions of change do not realise quite how traumatic its effects can be on people who have been performing the same job in the same way for a number of years.

It is also often the case that those of whom change is being asked do not feel able to ask for help, so that the 'implementors' can sometimes only discover the stress which they are causing when something – or, sadly, someone – breaks. Foundry Insurance introduced its changes at a cost, and it depends upon one's viewpoint as to how close that cost came to being too high.

Conclusion

The discussion at the start of this chapter concerned the tactics for implementation of the changes and the effects of those tactics on the people involved. It is evident from the case studies that the two are very much linked in an iterative way. The more that link is appreciated when the implementation approach is determined, the better are the chances for the success of a radical process-based change initiative.

Each of our case studies began the process of change with the appointment of new chairmen. Suddenly there were people at the very top of the organisation who wanted to transform the business, to take the current status quo and drop it from a great height. We have already discussed how willingness to change is a vital part of a successful project, and in both cases the revolution started not only with a willingness to change but an eagerness to do so. That this eagerness was present at the very pinnacle of the organisation was fortunate for the companies concerned. In many businesses there will be individuals or pockets of people who want change, not because they are dissatisfied with their lot, but because they believe they can see how change would benefit the organisation. Since they do not have the formal authority or the political clout to initiate such changes themselves, though, they face an uphill battle which practically many of them will lose.

Convincing people of the drivers for change, as we saw in one of the earliest chapters, is the first and one of the most important prerequisites for a successful project. Here, of course, the managing director or chairman has a distinct advantage in that the first hurdle of initiation can be lowered by a direct command. But while it can be lowered it cannot be removed altogether. People will presume that adverse effects of the threats will impact upon others before them. They are doing a good job, aren't they and so are 'relatively' safe from the consequences of a threat. No one person on their own is going to be able to change a whole company no matter how powerful that person may be; they need the support of the people below them, starting with those directly below them.

Another advantage of being the boss is that, generally speaking, staff – particularly the ones below management level – will take their lead from the top. Those people do not define the 'top' as the one person at the pinnacle, however, but as the group steering the company. It is their intentions and behaviours as a group which will have influence. Staff are generally more aware of high-level conflict than the board would care to acknowledge, and edicts which are accepted on the surface but rejected in the hearts of the managers will not generate any enthusiasm in the staff. Coffee-machine comments, chance remarks in private, or any number of similar happenings, will make it very clear where the managers' real feelings lie, and those feelings will permeate through the ranks. It was therefore still vital for the chairmen to gain the support of the rest of their boards and senior managers.

In neither of the case studies was this something that could be done with the existing boards, who had too much to lose by adopting, or were unable to broaden their thinking to encompass, the envisaged changes. But in this situation the chairman has another advantage over 'lower' members of the organisation in gaining that initial acceptance of the drivers for change.

There are three ways in which acceptance will come.

First, people see that the change is going to benefit the company, and, regardless of personal implications, will therefore welcome it. These people range from sensible enthusiasts to martyrs, but their support is genuine.

Second, people realise that change is coming; they see that the pressure for change is great enough to make it a certainty. Or, possibly, that the pressure for change will become great enough if they put their own weight behind it in support of the chairman. They realise that the change, if supported by themselves, will be personally advantageous as a result of that support. Hopefully it will be good for the company as well, since the two things go together in the longer term, but support – acceptance of the drivers for change – is sometimes engendered by purely personal motivations. Such support may also be genuine, and questioning its motivation is little more than an excursion into psychology.

Both the above ways were no doubt present in the case studies, though people rarely admit to the second while claiming the first. But third, and also present in both case studies, is the more direct method open only to the head of the company, of appointing into positions of influence and formal power people who bring that acceptance with them, and, conversely, removing people whose acceptance will never be gained. The power struggle in Carton Carrier, and the fortuitous retirements in Foundry Insurance cleared the way for the views of the chairmen and the new senior board members to hold sway. Once this had been achieved it was possible for the radical change projects to move forwards. Without it, they would have been doomed to failure somewhere down the line.

It is worth considering what happens when the changes are proposed – potentially initiated – by a person or group of people further down the organisation's hierarchy. Why are these initiatives so rarely accepted? Many companies have suggestion boxes and / or quality programmes whereby staff can put forward their ideas. Some of these are adopted, but they rarely initiate radical change. Changing the orientation of a company from a functional basis to a process one is not something which happens as a result of suggestions from clerical, administrative or shopfloor manufacturing staff. But why? Certainly there are staff at such levels who are more than capable of seeing what is occurring in an organisation, whose focal length extends beyond their own functional departments. They are sometimes able to take a wider view of the shortfalls of their functional organisation than their managers because the latter are squeezed metaphorically into the point of the pyramid and cannot see across its breadth. Yet suggestions, no matter how well prepared, argued and based in sound business logic, will generally get very short shrift, or, more likely, an encouraging, almost patronising, comment on a yearly appraisal but little follow-up action.

The hierarchical positioning within a company is likely to have a lot to do with the stillborn nature of such lower-level suggestions. Managers may feel threatened by those beneath them who show signs of original thought, or they may be threatened by the implications of the suggestions. They may consider that those beneath them are incapable of making fundamental suggestions which are worthy of consideration. Or they may consider that it is their job to make strategic suggestions and therefore naturally disregard anything from a 'lesser' source. It may also be that the manager has sufficient political acumen to realise that the suggestion would meet with a variety of the other responses were it pushed up the line, and that there is therefore no point in doing so.

Whatever the reason – and this conclusion exempts any organisation which is open-minded enough to listen and sometimes act on such things – radical change is rarely initiated by the staff. While we have concluded that staff take their lead from the managers, it is very rare for managers to take any lead from their staff.

For example, a major oil company that wanted to innovate its production operations set up an 'ideas' scheme. Any employee who proposed an innovative idea which was subsequently accepted would receive a percentage of the productivity improvement. Yet after a year there were fewer than ten ideas received by the board. When one mid-level line manager decided to apply stakeholder and process principles to the 'ideas' scheme, he discovered that for any idea to reach the board it required seven 'Yes' votes; one from each level in the hierarchy. Yet a single 'No' from any level consigned the idea to the trash can.

How many opportunities were thereby missed and which are being missed in similar situations within different companies is a matter for speculation. It is, though, a matter which a manager would do well to ponder for a moment before putting a suggestion to one side on the basis of little more than its origin.

This will hold true to some extent and for various reasons all the way up the line, and by getting the senior managers and the boards behind them, through various means, the chairmen of both Carton Carrier and Foundry Insurance had overcome the first and potentially highest hurdle to moving the projects forwards.

Those who were then made responsible for seeing the changes through did not simply rely on the view that people would do what they were told or would reluctantly change once they saw which way the wind was blowing – as some do. The most important realisation, as regards the successful conclusion of the projects, was that a critical mass of staff had to be supportive of the changes, and would therefore be willing to implement them. Reluctant implementation – the 'kicking and screaming' mode of forward movement – would delay the changes, so much of the work subsequently undertaken by the senior managers was designed to capture the hearts and minds of the staff, to bring them, as the modern cliché has it, 'on board'. It was recognised, although not stated in these specific terms, that in order for the radical initiatives to be successful, the managers had to engender in the staff that willingness to implement the changes.

Many projects start with the notion of making 'quick wins', that is gaining financial or operational benefits fast. Often this is described as 'gathering the low hanging fruit'. Certainly, some projects identify the quick wins to improve the return on investment of the overall project, so much so that without these benefits the strict cost-benefit case which has been put forward to support the project will not stand up. Consequently, the project will not be approved or will be cancelled. A point that is often overlooked is that 'quick wins' are gained only once a change is implemented.

Both Carton Carrier and Foundry Insurance made some early changes, and, for the most part, these did not bring financial benefits, but despite that they definitely fell under the description of 'quick wins'. Both companies had the foresight to realise that there are effects of equal and greater importance than limited early financial gain. Carton Carrier broke a hole through the depot wall, and introduced more modern phones, to say nothing of the flowers! The senior managers in Foundry Insurance started addressing, and being addressed by, people on a first name basis, and the class distinction of the restaurants was removed. The cost to Carton Carrier was low and to Foundry Insurance virtually zero, and yet the effects of these changes should not be underestimated. They send powerful messages about the senior management's intention to act, and to make changes, and, more importantly, they started to change the culture of the organisations, and to introduce that feeling of cross functional collaboration which has come up so often in this and previous chapters. That teamwork, and the initial impression – an accurate one – that things were likely to improve initiated the willingness to implement the changes which would be needed further down the project path.

This is not to denigrate the other benefits of so called 'quick wins'. If there are changes which can be made which bring benefits and which do not adversely affect longer term objectives such that those benefits are outweighed by future costs (or delays in the realisation of future benefits) then of course they should be sought. Similarly, immediate changes which are required to put out some of the fires which are currently burning must be made. The marketplace will not wait for a strategic change programme to be completed; customers rarely agree to give you a breathing space before taking their trade elsewhere. Hence the implementation of the change in Foundry Insurance whereby engineers were put up in London hotels. But, again, this was done in such a way that it added to the positive aspects of the overall programme – problems were being addressed, but so too were the needs of the engineers who were seconded to the capital. We are a team, the actions said, we are not just ordering you to do something with thought for nothing but the bottom line.

Cross functional collaboration is linked with ownership and responsibility. If members of a team feel no modicum of ownership and no sense of responsibility for what they are doing, then it is not a team, it is a hierarchy with the power, the decision making and the kudos or blame at the top. Ownership of the changes that were required in both Carton Carrier and Foundry Insurance was engendered by, and in its turn facilitated, that concept of willingness to implement change which we have discussed. The cross-functional teams which were set up involved people from all levels; the discussions held between board members, managers and their staff resulted in changes being made; the IT implementation teams in Foundry Insurance were given support along with the responsibility for their projects. All the actions taken by the board and the senior managers brought their staff 'on board', or 'into the fold' is perhaps a better way of describing it. While, of course, there was still a hierarchy, the perceived gap between top and bottom was drastically reduced, and the feeling of ownership of the systems, of responsibility for the ultimate customer service was spread throughout the organisations.

Ownership, as we mentioned in the Carton Carrier case study, does bring responsibility with it, as well as the factors of the previous paragraph. Changes which are led by outside influences, especially those from outside the company rather than simply outside one's own department or region, not only do not have the feeling of ownership but are easy to disown once the influences have gone. Placing the blame for failure of any initiative, any new way of working, on some external agency which is no longer there to suggest any sort of contrary opinion is a useful way of retracing the steps back to the previous position. Indeed, some managers will suggest the use of external consultants because of, from their point of view, this happy possibility.

To redress the balance of that discussion, external parties will often be able to bring experience of similar situations in other companies and will be able to stimulate ideas not only through that experience, but also through asking the sort of questions which, for various reasons, would not be raised internally. There is great value to be had from using such aid and experience, so long as the ownership of the initiative remains very firmly within the company. Ownership generates responsibility and, if handled correctly, should also generate an eagerness to introduce the change. The deputy managing director of Software Inc. discovered this in a Damascene flash of inspiration.

Initially the issues which were to be the subject of radical changes were sought through plenary discussion. Up to 50 of the managers who reported to the senior management team spent 2 days, along with their seniors, discussing what should be on the change agenda. Many ideas were forthcoming. Action points were put against each of these items with specific dates by which the actions were to be completed. They were followed through in the ensuing weeks before the team came back together once more. What was expected by the attendees of that next session was that they would be told what had been the outcome of the off-line actions, and therefore what changes were going to be made. They had all had an input into the formulation of the questions, but, as the managing director realised, they had not all contributed to the answers. While they would be happy to sit and listen to the considered instructions of others, they would not have been owning the change project themselves. They would be presented with a project plan formulated by others, admittedly in response to their own identified issues, but not of their own devising. The managing director's words below describe his own change of position, and how that then kicked off the successful project.

> *It suddenly dawned on me that this was totally the wrong way to do it. The way to do it was actually to force the managers of the various divisions to come up with their own project plans.*
>
> *What I did was I gave them an external project manager to help them do it all in the same format so that we could amalgamate the various plans into one overall plan, so he took with him software, an approach and effectively helped them to facilitate their own project plans. In that way it forced them to be up-front and say or show how they were managing their own activities to meet the overall objectives.*
>
> *That was probably one of the most effective decisions I took because up until that point there was always the risk of non-engagement, of neutrality, of hedge-sitting.*
>
> *I suddenly turned it round by saying 'right, you all think that I have got you in here today to present to you the plans. Mistake number one. So what am I going to do? I am going*

to get you to go away now and present your own plans as to how you are going to achieve the objectives, and you are going to present those back to us in two weeks time.' The whole of the company board would sit there and have it presented to them. 'I have a project manager here, he has some software, he has an approach, he has a methodology. He will show you that in the next two days. After that you go away and you work it out. If you need any help from him he will be there to help you.'

I can assure you that after two weeks we had a complete set of presentations, which were excellent, showing all the different levels of commitment. They all knew they had to perform and they were not going to fail. That probably was more important than anything in getting the message across.

The 'workshops' which Software Inc. ran were designed, as are many in many different companies, to address specific issues and come up with answers. They are supposed to be '*work*' shops, and not talking shops. Yet in a number of cases what happens is that the attendees sit and listen to presentations by people who have performed the actual work already, off-line. Those in attendance may nod and give verbal support, but they will rarely own the output. It is only when they themselves have become personally involved in the actual 'work' that ownership is engendered. And in the case of radical change, performing that work of addressing the issues begins to engender the personal willingness to implement the changes which is so important for success.

Willingness to implement the changes will reduce the stress involved, but cannot remove it altogether. The boards of both our main case study companies recognised this, but also recognised that there was a limit to what they could do to help people through the changes. Communication, culture change, support and encourage-ment are all important and were all used, but when push came to shove the changes did have to be made – the survival of the companies was more important than the staff within them. We have already seen in this summary how some obstacles to change at the highest level of the companies were removed, and the same approach was taken with the rest of the staff. Everyone was given as much chance to embrace the changes as the management could provide, from owning and designing the changes to being trained in the use of the new systems and having a high level of support from the managers. But if this was not enough, then the companies would move on and leave behind those staff unable or unwilling to follow.

At all stages of the change programmes there had to exist what we might term a 'critical mass' of people before success could be assured. Once the chairmen had engineered a critical mass of support among the board members, then the changes could go ahead, and their successful implementation ultimately depended on achieving a critical mass of staff willing to implement and adopt the new processes. In order to gain that critical mass the willingness to change must be engendered in the ways we have seen.

This concept of 'willingness to implement change' underlies the success of both Carton Carrier and Foundry Insurance, and it is important to consider the characteristics which it must display for a radical change programme to be successful. Our case studies suggest that we can look at the characteristics of 'willingness to implement change' under four headings.

- **Levels**: willingness needs to exist at all levels of the hierarchy, from board members to employees.
- **Critical mass**: not everyone has to be willing to implement the issues to be managed, but key people at each level need to be willing.
- **Action orientation**: for any particular tactic to be implemented, people either are or are not willing to complete the issues to be managed.
- **Choice**: in a choice between two or more actions people may be willing to implement some but not all the actions. These need to be separated and the impact upon the change programme understood.

In a perfect world a willingness to implement the identified changes would be induced through communication of the potential threats and opportunities and the desired objectives, and everyone would buy in without exception. In the real world there are many reasons why the carrot approach will not be sufficient, although hopefully it will go the vast majority of the way. But even if the stick is needed in some situations, we can conclude:

Axiom for change: 8
Radical process-based change is more likely to be achieved when ownership and a willingness to implement the changes is engendered throughout the organisation by company-spanning actions.

Where does your Company stand?

- What lead are the staff taking from those at the top of the organisation?
- Is there an identifiable 'pocket' of potential resistance, such as managers who will become 'losers' through the change?
- Do those willing to change represent a critical mass within the organisation?
- Are managers – or anyone – undermining in private what they are saying in public?
- Are there any early, perhaps symbolic, changes which can be made which will positively affect the perception of the other changes to come?
- Is the change project owned by those whom it will affect?
- Are those people responsible for identifying and implementing the changes?
- Is the potential trauma of change being properly and sufficiently addressed?

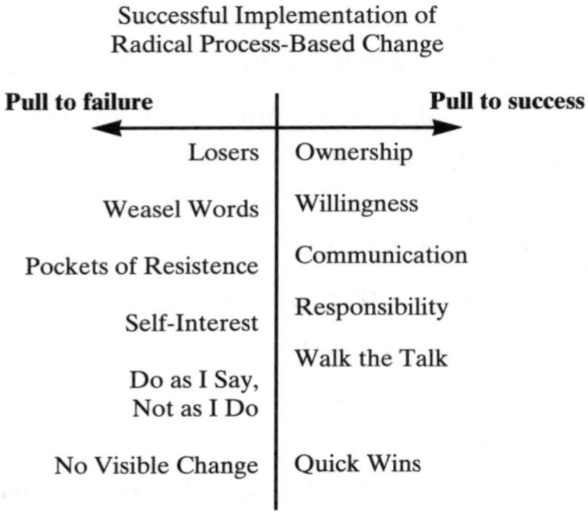

Successful Implementation of
Radical Process-Based Change

Pull to failure	Pull to success
←	→
Losers	Ownership
Weasel Words	Willingness
Pockets of Resistence	Communication
Self-Interest	Responsibility
	Walk the Talk
Do as I Say, Not as I Do	
No Visible Change	Quick Wins

Figure 9.1 *'Force-field' analysis of factors influencing success*

- In terms of the force-field diagram of Figure 9.1, where positive factors are encouraging successful change, and negative factors detract from it, which way are you being pulled?
- Do senior managers recognise that change has to precede any 'quick win'?

T E N

Give and Take

Jester Harrold was whistling a tune to himself as he arrived at work on that Monday morning. The weekend had been good to him, with his football team winning its first game of the season and his girlfriend finally agreeing to a goodbye kiss after their visit to the cinema. He gingerly touched his front tooth to see if it still wobbled after his somewhat overeager reaction to her relaxation of the rules. It did, but he shrugged; at least it proved that her braces were made of solid material.

Yes, it had been a good weekend. And now for a good week, back in his old job. Jester felt happy.

Although he had definitely enjoyed the last couple of months working with Alan Parsons and the rest of the team, there had been times when he had felt just a little uncomfortable with what he was doing; as though he were a touch out of his depth. He was actually telling directors – real directors – what they should be doing in the new organisational set-up; how their departments, and they themselves, interacted with the processes which were so important to the future of Downs Tools. They had been nice people, the directors, some of them practically human, but he still felt a bit like Anne Boleyn advising the hooded man next to her on the best way to grip an axe.

Oh, they had taken it well enough, he had to admit that. Not that they had any choice really, once old man Downs had chosen to go with Alan's recommendations. But you could see that some of them were smiling through teeth so gritted that they would probably suffer more damage than Jester had from yesterday's passionate head-butt.

The staff had been pretty good about it too, though Jester knew he was no man manager. It was just that having things explained to them was such a refreshing change in Downs Tools that they would have done anything. They were being treated like real people rather than the more usual mushroom approach, where they were kept in the dark and occasionally buried under a load of …

Well, never mind what they were buried under. This time they weren't, and they were grateful for it.

Still, Jester was pleased to be getting back to what he did best, with his head down in a corner and several long lists of numbers on the screen in front of him. Numbers were nice things; they obeyed rules which never changed. They didn't periodically do the unexpected just to be bloody minded. They didn't demand that the union should be in full and triplicate agreement before they reluctantly conceded that two plus two was the same as one plus three.

The corridor was a pleasing grey colour – the excesses of the board room were not for Jester – and the door to his small office was all the more welcoming for being shut. Behind it Sara and Joel would be waiting, each at their desks facing the wall, hunched over their machines.

He would speak upon entering, Jester decided. He would say good morning. Cheerily. It was not the way things were done in accounts, but he would do it anyway, just to show that he was pleased to see them.

Resolution drained from him as he grasped the handle, but he took a deep breath and turned it. He pushed open the door, and there, inside, was … nothing. No desks. No four-wheeled swivel chairs held together with tape and grime. No adding machines with little handles on the sides to make that 'mathematical' sound when you pulled them. There was nothing but a small white envelope in the middle of an otherwise bare floor.

Jester's hand dropped from the handle as his bottom jaw dropped from its partner. He stepped into the room and picked up the envelope, seeing his name on the front. He opened it and read. Realisation dropped into place.

'Dear Jester. If you are reading this it means you have forgotten that the changes we designed reached even into the heart of accounts, should there be such a thing. (Joke!) I thought you might.

Try the next door down the corridor, and welcome to the future. All the best. See you for lunch. Alan.'

* * *

Introduction

The people involved with the completion of a radical process-based change initiative are split, in logic and literature, between those who plan and devise it, and those to whom it happens. To give them each a title, we could call the former group the 'Implementors' and the latter the 'Recipients'. Kettinger and Teng[47] describe the roles people are expected to fulfil:

> *Based on the new process design, new organisational structures and job assignments must be conveyed to the affected employees outlining their future roles and performance expectations. … [such] dramatic changes during this step will cause anxiety that must be addressed by continual communication between top management, the regeneration team, and employees.*

The assumption is clear. The top managers and the implementation team – whatever that might be called – are the ones who dish out the changes, and the employees at the 'bottom' of the organisation[48] are the ones who have to accept it. As we have seen in earlier chapters, that acceptance can be facilitated by various behaviours and actions which generate a willingness to change, but willing or not, the lower ranking staff are the ones who must adopt, and adapt to, the new processes.

But while that may seem logical at first sight, from what we have already seen of Carton Carrier and Foundry Insurance it is surely only a superficial description of what is a more complicated procedure. When behaviours throughout an organisation are required to change, when teamwork is engendered from chairman to chairman and when due regard is given to cross-functional process orientation, there is a fundamental incompatibility about the notion of a split into two distinct camps of Implementors and Recipients. Are we not all in this together? Let us study the subject of Recipients and Implementors in more detail through those case studies.

CASE STUDIES

CARTON CARRIER

Before the change initiative got under way, as we have seen, the new chairman arrived from Home Merchandise. He soon brought some of his fellow directors with him to the exclusion of those already at Carton Carrier. By the end of the initiative, the directors were viewed in three distinct 'groups' by those below them. In one group was the chairman himself, alone. Wielding much of the power in the organisation were those in the second group, which included the managing director, the commercial director and the warehouse director, all of whom had been introduced from Home Merchandise. In a third group were those directors who had been, and remained, with Carton Carrier.

The power base, with the support of the directors who had been retained, determined that the responsibility for decision making should be extended downwards in the company hierarchy, and the regional managers were brought far more into the decision-making process. Regional managers became associate directors, raising their status within the company, and according to one of them:

> *The team of eight or nine people in the regions now wielded very considerable amounts of power, if only on a day-to-day basis.*

The regional power brokers, for their part, sought to extend the responsibility for service quality and profitability down to the depot managers and beyond, to the drivers themselves. That delegation of responsibility was effected and enforced by introducing regular reviews which measured achievements.

The new process and its supporting activities were first introduced into the Malham depot, and were then rolled out to the other depots, with implementation teams including people who had already undergone the transition. In some areas it met with resistance, most particularly in Liverpool, where the trade union was accustomed to holding the reins of power, having stepped over time into the vacuum at the shopfloor-level of the company. Although this power was not officially recognised in that it was not a part of the company hierarchy, it did conform to that which we have discussed in earlier chapters. The power base was something which the union officials had achieved, and which they were loath to concede. The suggestion of a new process where greater management control was exercised over the delivery of parcels was a direct assault on that power base. There was even an allegation, although doubtless unfounded, that greater control of the parcels' movements was being resisted because it would restrict the possibility of theft, but one hopes that this suggestion was more indicative of the tensions between the would-be implementors and the reluctant recipients than a statement of fact. For whatever reason, those who had successfully implemented the process at the Malham depot encountered great difficulty in transferring it to some others, despite the prior agreement of the trade union to all aspects of the new arrangements. Eventually, in Liverpool and a few other regions, the changes had to be imposed via the formal authoritative hierarchy.

The control of the overall parcel delivery process, and its wider implications in terms of employee development and collective responsibility, required that the depot managers learned new skills. The appraisals were an important part of the new process, and the ability to carry these out effectively was a new requirement of the depot managers and their assistants. Similarly, the parcel delivery managers required training in their new responsibilities, which now centred on the day-to-day control of the delivery process through a team of 10 to 15 drivers. Each parcel delivery manager was responsible not only for the daily delivery route-planning in his or her designated geographical area, but also for driver performance, training, development, disciplinary and grievance procedures.

New skills were required in the services department, but more important was a new role of specification, co-ordination and management of the required IT developments. The role was one of tremendous importance to the successful implementation of the new parcel delivery process, dependent as that was on computer system support, but it was also one which had to be controlled in such a way that it did not represent a threat to the responsibilities – the newly created powerbase – of the operational departments. A fine line was identified between the interpretation of business requirements and the virtual imposition of them, and having identified it, the managers succeeded in ensuring that it was not crossed. The new team-working behaviours allowed the gathering and interpretation of requirements from all departments to be seen for what it was – a co-ordinated approach to the implementation of the complete parcel delivery process across the companies.

Whenever modules of the new computer systems were developed and implemented, a training package was provided. Professional trainers were used to train the managers, and the managers in their turn trained the staff. It would, of course, have been possible to have the 'professionals' training all staff, but, as we discussed in the last chapter, outside agencies necessarily reduce the feeling of ownership, both of the managers and the staff beneath them, and increase the possibility that the system implementation is seen as an imposition.

FOUNDRY INSURANCE

In Foundry Insurance the start of the change initiative also arose through the appointment of a new managing director, and as in Carton Carrier, the behavioural change cascaded down the management line. Previously the managing director had taken all important and many unimportant decisions, while the managers beneath him simply maintained the status quo in their functional silos. Such – largely trivial – decisions as were left to the managers were guarded jealously, but had to be taken within strict and unchanging guide-lines. Stagnation emanated from the top and gradually the whole organisation was beginning to atrophy. The fresh air which blew through the company released the responsibility which had been dammed right at the top of the hierarchy and demanded that it be passed down the line. The managers did not have to hold onto what meagre empowerment they had because they were now asked to manage, to consider their department's role in the wider satisfaction of customer requirements. The day-to-day decisions could then be pushed down to the levels where it was appropriate for them to be taken while the greater responsibility for implementing change to support the company's overall strategic direction was located where it belonged, with the senior managers.

To stretch a mixed metaphor well beyond breaking point – the board realised that where a wind of change was blowing, and the removal of a dam had started a cascade, some people were going to catch cold! In order to cope with the newly devolved responsibilities, people required training and preparation. It was recognised that some people would have difficulty, both in terms of skills require-ments and in terms of the willingness to accept change. Compliance with instructions from on high was a well-established tradition in Foundry Insurance, but the board wanted commitment rather than compliance. Support was therefore given, but the recognition of problems with the changes by senior management did not go so far as to allow a possibility that those changes were not going to happen.

Managers, engineers and team leaders had to accept that their understanding of the wider aspects of the inspection process was important, and to realise that their activity could no longer be managed or performed in isolation of other activities in the inspection process. Functional specialists were required to take on a wider range of responsibilities; for example people who dealt only with internal staff began dealing with external customers as well. The training required was extensive, because long years in one functional area had left many people with outdated and incomplete skills. Through cross-functional movement, however, the situation was gradually changed so that eventually the understanding of the wider inspection process was engendered in the functions, and customer needs could at last be brought to the fore.

Conclusion

It is not difficult to see that a number of people in both companies undertook implementor roles and, at the same time or at different stages in the change initiatives, also became recipients of change.

In both cases the changes started at the top, and the new chairmen and managing directors began as implementors. The managers directly below them were the first of the recipients – their behaviours were required to change. If they were unable to effect this change then they were removed from the organisations. But the next step was for those senior managers to cascade the changes to the managers and staff beneath them, so they quickly became implementors. Indeed, the *role* of chairman underwent change, and each of them could be classed as a recipient in that way. The way that the role was made to change was through the appointment of a new chairman, but the point is already starting to be made. The successful change initiatives in both companies required that the changes started upon individuals right at the top and were then cascaded down the organisation. In both cases the roles of the managers changed such that their former responsibilities were pushed down to a wider level of the hierarchy. At every level of management, therefore, we are going to see a situation where managers are recipients of change, and then become implementors of change to others. A distinction between roles cannot generally be made at this level through movement between recipient and implementor, since most managers would be undertaking both at the same time, changing those beneath them through changing themselves.

The movement between the roles can be seen in many places in the case study examples. Those in Carton Carrier's Malham depot had first to be recipients of the new order fulfilment process and then in turn became implementors when they formed part of the teams in other depots which implemented the new process. Managers, as change recipients, had to learn how to undertake new appraisals within the company, and as implementors they had to undertake those appraisals. In other instances in both companies, staff had to learn new skills and then use those skills to support or monitor or simply to interact with other staff in new ways. In all these examples we see recipient and implementor roles being undertaken either in sequence or in parallel.

It is only at those levels of the company where there is no staff responsibility that we can expect to see only the recipient role being played, and that is only the case where the staff are not co-opted onto implementation teams where clearly the other role is integral. The cascade effect of a change which starts at the top of an organisation demands that most people are both implementors and recipients. Any organisation which can point to a high-level split between implementors and recipients is one where the change has not been all encompassing. All too often it will be a case of the senior management imposing changes on those below them while protecting their own positions. One example of that comes from a large financial organisation which decreed that the levels of management within the hierarchy were too many and varied, and should be reduced. The edict began at the board level, and was passed down to the next level for implementation. That level, of course, was not one of those to be removed, and therefore passed the edict down another level. That level could easily point to any number of exceptional reasons why the hierarchy was in place at their own level for good business reasons, and how changing it would be to weaken the company. The edict was therefore passed down another level – and so on until maybe the odd token change was imposed on those who had insufficient clout or fleetness of thought to avoid it, and the general look of the hierarchical structure changed not a bit.

Another example is that of the encouragement of more open behaviour by the newly appointed chief operations officer of an international technology-based company. He repeatedly stated in open forums that what he wanted was good, open, honest discussion of problems and possible solutions, and a greater degree of responsibility being taken by his subordinate managers. His own behaviours, however, remained intensely command and control, and it was plain that anyone who made the slightest suggestion which was contrary to his wishes and mind-set was to be marked down. Far from engendering a culture of openness and discussion – which he really did want to do in those beneath himself – within a month of his appointment he had created one of fear and distrust.

If change is to be encompassing – and if radical change is to be successful – then it has to start at the top. The imposition of change without the willingness of the implementors to undergo change themselves generates feelings of unfairness on top of all the others which we have discussed in earlier chapters. And as suggested in the above example, the notion that 'Do as I say, not as I do' will actually work, is a delusional one.

We have discussed in earlier chapters how the willingness to change must be addressed, and how in general terms change is seen as threatening and unwelcome. It would follow, then, that of the two roles, the implementor one will be much more readily accepted than that of recipient. Changing others is not as scary as having to change oneself. For the most part, such a comparison would doubtless produce a preference for the implementor role, but it is not always the case. Those in Carton Carrier who tried to implement the new process in the Liverpool depot found considerable resistance from the union representatives (who did not want to be recipients). Some of those implementors stated quite explicitly that while they welcomed the changes to their own roles, they definitely did not relish the prospect of introducing them elsewhere.

The research behind this book has led to the conclusion that people have to deal with the inherent contradictions of implementor and recipient roles. The ability of individuals to deal with the paradoxes created can have a major impact on the success or failure of a radical process-based change initiative. We have identified four potential roles that people can assume during such an initiative. They are summarised in Figure 10.1.

Obstructors are people who want to be neither implementors nor recipients. These people often play a passive role, hoping the change

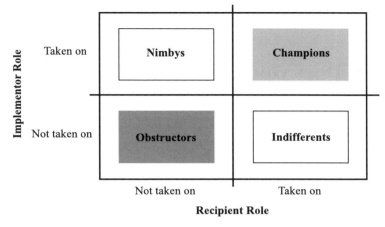

Figure 10.1 *Roles adopted during radical process-based change initiatives*

initiative will simply go away. Alternatively they may proactively, but covertly, make moves to kill off the project.

Nimbys (not in my back yard) are people who want to implement change but do not want to change themselves or see change happen in their department or function. These people are easy to spot as they preach change but will quickly find several plausible reasons for not having the same changes visited upon themselves.

Indifferents are people who are willing to take on change but are unwilling to implement it elsewhere. This can result in changes petering out after a good start as momentum is lost. Indifferents manifest themselves through lack of commitment to the change, lack of personal confidence, or perhaps poor communication skills.

Champions are people who, as described in this chapter, are willing to take on both implementor and recipient roles.

The conclusion we can draw is summed up as:

Axiom for change: 9
Radical business change is more likely to be achieved when implementors and recipients accept these roles as reciprocal, and enact both roles.

Where Does your Company stand?

- Is there a clearly defined split between implementors and recipients?
- Is as much attention being given to problems faced by implementors as to those faced by recipients?
- Make a list of key players in your change programme. Classify which are Nimbys, Obstructors, Indifferents and Champions.
- What further training or support will move Indifferents to Champions?
- What tactics are available for dealing with Nimbys and Obstructors?
- Do senior managers recognise that they too will be recipients of change?

ELEVEN

Achieving Change

Alan Parsons leaned back in his chair and breathed a sigh. Then he took a few moments to determine what the sigh was for. Relief? Certainly there was some of that in it. The projects had pretty much been delivered. The major processes of Downs Tools had been identified, documented, adopted, implemented and even tweaked to make them better based on suggestions from the staff. IT systems had been built to support them, and in record time thanks to the way the business people and the IT professionals worked so well together on them, all with a common understanding of what was wanted. (Who said miracles didn't still happen?) And thanks to the time-boxing method of development. Not to forget the great bonuses which were available if the targets were met.

So was that it? A sigh of relief?

No, not entirely.

A knock on the open door derailed his train of thought and Peter Window came into the room.

'Have you got your diary handy, Alan?' he asked.

'Always. I'm thinking of starting a society that places one in every hotel bedroom for the travelling executive.'

'I need to book some time for the first post-implementation review session.'

'Fair enough. What are we going to do at that?'

'We're going to work out what the content of the post-implementation review is going to be, for starters. I think this one might be a little different from most.'

'How so?'

'Well in Downs Tools, as a rule ... no pun intended ...'

'... and none achieved ...'

'... we usually spend the weeks after a project in covering our own backs, placing the blame on those who are least able to defend themselves and eventually punishing the innocent. Unless we're lucky enough to have someone resign, because they then become responsible for everything from late IT system delivery to the latest Middle East crisis. But this time it's a little unusual in that we seem to have succeeded.'

'Despite our best efforts, you mean?'

Window smiled briefly, but then looked serious. 'It's strange. You know you have been saying all through this that we have to be aware of people's comfort zones? How different is bad, and the same is good?'

'Yes.'

'Well, I think in a way we have got so used to the failure of our projects, whatever they are, that we have grown comfortable with that. We're quite happy analysing where things went wrong because we expect them to go wrong. I'm not saying that success is scary, but it makes you look back on the past and ask some serious questions about our previous mind-sets.'

Parsons nodded. 'A lot of people have been asking questions about their mind-sets these past few months. And a lot of them haven't much liked the answers.'

'Do you think they've changed though? Can we trust what they say?'

Parsons shrugged. 'It's what they do that matters. They may be claiming a Damascene change while keeping their spots ...'

'A leopard on the road to Damascus?'

'Don't try, Peter; when I mix a metaphor it takes a week to unravel it. But the point is it doesn't matter what they think so long as they act the right way, and don't revert.'

'That's what it's about isn't it. The future. We've done the best we can; now it's up to the people out there.'

Parsons nodded, and realised what the sigh was for. The projects were just about over, and their success was a recognised fact. He felt like he had run a marathon, and so had many of those in the company. They could all do with a rest, and they all deserved one.

And what would the customers do while they were resting?

Go somewhere else, the ingrates!

Never mind the wicked, there was no peace for the not-too-bad, either!

*   *   *

Introduction

We stated when introducing the case studies that both Carton Carrier and Foundry Insurance had been successful in their implementation of radical process-based change. We have seen in succeeding chapters how that success was achieved, and the various difficulties which had to be overcome on the way. But how is that success measured? When we look at the two companies to determine whether or not they really have been successful, what do we look at?

As in many instances through this study, the answer seems reasonably straightforward, and the method is used in most companies across the world when evaluating a project. Benefits versus cost is the accepted basis, with figures forming the bottom line. But in many projects it is not just the numbers that matter – 'How much did this computer system cost us to build, and how much saving had we made from it?' Unquantifiable benefits are often brought into the equation, and in both case studies these had a large part to play. When a company is faced with possible extinction it is difficult to put a figure on the benefits of staving off that circumstance. At the start of the case studies we saw that both companies were in severe trouble, and the symptoms included factors which would have led to destruction. The symptoms were just that, though, and while the crises finally made people wake up to what was happening, they were merely indicative of deeper problems, of causes. Let us visit the case studies just once more and look back over what they achieved, and what they did not achieve, in terms of addressing the symptoms, the crises, and the underlying causes.

CASE STUDIES

CARTON CARRIER

Carton Carrier had 35 depots spread across the country, and needed the new order fulfilment process to be introduced into all of those depots if the programme was to be successful. This meant not only the roll-out from the Malham depot where the new process was first implemented, but the prior documentation of that process so that it could be replicated with minimal variation. After the changes every depot followed the rules laid down in that documentation in a consistent manner, such that anyone moving from one depot to another would find the same procedures and activities, and would be able to fit in with no change in working practice. It was not that great movement *would* take place within the company – although there was some – but rather that management control was only possible if there were not vast regional differences in the way things are done. (Picture the individual restaurants in the McDonald's chain each operating to different criteria and imagine the management difficulties which would be encountered.)

Evidence of the successful operation of the new process, and its replication across all of Carton Carrier's depots, came from the company's entry into the external market for parcel deliveries. Prior to the changes, they had made one or two forays into that marketplace, taking on the delivery of parcels for companies other than Home Merchandise. The promises of service levels which had to be given in order to secure such business, however, were quickly shown to be empty ones. A manager from a large international electronics and manufacturing company recalls her experience with Carton Carrier prior to implementation of the process.

> We tried Carton Carrier because they promised us next day delivery. Then not only did the shipment not arrive but when we phoned to find out what had happened to it they didn't have the faintest idea where it was.

Whereas Home Merchandise could not just walk away to a different distributor, the other customers could, and the sound of rapidly receding footsteps was commonly heard very soon after the business was first secured.

After the new process had been put in place across the company external customers were once again sought – presumably ones with short memories! This time, however, the promises were based not on hope but on a well-controlled, robust process. A spectacular testimony to the success of the change project is that within 5 years of its completion some 30% of Carton Carrier's deliveries were for companies other than Home Merchandise.

Those factors which had prevented the earlier successful foray into the external market became the drivers for change within Carton Carrier. There was no consistency of delivery times, no management control over the process, no tracking or information on parcel status, and no notion of customer service.

After the changes, there was control over every individual parcel which passed through the company's hands. A consistent delivery period of between 1 and 3 days was achieved, and this was used as the basis for the improved customer service. Behavioural change also entered into the customer service equation so that customers were treated as such and had their parcels delivered by hand, on time. Even if they lived in a penthouse with a pair of Dobermans!

It sounds very like a 'happy ever after' ending, but there is still some disquiet in the company, and maybe a residue of the old organisation. As one depot manager says:

> *It's still a dictatorship. Whilst we had some input on things, at the end of the day it was driven from the top. It was going to happen whether I wanted it to happen, whether I'd allowed it to happen, or whatever. To a certain extent, we felt that we were a part of it. The company is a dictatorship, but I think that within that it has flexed a little bit. It's not quite such a rigid dictatorship as it used to be.*

FOUNDRY INSURANCE

Foundry Insurance faced similar problems to those within Carton Carrier – poor customer service meant that customers did not know

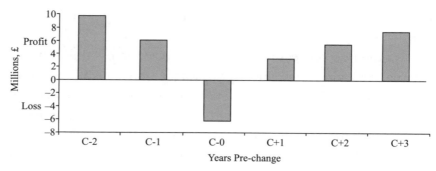

Figure 11.1 *Foundry Insurance profit/loss*

how long it would take to get their reports issued once an inspection, itself often overdue, had been carried out. Up to 25% of customers were let down on timing, and eventually this led to some of the major clients leaving. Following the implementation of the new inspection process, the percentage of late inspections fell to between 1 and 2% and reports were issued between 1 and 3 days following the inspection, and always within 24 hours of receipt at head office.

We saw in an early chapter that it was not only the loss of a major customer which created the (threatening) drivers for change within Foundry Insurance, but the first ever year-end loss. The managing director reckoned that there were no more than 2 years available to turn the company round. As Figure 11.1 indicates, in the event it took only one, after which the improvements were maintained.

A significant contributor to the original problems within Foundry Insurance, and a significant contributor to their solution, once the focus had been shifted to the process as a whole rather than the individual activities within it, came from the IT infrastructure. Prior to the change initiative, there was very little. Afterwards, through the radical changes which had been made to the organisational structure and the innovative development techniques, IT was one of Foundry Insurance's strong suits. This point was proven during the height of the IRA terrorist campaign in London, when the insurance industry as a whole was facing considerable problems through the increased exposure to massive claims. Foundry Insurance, like many other similar companies, were forced to put a clause in their policies effectively excluding terrorist activity. Leaving aside the procedure which is required to amend policy wording – generally a lengthy and complicated affair, taking weeks if not months. Foundry Insurance agreed the wording change, and it was implemented into every one of their policies that same day. So good, in fact, were Foundry's systems that they actually won several awards.

What was never forgotten, importantly, was that the systems were there to support the processes, and not to drive them. A major failing of the old company was that managers had very little control over the activities that people performed to deliver the inspection process to the customers. Information became available which gave an accurate picture of the state of the various regions in terms of timely inspections and the production of reports and policies. Such things could have been produced before but only through a massive manual effort which would have further detracted from the important customer-facing inspection process. Control over the process gave the company enormous benefits. As the customer services manager described:

> *Support of the process streamlined the service that we provided, improved turnaround times, reducing surveyors' reports delivery from three to four weeks, to three to four days. From the customer service point of view, and a quality point of view, that was a phenomenal benefit to us.*

So, happy ever after? As with Carton Carrier, and with everything else in the real world; not quite. The drive to improve the systems in a very short timescale led to a decision to use four different IT suppliers (Wang, SUN, Ingres and Compaq). And hindsight is a wonderful thing.

> *In hindsight we wouldn't have done some of the things that we've done. Well, we have issues, we've got problems. We've got systems on three different platforms for example. It seemed the right thing to do at the time. It probably was the right thing, but one has to ask the question. (customer services manager)*

It is very easy to point the finger at decisions taken when the company was sinking fast and needed rapid action, and maybe the question should be asked, as the customer services manager suggests. But the judgement should not be too harsh.

One other remaining problem became apparent during the study, though. Backlogs of work are still a problem within Foundry Insurance, although to nowhere near the extent that they were prior to the change initiative. The point is made, and the reasons given, quite clearly by the deputy managing director, and his words are reproduced here because they say it all.

In the customer services area, I keep worrying about the fact that they have a backlog. There's always good reasons but I have difficulty in seeing somebody saying 'Let's own this, let's get it down'. I suspect behind it is this fear of job reduction. So there's this reluctance to keep simplifying the process or eradicating certain steps, or getting rid of unnecessary activities. ... And I think that actually applies at the middle-level management, because they don't like to be the hard-hearted people. They forget the bottom line that we have to aim for. They'd rather have stability and settle at many levels because they've been going through three or four years of change and seeing people leave and they feel uncomfortable.

Conclusion

The drivers for change which were considered as threats in Carton Carrier and Foundry Insurance were:

- Deep flaws in the previous process
- Stakeholders becoming intolerant of poor service levels
- A major financial or operational crisis

The driver for change interpreted as an opportunity in both companies was that of activities which affected customer service being brought under management's control.

Carton Carrier implemented the parcel delivery process, to complete the order fulfilment process, in all of its depots. Foundry Insurance implemented the inspection process across the whole organisation. Both companies addressed and removed the deep flaws in the previous process.

Service levels were dramatically improved in each organisation. Carton Carrier retained its traditional Home Merchandise customer base and was able to expand its operations into new third party markets. Foundry Insurance's customers are no longer leaving them, and they are able to react quicker than their competition to changes in the marketplace.

The crisis of end-of-year loss was removed by Foundry Insurance and turned into a profit which has since grown year on year. Overdue inspections were reduced significantly, such that 95% of reports are issued within 24 hours, while the rest rarely take longer than 3 days.

The Malham depot's stockpile of a significant proportion of the UK's undelivered parcel mountain has been resolved, as witnessed by that entry into the third party markets. Customers now trust the company to keep its promises to deliver consistently, and on time. In most areas of the UK the customers receive their parcels on a regular 3-day cycle.

As far as the identified opportunity is concerned, the management of both organisations has regained control over the key activities in their processes.

Performance has improved, as we have seen, and for many organisations that is the only measure which is considered when judging the success or failure of a radical process-based change initiative. But while that is certainly of great importance, it does not address the fundamental objectives of the project, which were to remove the drivers for change without which the projects would not have been initiated. If the symptoms of a chronic illness are treated, then the patient will feel better, but the underlying causes are still present and will re-emerge if treatment is not continued. In the case of significant drivers for change in business, as with such illnesses, it is sometimes much easier to treat only the symptoms, and we have seen many reasons why that is the case in the preceding chapters. It is further evidenced by the comments which were reported at the conclusion of each of the case studies in this chapter.

As we saw above, the depot manager in Carton Carrier said:

> *It's still a dictatorship. Whilst we had some input on things, at the end of the day it was driven from the top. It was going to happen whether I wanted it to happen, whether I'd allowed it to happen, or whatever. To a certain extent, we felt that we were a part of it. The company is a dictatorship, but I think that within that it has flexed a little bit. It's not quite such a rigid dictatorship as it used to be.*

Now a part of what he said is to be expected in any hierarchical organisation. Unless the company is run on a collective basis there must be an ultimate decision-making point, and various other levels of responsibility throughout the organisation. Carton Carrier were keen to spread the responsibility, but there was never an aim to spread it equally across every member of staff. Their objective has certainly been achieved, from what we have seen earlier. We talked, though, about the acceptance of the need for change, and how that acceptance is achieved.

In chapter five above, we argued that acceptance can be grudging, so long as it is acceptance. It is not terminal if, privately, those who have to implement the changes are not completely convinced so long as the acceptance is achieved. Some people – not necessarily a small minority – will see the direction of the change as it develops and will plan their career route accordingly. Certainly willing acceptance is better than grudging acceptance, because the implementation is undertaken with more enthusiasm. But by the same argument as above, those who know which side their bread is buttered will adopt the appropriate approach when it comes to implementation, so the type of acceptance achieved may not matter at all.

In the words of the depot manager we see that acceptance of the need for change was in some cases based on knowing what is good for you, as well as – or rather than? – what is good for the company.

What it shows graphically, however, is how difficult it is to change the behaviours within an organisation, and particularly those behaviours which have built up over many years and 'calcified'. In this case at least, there is clearly not full acceptance that what was being done within Carton Carrier was the right, inevitable, only and welcome way to go. The mind-set of the depot manager has still some way to go before his prime concern is the satisfaction of, or better yet, exceeding, customer expectations. He will do it because he is told to.

In Foundry Insurance we saw that backlogs are still a problem, although a much smaller one. The reasons given are revealing of the same problem – that of shifting behaviours, of redirecting the mind-sets.

> *I suspect behind it is this fear of job reduction. So there's this reluctance to keep simplifying the process or eradicating certain steps, or getting rid of unnecessary activities .... And I think that actually applies at the middle-level management, because they don't like to be the hard-hearted people. They forget the bottom line that we've to aim for. They'd rather have stability ...*

Those staff who allow the backlogs to grow have seen change in the company, and so far they have 'survived' it. How often is that description used when radical change is being discussed, either as a forthcoming event or in retrospect. Change is scary, and change has been seen in Foundry Insurance to lead to the reduction in staff numbers. Some of those who remain, despite the fact that the company is on a far better footing thanks to the initiative, and despite the work undertaken to prepare them for change, remain traumatised by it. They do not feel safe, and seek a greater feeling of safety – albeit perhaps an illusory one – through allowing the work to build up. As soon as the work reduces, they argue, so too does the number of staff needed to complete it.

Some of the middle managers have maybe had their fill of being change implementors. The period of radical change is over as far as they are concerned. Their comfort zones have been stretched and moulded into new forms, and they would like a little time to get used to the fit.

That second factor is one which is perhaps a passing consideration, and almost certainly a lesser one. Change implementation is easier than change reception, and it is certainly less traumatic. Behaviours can be changed, albeit very slowly. Most companies, regardless of their size, have the same problems as turning supertankers when behavioural – or 'cultural' – issues are addressed. Where those issues go to the very heart of what makes a person what he or she is, regardless of the company context, then they become virtually unchangeable, and this should be remembered by anyone undertaking a radical change initiative. It is not sensible to expect that staff at any level can be altered so that ever after they welcome change and embrace uncertainty. All that can be done in the context of radical change is to determine how the behavioural issues which contributed to the change drivers have been addressed, and whether the new behaviours still pose a threat. That is likely to be a judgement call, and one that must also take into effect the proximity of the last change project before it concludes that what the company needs is another one.

Those considerations apart, though, what we have seen in this chapter is that the successful completion of a radical process-based change initiative is not solely judged by the improvements in performance which are achieved, but rather by looking at the underlying issues which instigated the project in the first place.

> **Axiom for change: 10**
> **The achievement of radical process orientation needs to be assessed in terms of whether or not the drivers for change were removed and the extent to which behaviours are changed, or unchanged.**

Where does your Company stand?

- Is the project marked as a success on the basis of performance improvements it has brought about?
- Are the underlying drivers for change completely removed?

- What positive aspects of the 'old' organisation remain?
- What 'traditional' aspects remain?
- Have the drivers for change been removed?
- Are new and/or different behaviours noticeable?
- Do people in different functions collaborate and work together more effectively?
- Is the organisation more stakeholder focused?

TWELVE

Summary

One of the most common ways of representing an organisation, on paper, is to draw its structure chart. This typically has the chief executive at the head of the organisation with functional directors in control of their own vertical areas. The principles for managing this functional structure were formalised at the beginning of the twentieth century and they have been developed in waves throughout the last century. Each wave attempted to assist managers to take decisions to allocate resources, determine responsibilities, and establish appropriate levels of control and authority within each function. Each wave reinforced the structure until it became more than a tradition, but reached the level of something which was barely noticed, let alone questioned.

More recently though, the idea of business process orientation focused management's attention on the need to identify and manage the organisation's processes that cut horizontally across the functional boundaries. In the past, the management of business processes received scant attention. Then, exemplar organisations that had implemented business process-based changes were identified and held out as models for others to follow,[49,50] and orientation according to business processes was shown to deliver significant performance improvements.[21] For example, business processes were identified as being the basis for sustainable competitive advantage.[51] And orientation according to those processes was shown to be important in integrating information systems across functions.[52]

Many organisations have attempted to implement business process-based change expecting to achieve significant performance improvements, but many failed to achieve their expectations.[42] One of the main reasons for this failure is that organisations begin their initiatives with the intention of making fundamental organisational changes to achieve large-scale improvements. However because these fundamental changes are only partially implemented, the really significant performance improvements are not realised.[14] Partial implementation results mainly because the movement away from functional orientation is simply too big a step to take. It not only challenges an assumption of the way companies should be organised which is thought to be immutable, but in doing so it threatens disruption to the lives of the majority of staff within the organisations, and to the power bases and career aspirations of those in the higher positions of responsibility. Hence there are forces arrayed against many process-based change initiatives which are just too great to overcome.

The answer, though, was not, and is not, to abandon the idea of process orientation, but to consider how we can address the inherent tensions between the functional structure (including the people within it) and the business process. Those tensions have significant implications for the satisfaction of customer or stakeholder expectations and the commercial success of a business; the two being the same thing. The functions control and define activities, resources and responsibilities, yet a single function rarely satisfies any one stakeholder expectation. Business processes, namely activities that are integrated across different functions to create outputs that are of value to the stakeholder, fulfil stakeholder expectations. More often than not business processes are barely managed, as each function focuses upon its own priorities, often to the detriment of the process. Recently, the tensions between the functional structure and the business process have been exacerbated, as stakeholders, especially customers, become more demanding and sophisticated.

Addressing the expectations of the stakeholders has never been more important, and with the explosion of technology making those expectations ever more varied and sophisticated, failure to do so is becoming ever more dangerous. But trying to satisfy stakeholders within a functionally based organisation is fraught with sufficient difficulties as to make it virtually impossible. Changes internal to a function may appear to be improvements, but might damage the process of which the functional activities form a part, resulting in a reduction in the satisfaction of customer expectations. Furthermore, those within the company will find it very difficult to pinpoint how this could have been the case since their investigations will focus on the functions in the same way as did their previous change initiatives.

In this book we have considered how a radical change initiative based on business processes may be successfully concluded. We have not proposed altering the organisational structure of a company, recognising that this was the rock on which so many earlier projects have foundered. What a company must do is encourage a holistic approach whereby those in the functional domains – in the silos – increase their focal length so that they recognise the processes to which their activities contribute. Those activities can then be designed such that they support the processes. The processes can be designed such that they address the most important expectations of those stakeholders whom the company board have deemed to be their top priorities. And those stakeholders will then enable or frustrate the achievement of the organisation's business objectives. If all the individual factors are aligned in such a way, then the activities that people perform within the company is directly contributing to that company's success.

On paper it appears easy. But those three or four sentences sum up what is a tremendously difficult task – taking a company with all its historical momentum behind it, and getting it to change its direction. Getting tens, hundreds, thousands of people to study their own mind-sets and to reshape their thinking. Getting the most influential people in the organisation, with, seemingly, the most to lose, to recognise that making the changes is really the only way to win. Many try, but few succeed. By following the axioms set out in this book, the chances of success will be greatly increased.

We can sum up those axioms in the four parts of the project into which they fit.

1 *Commencement*. This begins with the rationale that underpins the initiation of a radical process-based change initiative. Success is more likely when people accept the organisation's drivers for

change, which can be opportunities or threats (*axiom one*). In our two main cases studies we saw threats including:

- a breakdown in the organisation's existing process;
- key stakeholders changing their existing relationship with the organisation; and
- operational and financial crises.

In both cases the opportunity identified was the organisation's ability to bring activities in different functions under management's control.

The commencement phase also suggests that once drivers for change are identified, radical process-based change is more likely to be achieved when people establish the specific need for such a change rather than another type (*axiom two*). This axiom suggests that organisations recognise explicitly that they have a choice of change initiatives with which to address drivers for change, and that radical process-based change may be inappropriate to their specific circumstances. The need for radical process orientation is greater when the drivers for change require an organisation to:

- co-ordinate changes across several functions; and
- increase levels of managerial and operational interdependence between the activities in those functions.

2   *Changes that need to occur.* This part of the project deals with the changes an organisation experiences during a successful radical process-based change initiative. We conclude that radical process-based change is more likely to be achieved when people recognise that organisational elements, namely:

- strategy
- structure
- people's responsibilities
- appraisal criteria
- collaborative behaviours, and
- information systems

will change and that these elements will align to a function *and* process orientation (*axiom three*).

It is also vital that people accept the changes that *actually* need to occur in the organisation (*axiom four*). The option to pick and choose is no option. This is particularly essential at the board and senior management levels. Where they do not accept that a change *actually* needs to occur in the organisation that change is rarely implemented and the success of the project is threatened as a result.

This part of the project 'domain' also suggests that people impacted by the changes should be willing to allow the actual changes to affect them. Without that willingness, the chances of success are reduced (*axiom five*).

3   *Issues that need to be managed*. This part refers to the issues that enable the implementation of the changes that need to occur. Radical process-based change is more likely to be achieved when people specifically link the issues to be managed to the changes that need to occur (*axiom six*). The case study organisations did not follow a prescriptive methodology, and there cannot be one for any specific project. Instead they focused the issues they managed to the identified changes that needed to occur.

The modes for deployment of the changes were both radical and evolutionary (*axiom seven*), since, again, no prescriptive approach can be used. Every project is different, as is every issue within it.

Axiom eight considered the willingness of people to implement the required changes, and the actions which should be taken early in the project to engender that willingness. The more that can be done to prepare the way, the better.

Axiom nine determined that many people will be required to be implementors of change as well as recipients of it. Due attention should be given to each of the roles, to the need for people to make the transition from one to the other, and to the tension that individuals will feel when fulfilling both roles concurrently.

4   *Effects of radical process orientation*. The achievement of radical process-based change needs to be assessed in terms of whether or not the drivers for change have been removed and the extent to

which vestiges of the old behaviours and structural bias – the short focal length – are unchanged (*axiom ten*). The case study organisations were able to align their processes to the objectives set out by the board, retain their customers by increasing service levels, remove the crises they faced and bring activities in the processes under management's control. Nothing, though, is perfect, and they will need to keep addressing the remnants of those issues which have not been completely resolved.

The axioms are reproduced in Table 12.1.

Table 12.1   *Summary of the axioms developed from case-study evidence*

Axiom number	Axiom
1	**Radical process-based change is more likely to be achieved when people accept the organisation's drivers for change, which can be both opportunities and threats.**
2	**The successful implementation of radical process-based change is only possible when people establish the need for a transformational cross-functional response to change drivers rather than any other type of change initiative.**
3	**Radical process-based change is more likely to be achieved when people recognise that organisational elements, namely strategy, structure, people's responsibilities and appraisal criteria, collaborative behaviours, and information systems, will change and that these elements should align to a function *and* process orientation.**
4	**Radical process-based change is more likely to be achieved when people identify and accept all the changes that actually need to occur in the organisation.**
5	**Radical process orientation is more likely to be achieved when people, including board members, senior managers, middle managers and employees, are willing to allow the changes to affect them.**
6	**Radical process-based change is more likely to be achieved when people identify the specific issues which**

need to be managed and link those to the actual changes that need to occur.

7   Radical process-based change is more likely to be achieved when both radical *and* evolutionary implementation methods are adopted depending on the individual issue being managed.

8   Radical process-based change is more likely to be achieved when ownership and a willingness to implement the changes is engendered throughout the organisation by preliminary company-spanning actions.

9   Radical process-based change is more likely to be achieved when implementors and recipients accept these roles as reciprocal, and enact both roles.

10   The achievement of radical process orientation needs to be assessed in terms of whether or not the drivers for change were removed and the extent to which behaviours are changed, or unchanged.

AXIOMS AND CHECKLIST FOR SUCCESSFUL PROCESS-BASED CHANGE

1 **Radical process-based change is more likely to be achieved when people accept the organisation's drivers for change, which can be both opportunities and threats.**

- Are the drivers for change in your company mainly threats? It is often easier to see the threats, because they show themselves, whereas opportunities have to be sought out. It is easier to disregard potential opportunities because they may not be seen as business critical, but the company which stands still today will soon fail.
- Have you tried to identify any opportunities which might also be present? On their own the threats might not be enough to persuade a sufficient 'mass' within the company that change is needed. Identified opportunities may tip the balance in favour of a change initiative which the company does really need to thrive.
- In addressing the threats do any opportunities present themselves? The resolution of threatening change drivers through the

concentration on business processes allows the benefits of such an approach to be gained as well as removing the threat.

- Are the drivers for change widely recognised in the company? A critical mass of opinion and power must be convinced of the need for change before it can happen.
- Are they recognised at a level high enough to instigate some action? A department head can influence his or her own department, but generally will not be able to influence a process which crosses functional boundaries. Unless the recognition of the need for change is at a level sufficiently high to have control over the whole process, the initiative is unlikely to succeed.
- Are the drivers for change sufficient to initiate a radical change initiative? Or will managers be able feasibly to suggest less radical changes to address the problem, such as intrafunctional quality initiatives, or a new computer system?
- Once that suggestion is mooted, will the acceptance of the change drivers be strong enough to withstand the initial, probably adverse reaction to proposed change? The more far-reaching the proposed change, the more likely that a kneejerk reaction will catch it on the chin and knock it out! The commitment will be tested at this point.
- By stressing the opportunities as well as the threats, will that tip the balance in favour of acceptance?

2 **The successful implementation of radical process-based change is only possible when people establish the need for a transformational cross-functional response to change drivers rather than any other type of change initiative.**

- Do your company strategy and business objectives give sufficient weight to customer satisfaction, or do they concentrate on cost reduction and profit increase? If the latter, there will be less incentive to consider the business processes and more on the intrafunctional activities.
- Is customer service suffering because the processes are being disrupted by the internal functional requirements? Do you actually know why customer service is suffering?

- Is there more emphasis placed on people's 'day jobs' rather than on satisfying customer expectations? The more ingrained the functional organisation the shorter will be the focal length of the staff from 'shopfloor' to management.
- Do people see and describe themselves in terms of the departments in which they work or do they include the processes of which they form a part?
- Which are more important to them?
- Are managerial bonuses dependent on departmental performance rather than on end-customer satisfaction? If so, then it is reinforcing the functional viewpoint and actively hindering process orientation.
- Is there sufficient knowledge of what happens across functional boundaries to guarantee that all activities are contributing positively to the process, and in a timely, efficient manner?
- Are all the managers directly responsible for end-customer satisfaction, and not just those with direct contact? Their departmental activities all contribute to or detract from it, yet many are not held accountable.
- Do you actually know what your processes are, and what activities they should contain (rather than what they *do* contain)? Many people think they know what a process is and can name half a dozen. They are more likely, though, to be single activities or random collections of them.

3 **Radical process-based change is more likely to be achieved when people recognise that organisational elements, namely strategy, structure, people's responsibilities and appraisal criteria, collaborative behaviours, and information systems, will change and that these elements should align to a function *and* process orientation.**

- Has the company strategy changed to reflect the objectives for the achievement of which the project was initiated? If not (assuming change was needed) then there may be insufficient support for the radical changes required.

- What behaviours contributed to the current situation or need changing in order to achieve the objectives?
- Whose behaviours are they and are they aware of the changes required?
- Are they able to make the changes required? It may be a subjective judgement, but some people cannot change deep-seated habits, channels of thought or modes of behaviour.
- Is there a feeling of teamwork being built up along the lines of the processes which ultimately lead to satisfaction of customer expectations? The less teamwork there is, the more the customer will suffer, and that will reflect on the company.
- Is the internal appraisal system being used to devolve the changes throughout the organisation? It is an effective tool, and should be used to support and develop the business processes wherein the appraisee's activities reside.
- Should the remuneration package be amended in order to encourage and reinforce the required changes in activity and behaviour? It is a powerful tool, and not using it will leave the move towards a process-oriented mind-set with less of a chance of success.
- Have you tried to shift the organisational structure to a process basis, or is the emphasis going to be on people's mind-sets while leaving the structure as it is? If you are trying to change the structural organisation, that may well be an overambitious step. Many companies find themselves unable to make this revolutionary change, and failure in the attempt may sound the death knell for other change which would be feasible.

4 **Radical process-based change is more likely to be achieved when people identify and accept all the changes that actually need to occur in the organisation.**

- Are the changes which are required supported by the chairman, CEO and / or managing director? If not, then radical changes will fail.
- Do the senior managers support the changes? They will steer the project and have the power to kill it.

- Is that support genuine? Is it from the heart, from the head, or is it only skin deep? Whether from the head or the heart may not matter so long as the support is not merely a veneer which will crack when the heat increases!

- Has your company attempted radical change before and failed or given up on it? If so, do the managers expect anything different this time around? If they don't then the support for the changes is likely to be less than whole-hearted – they are waiting for the monthly fad to pass. When it does not, unexpected resistance may surface.

- Are there some changes which (some of) the managers simply will not or cannot accept?

- Will all of the managers make it into the 'new world'? Some may not. It can be a choice between the changes surviving, or the managers.

- Are you shying away from some of the required changes because they would 'never be accepted', or because they are 'too difficult'? Those problems which are quietly put on one side will come back to bite the project at a later stage and will by then be much harder to resolve.

- Have you really identified all of the changes that need to take place, or has your own thinking been constrained by its historical perspective? People external to the unit of analysis – maybe external to the whole company – may well be able to ask questions about the trees which simply do not occur to those in the midst of the wood.

5 **Radical process orientation is more likely to be achieved when people, including board members, senior managers, middle managers and employees, are willing to allow the changes to affect them.**

- Is the company one where change is frequent (and therefore causes less disruption to comfort zones), or rare (and therefore causes more)?

- Are people willing to allow the changes to affect them?

- How much communication and explanation has taken and is taking place? The more the better (within reason), even when not all of the news is good.
- Are jobs at risk, and is this known? Clearly the greater the threat the greater will be the possible resistance. While people would be more willing to experience change within their job than to lose it, they would probably prefer just to see the threatened change go away.
- Is there a swell of opinion that 'what we need is a new / updated computer system' from people who are seeking to deflect the changes that affect people, especially themselves? It is the easiest way to stop real change from happening, and it is also the first thing that occurs to people when solutions for bad service are sought. It is almost always the wrong answer.
- Is the sponsorship of the change project at a high enough level to ensure that willingness to change can be engendered in all those who need to do so? Some people will need to be coerced, and while not the ideal way of generating 'willingness', it sometimes has to suffice.
- Are managerial power bases being affected in such a way as to create 'losers', and therefore resistance?
- Are some managers using tactics to delay or deflect the impact of the required changes?
- Are the managers displaying the behaviours which they are requiring of their staff? If not, then their requirements will not be satisfied, and, ultimately, neither will those of the end customers.

6 **Radical process-based change is more likely to be achieved when people identify the specific issues which need to be managed and link those to the actual changes that need to occur.**

- Are you attempting to follow what may be a restrictive, perhaps proprietary, methodology? While useful, any prescriptive, step-by-step guide is unlikely exactly to fit any specific project. The issues within each project will be in some part unique, if only because so many concern real people, not literature stereotypes.

- Have you identified all the issues which require resolution in order to address the drivers for change?
- Have you identified all the secondary issues which then prevent the required resolutions of the primary issues? It is not just a question of saying, 'We must do *that*', because there is likely to be something else stopping you doing '*that*', which must also be addressed.
- Does the steering committee (however it is designated) still support the project? They are the ship's engine and rudder. Without them, rocks lie in wait for the project.
- Is that steering body aware that further issues may arise before the completion of the project? Or do they believe an earlier (and premature) estimate of the project duration and required resources?
- Are mutterings beginning? Is the support waning? It is natural for it to do so as more issues arise, but the continued support and concentration on the end goals is vital to overall success. Any temptation to try to reach the goals via a short cut which leaves some issues unaddressed must be resisted.

7 **Radical process-based change is more likely to be achieved when both radical *and* evolutionary implementation methods are adopted depending on the individual issue being managed.**

- Are you trying to employ either solely revolutionary *or* evolutionary implementation methods when a mixture is more appropriate? It is unlikely that one or the other is exclusively right for all the issues.
- Do the behaviours of a significant part of the organisation need to change as part of the change programme? If so, then this is something that is unlikely to be achieved with a massive revolutionary change. Behaviours change only gradually, usually through taking a lead from others.
- Is there sufficient resistance to indicate that a clean break is the only way of inducing movement? Sometimes changes simply have to be imposed, especially when gradual stretching of the comfort zone sees only a snapping back to the original position.

- Are new computer systems needed, or can current ones be used or easily amended? IT systems always take some time to build, and usually a long time. In order to keep things moving, look at amendment of the existing systems – and maybe of the newly designed process – as an interim and temporary step. Do not let the temporary amendments become established.

- Are there interim steps which can profitably be taken without providing an opportunity for the programme to be halted early? Quick wins are good for maintaining enthusiasm, teamwork and project momentum, but they can be used as an artificial end-point by those keen to avoid the longer term changes.

- Are the current methods of development or change *capable* of taking the company to the 'new world'? If not, then completely new ones must be adopted, or the company will stay in the 'old world' and suffer the consequences.

8 **Radical process-based change is more likely to be achieved when ownership and a willingness to implement the changes is engendered throughout the organisation by preliminary company-spanning action.**

- What lead are the staff taking from those at the top of the organisation? Because that is where the lead should come from. Do not underestimate its influence.

- Is there an identifiable 'pocket' of potential resistance, such as managers who will become 'losers' through the change? If so it must be tackled, and as early in the project as possible. 'Tackled' can mean education, persuasion, force or ejection.

- Do those willing to change represent a critical mass within the organisation? The critical mass is a weighted calculation, but without it the impetus for change will be lost.

- Are managers – or anyone – undermining in private what they are saying in public? Hearts and minds need to be behind the need for change, and not just public mouths. The critical mass of an iceberg is that below the surface, and the same applies to the support for change.

- Are there any early, perhaps symbolic, changes which can be made which will positively affect the perception of the other changes to come? If so, make those changes. Nothing succeeds like success.
- Is the change project owned by those whom it will affect? If not then it will be harder to implement and it will be a lot easier and more tempting to 'un-implement' again!
- Who is responsible for identifying and implementing the changes? If changes are designed by the people who will be affected by them then they stand a much better chance of success, both because of a natural affiliation with what one has built with one's own mind and hands, and also because there is no easy back door.
- Is the potential trauma of change being properly and sufficiently addressed? Don't underestimate it. Ask the questions during the communications. Change is about people, and so are companies. Look after them.

9 **Radical process-based change is more likely to be achieved when implementors and recipients accept these roles as reciprocal, and enact both roles.**

- Is there a clearly defined split between implementors and recipients? If there is then the changes are not affecting the whole company. Are they therefore as wide-ranging as they were intended to be? And why should those lower down change if they see those above making no effort to do the same?
- Is as much attention being given to problems faced by implementors as to those faced by recipients? People find it hard to enforce changes as well as to receive them, but both need to be done if the project is to succeed.
- Are there identifiable Nimbys, Obstructors, Indifferents and Champions? Knowing which are which, and how much influence they wield within the management and the project structures will allow action to be taken. Positives can be accentuated and potential pitfalls circumnavigated.

10 **The achievement of radical process orientation needs to be assessed in terms of whether or not the drivers for change were removed and the extent to which behaviours are changed, or unchanged.**

- Is the project marked as a success on the basis of performance improvements it has brought about? Hopefully it is, but hopefully it has also removed the drivers for change which provided the impetus for its creation.
- Are the underlying drivers for change completely removed, or do vestiges remain? The weed which is snapped off where it leaves the soil will grow again. Maybe not today, maybe not tomorrow ...

Closure

The achievement of radical process-based change is complex, painstaking and laborious. It requires people, from different functions and hierarchical levels, to construct a shared perspective of the need for radical process-based change, the changes that need to occur, and the issues that need to be managed.

In reaching this consensus individuals reflect upon their own beliefs about the organisation and about their personal position within it. They fall back on their own knowledge and prior experience. At some point in time they realise that these very things, so integral to each one of them as individuals, have to be adjusted in order to reach some common ground with colleagues.

It is at this point that the successful achievement of radical process-based change begins. If the point is not reached, or the realisation is rejected, then the initiative will simply peter out into small adaptive changes to the status quo. Where people let go of their preconceptions, prejudices, and fears, when they are prepared to leave behind the baggage that years of functional orientation has built up and to embrace the challenges presented by radical process-based change, then it has the real potential to succeed.

The research and conclusions of this work will assist people in organisations to establish the shared perspective that is vital to the achievement of such radical change. Good luck to all who try.

References

1. Ghoshal S, Bartlett CA. Changing the role of top management: beyond structure to processes. *Harvard Business Review*, 1995; **73**(1): 86 (11).
2. Dixon JR, Arnold P, Heineke J, Kim JS, Mulligan P. Business process reengineering: Improving in new strategic directions. *California Management Review*, 1994; **36**(4): 93–108.
3. Ascari A, Rock M, Dutta S. Reengineering and organizational change: Lessons from a comparative analysis of company experiences. *European Management Journal*, 1995; **13**(1): 1–30.
4. Teng JTC, Grover V, Fiedler K. Re-designing business process using information technology. *Long Range Planning*, 1994; **27**(1): 95–106.
5. Buchanan DA. The limitations and opportunities of business process re-engineering in a politicized organizational climate. *Human Relations*, 1997; **50**(1): 51–72.
6. Ayers JB. What smokestack industries can tell us about reengineering. *Information Strategy: The Executive's Journal*, 1995; Winter: 20–6.
7. Hamel G, Prahalad CK. *Competing for the Future*. Boston: Harvard Business School Press, 1994.
8. Gerwin D, Guild P. Redefining the new product introduction process. *International Journal of Technology Management*, Special Issue on Technological Responses to Increasing Competition, 1994; **9**(5/6/7): 678–90.
9. Gouillart FJ, Sturdivant FD. Spend a day in the life of your customers. *Harvard Business Review*, 1994; **72**(1): 116–25.
10. Markides CC. Diversification, restructuring and economic performance. *Strategic Management Journal*, 1995; **16**(2): 101–18.

11. Cheon MJ, Grover V, Teng JTC. Theoretical perspectives on the outsourcing of information systems. *Journal of Information Technology*, 1995; **10**(4): 209–19.

12. Carr DK, Johansson HJ. *Best Practices in Reengineering: What Works and What Doesn't in the Reengineering Process*. New York: McGraw-Hill, 1995, 235pp.

13. Hammer M, Champy J. *Re-engineering the Corporation: A Manifesto for Business Revolution*. London: Nicholas Brealey Publishing, 1993.

14. Currie WL, Willcocks L. The New Branch Columbus project at Royal Bank of Scotland: The implementation of large-scale business process re-engineering. *Journal of Strategic Information Systems*, 1996; **5**(3): 213–36.

15. Stoddard DB, Jarvenpaa SL. Business process redesign: Tactics for managing radical change. *Journal of Management Information Systems*, 1995; **12**(1)(July): 81–107.

16. Stoddard DB, Jarvenpaa SL, Littlejohn M. The reality of business reengineering. *California Management Review*, 1996; **38**(3): 57–76.

17. Davenport TH. *Process Innovation: Reengineering Work through Information Technology*. Boston: Harvard Business School Press, 1993.

18. Tushman ML, Newman WH, Romanelli E. Convergence and upheaval: Managing the unsteady pace of organizational evolution. *California Management Review*, 1986; **29**(1): 29–44.

19. Grover V, Jeong SR, Teng JTC. Survey of reengineering challenges. *Information Systems Management*, 1998; **15**(2): 53–9.

20. Kaplan RB, Murdock L. Rethinking the corporation: Core process redesign. *McKinsey Quarterly*, 1991; **2**: 27–43.

21. Hall EA, Rosenthal J, Wade J. How to make reengineering really work. *McKinsey Quarterly*, 1994; **2**: 107–28.

22. Hagel III J. Core process redesign: Keeping CPR on track. *McKinsey Quarterly*, 1993; **1**: 59–72.

23. Grover V, Jeong SR, Kettinger WJ, Teng JTC. The implementation of business process reengineering. *Journal of Management Information Systems*, 1995; **12**(1): 109–44.

24. Earl MJ, Sampler JL, Short JE. Strategies for business process reengineering: Evidence from field studies. *Journal of Management Information Systems*, 1995; **12**(1): 31–56.

25. Davenport TH, Nohria N. Case management and the integration of labor. *Sloan Management Review*, 1994; **35**(2): 11–23.

26. Caron JR, Jarvenpaa SL, Stoddard DB. Business reengineering at CIGNA Corporation: Experiences and lessons learned from the first five years. *MIS Quarterly*, 1994; **18**(3): 233–50.

27. Asamoah A, Duncan A. Business Process Redesign: Case Study Report. 1993.

28. Kilmann R. A holistic program and critical success factors for corporate transformation. *European Management Journal*, 1995; **13**(2): 175–86.

29. Earl M, Khan B. How new is business process redesign? *European Management Journal*, 1994; **12**(1): 20–30.

30. Anon. State of Reengineering Report. Cambridge, MA. CSC Index. 1994.

31. Grint K, Willcocks L. Business process re-engineering in theory and practice: Business paradise regained? *New Technology, Work and Employment*, 1995; **10**(2): 99–109.

32. Bashein BJ, Markus ML, Riley P. Preconditions for BPR success and how to prevent failures. *Information Systems Management*, 1994; **11**(2): 7–13.

33. Jarvenpaa SL, Stoddard DB. Business process redesign: Radical and evolutionary change. *Journal of Business Research*, 1998; **41**(1): 15–27.

34. Motwani J, Kumar A, Jiang J. Business process reengineering: A theoretical framework and an integrated model. *International Journal of Operations & Production Management*, 1998; **18**(9/10): 964–77.

35. Hammer M, Stanton S. *The Re-engineering Revolution: A Handbook*. New York: Harper Collins, 1995.

36. Petrozzo DP, Stepper JC. *Successful Reengineering*. New York: Van Nostrand Reinhold, 1994.

37. Armistead C, Rowland P. (eds). The role of people in process. In *Managing Business Processes: BPR and Beyond*. Chichester: John Wiley, 1996, pp. 61–71.

38. Smith G, Willcocks L, Grover V, Kettinger WJ, (eds). Business process reengineering, politics and management: From methodologies to processes. In *Business Process Change: Concepts, Methods and Technologies*. Harrisburg: Idea Publishing, 1995, pp. 493–525.

39. Jaffe DT, Scott CD. Reengineering in Practice. Where are the people? Where is the learning? *Journal of Applied Behavioral Science*, 1998; **34**(3): 250–67.

40. Morris D, Brandon J. *Re-engineering your Business*. New York: McGraw-Hill, 1993.

41. Braganza A, Myers A. Issues and dilemmas facing organizations in the effective implementation of BPR. *Business Change and Re-Engineering: The Journal of Corporate Transformation*, 1996; **3**(2): 38–51.

42. Davenport TH, Stoddard DB. Reengineering: Business change of mythic proportions. *MIS Quarterly*, 1994; **18**(2): 121–7.

43. Mumford E. Creative chaos or constructive change: Business process re-engineering versus socio-technical design? In *Examining Business Process Re-engineering*, Burke G, Peppard J, (eds). London: Kogan Page, 1995.

44. Robey D, Wishart NA, Rodriguez-Diaz AG. Merging the metaphors for organizational improvement: business process reengineering as a component of organizational learning. *Accounting, Management & Information Technology*, 1995; **5**(1): 23–39.

45. Carr NG. Redesigning business. *Harvard Business Review*, 1999; **77**(6): 19.

46. Cardarelli DP, Agarwal R, Tanniru M. Organizational pitfalls of reengineering. *Information Systems Management*, 1998; **15**(2): 34–9.

47. Kettinger WJ, Teng JTC. Aligning BPR to strategy: A framework for analysis. *Long Range Planning*, 1998; **31**(1): 93–107.

48. Moss Kanter R, Stein BA, Jick TD. *The Challenge of Organizational Change: How Companies Experience It and How Leaders Guide It*. New York: The Free Press, 1992, 535pp.

49. Hammer M. Reengineering work: Don't automate–obliterate. *Harvard Business Review*, 1990; **68**(4): 104–12.

50. Venkatraman N. Morton MS, (eds). IT-induced business reconfiguration: The new strategic management challenge. In *The Corporation of the 1990s*. New York: Oxford University Press, 1991.

51. Stalk G, Evans P, Shulman LE. Competing on capabilities: The new rules of corporate strategy. *Harvard Business Review*, 1992; **70**(2): 57–69.

52. Teng JTC, Grover V, Fielder KD. Business process reengineering: Charting a strategic path for the information age. *California Management Review*, 1994; Spring: 9–31.

Index